Edu̲ca̲ :
QUA̲

LIBRARY

Issues in Educational Research: QUALITATIVE METHODS

Edited by
Robert G. Burgess

 The Falmer Press
(A member of the Taylor & Francis Group)
London and Philadelphia

UK The Falmer Press, Falmer House, Barcombe, Lewes, East Sussex, BN8 5DL

USA The Falmer Press, Taylor & Francis Inc., 242 Cherry Street, Philadelphia, PA 19106-1906

First published 1985

Library of Congress Cataloging in Publication Data

Main entry under title:

Issues in educational research.

Includes index.
1. Education—Research—Addresses, essays, lectures.
2. Education—Research—Great Britain—Addresses, essays, lectures. I. Burgess, Robert G.
LB1028.I86 1985 370′.7′8 85-6754
ISBN 1-85000-036-0
ISBN 1-85000-035-2 (pbk.)

Jacket design by Leonard Williams

Typeset in 11/13 Garamond by Imago Publishing Ltd, Thame, Oxon.

Printed in Great Britain by Taylor & Francis (Printers) Ltd, Basingstoke

Contents

Contents

Part three: Issues in Teacher Research

Preface

There are now numerous texts and sets of readings that are devoted to social research methods in general and qualitative methods in particular. Common to much of this literature is the notion that 'method' is little more than an outline of techniques which can be used by the researcher. The result of such an approach is that the main issues discussed concern the practicalities associated with doing research. As a consequence, issues concerning the relationship between theory and method, between policy and practice and the use of methods in a variety of settings and circumstances are relatively hidden from view. Yet, no matter whether research is 'pure' or 'applied', these issues confront the researcher. Certainly in a field of study such as education where research may be related to theory, policy and practice, there is an urgent need for dialogue and debate about a range of issues that arise in the course of research practice.

The chapters in this book attempt to contribute to this dialogue by bringing material together from a number of individuals who have had first-hand experience of conducting educational research where qualitative methods have been used. For some of the researchers the main concern is with theoretical problems, while others are more concerned with policy and practice. Yet despite this range of work they are all concerned with issues in educational research that arise out of using qualitative methods of investigation in different research projects. The authors of these chapters discuss some of the problems involved in dealing with these issues and the ways in which they have attempted to come to terms with them.

All the chapters that are included in this volume were specifically commissioned from individuals who have had recent experience of conducting educational research projects where qualitative methods of investigation have been used. As a consequence all the issues that are discussed in this book are illustrated by reference to educational research projects of various kinds. It is, therefore, to be hoped that the material in this volume will contribute in some way to debates about social research in general, and qualitative research in particular; especially when conducted in educational settings. In particular the book has been designed not only to be used by undergraduate and postgraduate researchers, but also by teachers and policy makers who are now frequently concerned with the conduct and assessment of educational research projects where qualitative methods have been used.

The majority of chapters in this volume were originally presented at a three day workshop entitled 'Qualitative Methodology and the Study of Education' that was held at Whitelands College, London, in July 1983. This workshop brought together researchers and teachers who were concerned with the collection, analysis and use of qualitative data in educational research. All the workshop papers were pre-circulated so that the maximum amount of time could be devoted to discussion and debate. At the workshop, all the sessions were tape-recorded so that further material was available for authors to use in the course of redrafting their papers for publication. In addition, the session in which papers were presented by Andy Hargreaves, Peter Woods and Martyn Hammersley, John Scarth and Sue Webb was video-taped. A video of the original presentations of the material that is included in their papers can be hired free of charge from the editor of this volume at the Department of Sociology, University of Warwick, Coventry, CV4 7AL. These video-recordings also contain the discussion that followed the papers from other workshop participants. In addition to those individuals whose papers are included in this volume, contributions to the discussion were also made by Clem Adelman, Alison Andrew, Stephen Ball, Martin Bulmer, Brian Davies, Sara Delamont, Lee Enright, Tony Green, Ivor Goodson, Stephen Hester, Dave Hustler, Alan James, Saville Kushner, Colin Lacey, Lynda Measor, Andrew Pollard, June Purvis, Rene Saran, Marten Shipman, Helen Simons, Marie Stowell, Pat Sikes, Rob Walker and Mary Willes.

The workshop was made possible by a grant that I was awarded by the Education and Human Development Committee of the Social Science Research Council. In addition, I was also given a further grant by the Research, Resources and Methods Committee of the Social Science Research Council so that some of the sessions at this workshop could be video-recorded. I would, therefore, like to thank the members of these committees who supported my proposal for a workshop which would examine the use of qualitative methods in the study of education. I would also like to thank all the workshop participants; especially those who prepared papers and who have contributed to the shape and substance of this volume. In turn, we are all indebted to the domestic staff at Whitelands College and to the technical staff of the Roehampton Institute who worked very hard on our behalf and contributed to the success of the workshop. I am also indebted to all the contributors to this volume who have provided support and encouragement throughout the project. Finally, my thanks are due to Sue Turner who has provided first class secretarial support in preparing these papers for publication.

Robert Burgess
University of Warwick

1 Issues and Problems in Educational Research: An Introduction

Robert G. Burgess

What is educational research? Who conducts it? How and for what purpose? In answering these questions just over ten years ago contributors to a volume entitled *Research Perspectives in Education* (Taylor, 1973) indicated that educational research was confined to professional researchers located in higher education who might well conduct their research from a sociological, psychological, philosophical or historical perspective; or to professional researchers engaged by central or local government departments who were interested in collecting statistical data for future work in policy and planning. Subsequent developments in the last decade have resulted in a situation whereby educational research is no longer narrowly confined to higher education and government departments but is also conducted by teachers who have addressed fundamental issues concerned with curriculum development work in schools (*cf.* Stenhouse, 1975; Burgess, 1980; Nixon, 1981). But, we might ask, what do these researchers contribute to our understanding of education? What kinds of social and educational research do they conduct?

A simple answer might result in the suggestion that some investigators engage in pure research while others are involved in applied work. Indeed, simple dichotomies such as this abound in the world of social and educational investigation where distinctions are drawn between the pure and the applied, the strategic and the utilitarian and basic and applied research (*cf.* Rothschild, 1971). Yet, such distinctions have been shown to be unsatisfactory (*cf.* Dainton, 1971) as they imply an artificial division between different fields of investigation. Indeed, in educational studies research might simultaneously contribute to theory, policy and practice. Nevertheless, some investigations might be more concerned with contributing to theory or policy or practice but still have some contribution to make to other areas.

Accordingly, social scientists have found it useful to establish typologies of social research. One attempt to classify social research has been made by Martin Bulmer (1978) who proposes a five-fold classification: basic social science, strategic social science, specific problem orientated research, action research, and intelligence and monitoring. He indicates that the distinctions that he has proposed are not clear cut but may be thought of as a continuum in which all research may be classified. It is this five-fold division that has some relevance for educational studies and may be used to classify different types of educational research as follows:

1 *Basic educational research* which is principally concerned with advancing knowledge through testing, generating and developing theories. While such investigations may have some benefit for policy and practice this is not their prime purpose. In the sociology of education, for example, the work of Margaret Archer (1979 and 1981) is principally concerned with the theoretical study of educational systems. Nevertheless, her work has implications for our understanding of decision-making and educational policy making.

2 *Strategic educational research* which is based on an academic discipline but is oriented towards an educational problem. In sociological research, for example, work concerned with conceptual issues of sociology has in turn been concerned with practical problems. For example, studies on mixed ability teaching in comprehensive schools (*cf.* Ball, 1981; Corbishley *et al.*, 1981) have increased our understanding of a school-based issue whilst simultaneously contributing to theoretical developments in the knowledge base of the sociology of education.

3 *Specific problem-orientated research* which is designed to deal with a practical problem. Such work might be conducted on behalf of government departments or local authorities and might be concerned with topics such as the teaching of reading or with examination performance in schools (*cf.* Shipman, 1985; Mortimore and Byford, 1981).

4 *Action research* which involves research in a programme of planned change. This research is often designed to study the effects of change. In the field of education there have been a number of action research projects concerned with curriculum development (*cf.* Stenhouse, 1980; Sten-

house *et al.* 1982) as well as with educational priority areas (*cf.* Halsey, 1974). However, teachers have also been engaged in their own small-scale studies which have been seen by some commentators as a form of action research (*cf.* Nixon, 1981).

5   *Intelligence and monitoring* which involves the collection of statistical data on education by such bodies as the Office of Population, Censuses and Surveys. It is reported in the *General Household Survey* and *Social Trends* as well as in *Statistics of Education* (for commentaries on the use of this material in education see Burgess, 1984c and 1986).

This classification results in a very broad range of social and educational research which includes abstract theoretical work and basic fact finding but may also involve some contribution being made to policy and practice in education. However, we might ask how such research may be conducted.

As many basic texts reveal (*cf.* Cohen and Manion, 1980) educational research utilizes a range of methods of investigation although the main strategies that are used are: social surveys, experimental designs, historical sources and qualitative techniques. Much educational research appears to show a preference for social surveys but as Bechhofer (1967 and 1974) has shown, although the survey is an excellent way of obtaining some data it has limitations and has been over-used. This preference for survey methods is sometimes explained in terms of the strength and superiority of survey research compared with other techniques; especially qualitative methods which are regarded as lacking 'rigour' and presenting problems of reliability and validity (*cf.* Burgess, 1985a; Halfpenny, 1979; Zelditch, 1962). Nevertheless, some investigators (*cf.* Becker and Geer, 1957) have shown a preference for qualitative methods such as participant observation and unstructured interviews, but as Trow (1957) reminded them, it is not a question of the superiority of one method over another but the appropriateness of a method of investigation for a particular research problem. For Trow (1957) remarked:

> Let us be done with the arguments of 'participant observation' *versus* interviewing — as we have largely dispensed with the arguments for psychology *versus* sociology — and get on with the business of attacking our problems with the widest array of conceptual and methodological tools that we possess

and they demand. This does not preclude discussion and debate regarding the relative usefulness of different methods for the study of specific problems or types of problems. But that is very different from the assertion of the general and inherent superiority of one method over another on the basis of some intrinsic qualities it presumably possesses. (p. 35)

Such a perspective suggests that researchers should not rigidly apply methods of investigation but need to consider the theoretical and substantive problems involved and be flexible in their research approaches as Wax (1971) has warned:

Strict and rigid adherence to any method, technique or doctrinaire position may, for the fieldworker, become like confinement in a cage. If he is lucky or very cautious, a fieldworker may formulate a research problem so that he will find all the answers he needs within his cage. But if he finds himself in a field situation where he is limited by a particular method, theory, or technique he will do well to slip through the bars and try to find out what is really going on. (p. 10)

On this basis, researchers who have utilized a qualitative approach in their investigations have tended to use a range of methods, styles and strategies based upon social interaction with those whom they study, observation of people, situations and events, formal and informal interviewing, and the collection of documentary materials (*cf.* Burgess, 1982 and 1984a; Hammersley and Atkinson, 1983; Schatzman and Strauss, 1973).

In recent years there has been an increase in the popularity of qualitative methods in studying educational problems as reflected in studies of schools, classrooms and curricula[1] and the commentaries on research methods produced by investigators who have worked in education in Britain and the USA.[2] Although this work covers a range of different topics and utilizes a series of different methods there are a number of elements that they have in common. On this basis, it is important to establish the main characteristics associated with qualitative work in the field of education. Nevertheless, it should be stressed that there is no single attribute that is present in all studies. However, the following attributes are present to a greater or lesser degree in many qualitative projects:

1   The focus is on the observed present, but the findings are contextualized within a social, cultural and historical framework.
2   The research is conducted within a theoretical framework. While

there may only be a small number of questions to orientate a study, further questions may arise during the course of the investigation.

3 The research involves close, detailed intensive work. The researcher participates in the social situation under study.

4 The major research instrument is the researcher who attempts to obtain a participant's account of the social setting.

5 Unstructured or informal interviews in the form of extended conversations may complement the observational account.

6 Personal documents may give depth and background to the contemporary account.

7 Different methods of investigation may be used to complement qualitative methods with the result that different methodologies may be integrated by the researcher.

8 The decisions regarding the collection and analysis of data take place in the field and are products of the enquiry.

9 The researcher attempts to disturb the process of social life as little as possible.

10 The researcher has to consider the audience for whom he or she is producing a report and the main concerns to be included.

11 Research reports disseminate the knowledge which informants have provided without rendering harm to them, taking into account ethical problems that confront the researcher and the researched.

12 The researcher monitors the dissemination of materials and provides feedback to those who have been researched.

These characteristics are associated with a number of qualitative investigations whose investigators may be concerned to contribute to:

(a) the theoretical and methodological knowledge base in the study of education;

(b) the policies that may be initiated by central and local government and by individual schools;

(c) the practice of education within teachers' classrooms. In some situations this might involve action research projects by researchers from outside the institution or small scale investigations by teacher-researchers.

Robert G. Burgess

The Organization of the Book

The chapters in this volume have been contributed by researchers who have worked in a variety of educational settings: in the pre-school stage, in infant, junior, primary, middle and secondary schools, and in higher education. In some cases the researchers have been predominantly concerned with theoretical developments in the field of education, while others have been predominantly concerned with social policy and the practice of education. Accordingly the papers have been subdivided into three major sections.

1   Issues in Theory and Method

The chapters in this section all focus on different problems concerning the relationship between theory and method. The section opens with a paper from Andy Hargreaves who is concerned with a fundamental problem in sociology and the sociology of education, namely the relationship between microscopic and macroscopic modes of analysis. Among sociologists of education there has been much speculation about whether it is possible to build bridges between these two forms of analysis (Banks, 1978; Archer, 1981; Hammersley, 1984). Hargreaves suggests that if some synthesis is to occur further empirical work is required in order to make connections between micro and macro theory and between school and society.

As well as sociologists of education being confronted with the micro-macro problem they are also concerned with building and developing theories; a strategy that Hammersley and Atkinson (1983) have advocated should be uppermost in the minds of qualitative researchers. In their paper in this volume, Hammersley, Scarth and Webb point to the ways in which sociologists can develop and test theory; a situation that they illustrate by making reference to their research on examinations.

However, particular kinds of sociological theories used in the study of educational settings have implications for the strategy of research and the work of the investigator. In this context, Sue Scott draws on her research experience in investigating postgraduate education to look at the implications of feminist theory for qualitative research. Here, she discusses the implications not only for problems and methods, but also for the data that are generated on a particular project (*cf.* Roberts, 1981; Stanley and Wise, 1983).

It is this concern with data, with data analysis and the transmission of data that we turn to in the final paper in the first section where Peter Woods examines the relationship between data analysis and writing reports; a topic that is seldóm discussed in 'methods' books (although, for an exception see Hammersley and Atkinson, 1983) but which has considerable implications for the audience and for policy and practice.

2 *Issues in Policy and Practice*

Of all the fields of social policy, education, it is argued, has the potential to make a contribution to policy debates. However, as Glennerster and Hoyle (1973) remarked, there are doubts about the extent to which educational research has contributed to social policy. As far as they are concerned there are three main reasons for raising doubts about the contribution that educational research can make to policy:

> Firstly, social scientists have not yet adequately resolved the conflict between a disciplinary and a policy orientation. For example, the sociological approach to the study of educational organizations has been largely concerned with using schools as an area for testing hypotheses derived from more general organizational theories rather than with tackling the substantive problems of streaming, curriculum change and school management. Secondly, educational issues cannot as a rule be wholly explored from the standpoint of a single discipline. Thirdly, education has suffered from what might be called the non-disciplinary approach. Many examples of educational research use the tools of the social sciences — tests, surveys and so on, but have little theoretical basis. These studies are often useful at the level of description, but lack explanatory power. The administrator or politician is likely to welcome description, for this leaves him with a considerable degree of freedom to formulate his own policies. (pp. 214–5)

However, it does not end there as a further problem concerns the style and strategy that is used to conduct studies with a policy focus. A brief glance at the basic texts in the policy field (*cf*. Bulmer, 1978 and 1982) confirms the importance accorded to survey based and quantitative studies. Accordingly, Janet Finch argues the case for using qualitative research designs in the field of social and educational policy (*cf.* Rist, 1984) while Alison Kelly and Dave Ebbutt take up a similar theme in relation to action research projects with teachers. While Kelly discusses some definitions of action research drawing on different educational projects, Ebbutt focuses on particular concerns relating to qualitative strategies that were used in the teacher-pupil interaction and the quality of learning project which involved teachers conducting classroom based studies.

3   Issues in Teacher Research

One development that has occurred in recent years has been the importance attached to teachers systematically investigating and evaluating activities that occur in schools and classrooms (*cf.* Stenhouse, 1975; Nixon, 1981; McCormick *et al.*, 1982; McCormick and James, 1983). As Nixon (1981) indicates, the small-scale intensive studies conducted by teachers are most appropriately researched using qualitative methods. Indeed, in recent years teachers' classroom research has been associated with observation, interview and documentary evidence (*cf.* Elliott and Adelman, 1976; Pollard, 1985a). Accordingly the last section of this volume is concerned with issues and problems that arise when teachers use qualitative methods. In the first chapter in this section Hilary Burgess provides a commentary on the research process involved in studying the mathematics curriculum in a primary school. Here she shows that the issues involved are not merely concerned with research practicalities, but are also associated with conceptual questions and problems of dissemination. Meanwhile, Gordon Griffiths' paper on a research exercise in a comprehensive school focuses on the uses of a research diary in which he takes up some of the problems associated with recording items in the diary. Finally, Carol Cummings and Margaret Threadgold draw on research conducted in an infant school and in a comprehensive school, respectively. Here, both accounts are based on work in their own schools and point up the fact that research conducted by teachers is not merely concerned with day to day practice but is also associated with conceptual and methodological issues. Indeed, in different ways, they both bring us full circle by suggesting that a major issue is not just to have research done by individuals in higher education and further educational research conducted by teachers, but collaboration over investigations between teachers *and* researchers as the next logical step on the research agenda (*cf.* Burgess, 1985c).

    While each of these sections is concerned with a major issue relating to the use of qualitative methods there are also a number of issues and problems which arise in different papers that are located in different sections of the book. It is, therefore, appropriate at this stage to examine some of these issues with a view to setting them in a broader context.

Some Issues and Problems in Qualitative Educational Research Projects

Although all the contributors to this volume have used qualitative methods of social investigation in a variety of different educational settings there are a number of issues that arise in several of the projects.

A   Issues on Theory and Theorizing

Within qualitative research all investigations focus on a problem of study that is influenced by theoretical and conceptual issues. Among the key problems is the question of when theory is used and for what purpose (see the papers by Hargreaves and by Woods in this volume). For some researchers theoretical perspectives are used in the formulation of initial questions and in establishing working hypotheses (*cf.* Geer, 1964 and 1970), while for others the theory is generated from the data that are collected (*cf.* Glaser and Strauss, 1967; Glaser, 1978) but this is just to present two extreme cases where theory is used. For Goetz and LeCompte (1984) have shown how three levels of theory: theoretical models, formal or middle range theory and substantive theory influences the design of qualitative research projects. Indeed, in this collection of papers theory is not merely confined to those projects where the researchers set out to test or generate theory, as Janet Finch argues that theoretically grounded critical accounts are demanded in the study of social policy. Furthermore, Hilary Burgess and Carol Cummings illustrate how different conceptual frameworks helped to formulate the kinds of questions which they used in their classroom-based studies. In turn, Sue Scott's analysis of feminist research suggests that theory is not merely confined to the beginning or end of a research project when questions are framed and data analysis occurs, but that theoretical propositions constantly shape and reshape the whole of the research process.

Robert G. Burgess

B   *Issues in Data Collection*

In collecting data in educational settings researchers are often dealing with a familiar setting; a situation that especially arises when teachers collect data in their own schools and classrooms or in other school settings. In this situation, it is argued, there are distinct advantages as they will have a knowledge of local culture and a detailed knowledge of the setting will assist them in analyzing data (*cf.* Smith and Robbins, 1984). Yet, several investigators (Becker, 1971; Delamont, 1981; Spindler and Spindler, 1982) have warned of the problems of being too familiar with the setting under study. For example, Hilary Burgess and Carol Cummings both comment on the difficulties involved in teachers studying classroom settings and how easily assumptions can be made and situations taken for granted with the result that questions remain unanswered. Accordingly, they argue that research by teachers in classrooms provides opportunities to challenge what might normally be taken for granted in the day to day life of a school.

One aspect of her work that Hilary Burgess highlights is interviews conducted with peers. Here, she shows how it was essential to question statements that would normally have been taken for granted in a conversation with her teacher peers. In a similar way, Sue Scott argues that in interviewing women she found that she identified with the women as peers; a situation that calls for the researcher to think reflexively about the research process and the position that he or she takes in the conduct of an investigation (*cf.* Hammersley, 1983; Burgess, 1984b; Bell and Roberts, 1984).

It is this question of reflexivity on the part of the researcher that occurs in the discussion by Gordon Griffiths. Many classic investigators have indicated the importance that they attach to a research diary (*cf.* Malinowski, 1967; Webb and Webb, 1932) not only to record data but also to record their own actions and activities. It is in this sense that Griffiths uses a diary but he also points to the difficulties involved in working with a diary to study his own position in classroom and school (*cf.* Enright, 1981). Indeed, diaries are not easy for either the researcher or those who are researched, for Hilary Burgess indicates how the standard diary that has been advocated by several researchers (Burgess, 1981; Zimmerman and Wieder, 1977) cannot be applied simply to all educational settings but has to be modified to suit the situation at hand. Such evidence highlights the way in which the use of qualitative methods involves flexibility on the part of the researcher not only in collecting but also in analyzing data (see also Hammersley, Scarth and Webb, in this volume).

C   Issues in the Analysis and Dissemination of Data

In many texts and monographs devoted to qualitative methods it is relatively rare to find explicit discussions of the ways in which data are analyzed and in turn disseminated (for an exception see the papers in Blaxter, 1979). Such issues relate to the audience with whom the researcher is communicating and questions of writing style (*cf.* Hargreaves, 1982).

While Woods deals with issues concerning writing, several other of our researchers are concerned with relationships between the way in which data are analyzed and reported. Janet Finch, for example, discusses the need for the researcher to identify the audiences to which the research report will be directed, the ways in which the material can be used and the commitment of the researcher to those who are researched. Such issues are also dealt with in the papers by Sue Scott and by Alison Kelly who indicate the importance of maintaining good relationships between researcher and researched after the data collection is complete. However, Hilary Burgess shows that this is not always easy as the kinds of questions and styles of analysis used by the investigator may not be used by those who have participated in the study. Some researchers have argued that this problem may be overcome by means of respondent validation of the data that are collected (*cf.* Ball, 1984) or by giving those who are researched the right of veto over the dissemination of data. In these circumstances some compromise becomes essential. Among the proposals that exist in this volume is an idea advanced by Dave Ebbutt and by Margaret Threadgold for greater collaboration between researchers and teachers not merely over data collection but in establishing research questions at the start of a project and in analyzing data at other points in the research process; a situation that is illustrated in Carol Cummings' work. Meanwhile, Gordon Griffiths argues that teachers and researchers should not merely aim at collaboration but need to become partners in the research process (*cf.* Fujisaka and Grayzel, 1978). It is in such situations where alternative proposals arise that researchers are involved in compromise.

Robert G. Burgess

D   Issues of Compromise

Many of the issues that are discussed in the sections and in the papers in this volume search after solutions to research problems. Yet, at this point our researchers demonstrate that compromise is about all that remains for the researcher who utilizes qualitative methods (*cf.* Barnes, 1984). Among the points over which researchers need to work out compromises are:

(a) the role of theory in the research process;
(b) the relationship between theory, policy and practice;
(c) the relationship between data collection and data analysis;
(d) the question of dissemination and the ways in which research reports can be written for different audiences;
(e) the relationship between researchers and teachers who may work collaboratively or in partnership with each other.

Certainly, the papers that follow in this volume do not provide any instant answers to these issues. Nevertheless, it is to be hoped that the material which follows will contribute to debates about the place of qualitative methods in the study of education and to relationships between theory, policy and practice that might be brought closer together in qualitative projects devoted to the study of educational settings.

Notes

1 There have been a number of recent studies on primary and secondary schooling that use a qualitative approach. On the primary school see, for example, SHARP and GREEN (1975), HAMILTON (1977), KING (1978) GALTON and WILLCOCKS (1983), POLLARD (1985b). On secondary schools, see for example, HARGREAVES (1967), LACEY (1970), WOODS (1979), BALL (1981), TURNER (1982), BURGESS (1983). For examples of curriculum research using a qualitative approach see SHIPMAN (1974), GOODSON (1982).
2 In recent years there has been an increase in the number of books that specifically deal with qualitative methods in education.
   In Britain see SHIPMAN (1976), SIMONS (1980), ADELMAN (1981), HAMMERSLEY (1983), HAMMERSLEY and ATKINSON (1983), BURGESS (1984a, 1984b, 1985a and 1985b).
   In the USA see POPKEWITZ and TABACHNICK (1981), BOGDAN and BIKLEN (1982), SPINDLER (1982), FETTERMAN (1984), GOETZ and LE-COMPTE (1984).

Many of these books contain excellent bibliographies and should be consulted for detailed references to particular issues in the conduct of qualitative research.

References

ADELMAN, C. (Ed.) (1981) *Uttering, Muttering: Collecting Using and Reporting Talk for Social and Educational Research*, London, Grant McIntyre.

ARCHER, M.S. (1979) *The Social Origins of Educational Systems*, Beverley Hills, California, Sage.

ARCHER, M.S. (1981) 'Educational systems', *International Social Science Journal*, 33, 2, pp. 261–84

BALL, S.J. (1981) *Beachside Comprehensive: A Case Study of Secondary Schooling*, Cambridge, Cambridge University Press.

BALL, S.J. (1984) 'Beachside reconsidered: Reflections on a methodological apprenticeship', in BURGESS, R.G. (Ed.) *The Research Process in Educational Settings: Ten Case Studies*, Lewes, Falmer Press.

BANKS, O. (1978) 'School and society', in BARTON, L. and MEIGHAN, R. (Eds) *Sociological Interpretations of Schooling and Classrooms: A Reappraisal*, Driffield, Nafferton.

BARNES, J.A. (1984) 'Ethical and political compromises in social research', *Wisconsin Sociologist*, 21, 4, pp. 100–10.

BECHHOFER, F. (1967) 'Too many surveys', *New Society*, 245, pp. 838–9.

BECHHOFER, F. (1974) 'Current approaches to empirical research: Some central ideas', in REX, J. (Ed.) *Approaches to Sociology: An Introduction to Major Trends in British Sociology*, London, Routledge and Kegan Paul.

BECKER, H.S. (1971) 'Comment', in WAX, M., DIAMOND, S. and GEARING, F.O. (Eds) *Anthropological Perspectives on Education*, New York, Basic Books.

BECKER, H.S. and GEER, B. (1957) 'Participant observation and interviewing: A comparison', *Human Organization*, 16, pp. 28–32.

BELL, C. and ROBERTS, H. (Eds) (1984) *Social Researching: Politics, Problems, Practice*, London, Routledge and Kegan Paul.

BLAXTER, M. (Ed.) (1979) 'The analysis of qualitative data: A symposium', special issue of *Sociological Review*, 27, 4, pp. 649–827.

BOGDAN, R. and BIKLEN, S.K. (1982) *Qualitative Research for Education: An Introduction to Theory and Methods*, Boston, Allyn and Bacon.

BULMER, M. (Ed.) (1978) *Social Policy Research*, London, Macmillan.

BULMER, M. (1982) *The Uses of Social Research: Social Investigation in Public Policy Making*, London, Allen and Unwin.

BURGESS, R.G. (Ed.) (1980) 'Symposium on teacher based research', *Insight*, 3, 3.

BURGESS, R.G. (1981) 'Keeping a research diary', *Cambridge Journal of Education*, 11, 1, pp. 75–83.

Robert G. Burgess

BURGESS, R.G. (Ed.) (1982) *Field Research: A Sourcebook and Field Manual*, London, Allen and Unwin.

BURGESS, R. G. (1983) *Experiencing Comprehensive Education: A Study of Bishop McGregor School*, London, Methuen.

BURGESS, R.G. (1984a) *In the Field: An Introduction to Field Research*, London, Allen and Unwin.

BURGESS, R.G. (Ed.) (1984b) *The Research Process in Educational Settings: Ten Case Studies*, Lewes, Falmer Press.

BURGESS, R.G. (1984c) 'Patterns and processes of education in the United Kingdom', in ABRAMS, P. and BROWN, R. (Eds) *UK Society: Work, Urbanism and Inequality*, 2nd edn., London, Weidenfeld and Nicolson.

BURGESS, R.G. (Ed.) (1985a) *Field Methods in the Study of Education*, Lewes, Falmer Press.

BURGESS, R.G. (Ed.) (1985b) *Strategies of Educational Research: Qualitative Methods*, Lewes, Falmer Press.

BURGESS, R.G. (1985c) 'Documenting pastoral care: Strategies for teachers and researchers', in LANG, P. and MARLAND, M. (Eds) *New Directions in Pastoral Care*, Oxford, Basil Blackwell.

BURGESS, R.G. (1986) 'Education as a key variable', in BURGESS, R.G. (Ed.) *Key Variables in Social Investigation*, London, Routledge and Kegan Paul.

COHEN, L. and MANION, L. (1980) *Research Methods in Education*, London, Croom Helm.

CORBISHLEY, P. *et al.* (1981) 'Teacher strategies and pupil identities in mixed ability curricula: A note on concepts and some examples from maths', in BARTON, L. and WALKER, S. (Eds) *Schools, Teachers and Teaching* Lewes, Falmer Press.

DAINTON REPORT (1971) 'The future of the research council system', in *A Framework for Government Research and Development* (Cmnd 4184) London, HMSO.

DELAMONT, S. (1981) 'All too familiar? A decade of classroom research', *Educational Analysis*, 3, 1, pp. 69–83.

ELLIOTT, J. and ADELMAN, C. (1976) *Innovation at the Classroom Level: A Case Study of the Ford Teaching Project*, Unit 28 of the Curriculum Design and Development Course, Milton Keynes, Open University Press.

ENRIGHT, L. (1981) 'The diary of a classroom', in NIXON, J. (Ed.) *A Teacher's Guide to Action Research*, London, Grant McIntyre.

FETTERMAN, D. (Ed.) (1984) *Ethnography in Educational Evaluation*, Beverley Hills, California, Sage.

FUJISAKA, S. and GRAYZEL, J. (1978) 'Partnership research: A case of divergent ethnographic styles in prison research', *Human Organization* 37, 2, pp. 172–9.

GALTON, M. and WILLCOCKS, J. (Eds) (1983) *Moving From the Primary Classroom*, London, Routledge and Kegan Paul.

GEER, B. (1964) 'First days in the field', in HAMMOND, P. (Ed.) *Sociologists at Work*, New York, Basic Books.

GEER, B. (1970) 'Studying a college', in HABENSTEIN, R. (Ed.) *Pathways to Data*, Chicago, Aldine.

GLASER, B.G. (1978) *Theoretical Sensitivity*, San Fransisco, Sociology Press.

GLASER, B. and STRAUSS, A.L. (1967) *The Discovery of Grounded Theory*, London, Weidenfeld and Nicolson.

GLENNERSTER, H. and HOYLE, E. (1973) 'Educational research and educational policy', in TAYLOR, W. (Ed.) *Research Perspectives in Education*, London, Routledge and Kegan Paul.

GOETZ, J.P. and LECOMPTE, M.D. (1984) *Ethnography and Qualitative Design in Educational Research*, New York, Academic Press.

GOODSON, I.F. (1982) *School Subjects and Curriculum Change*, London, Croom Helm.

HALFPENNY, P. (1979) 'The analysis of qualitative data', *Sociological Review*, 27, 4, pp. 799–825.

HALSEY, A.H. (1974) 'Government against poverty in school and community', in WEDDERBURN, D. (Ed.) *Poverty, Inequality and Class Structure*, Cambridge, Cambridge University Press.

HAMILTON, D. (1977) *In Search of Structure*, London, Hodder and Stoughton.

HAMMERSLEY, M. (1983) *The Ethnography of Schooling*, Driffield, Nafferton.

HAMMERSLEY, M. (1984) 'Some reflections upon the macro-micro problem in the sociology of education', *Sociological Review*, 32, 2, pp. 316–24.

HAMMERSLEY, M. and ATKINSON, P. (1983) *Ethnography: Principles in Practice*, London, Tavistock.

HARGREAVES, D.H. (1967) *Social Relations in a Secondary School*, London, Routledge and Kegan Paul.

HARGREAVES, D.H. (1982) *The Challenge for the Comprehensive School: Class, Culture and Community*, London, Routledge and Kegan Paul.

KING, R. (1978) *All Things Bright and Beautiful? A Sociological Study of Infants' Classrooms*, London, Wiley.

LACEY, C. (1970) *Hightown Grammar: The School as a Social System*, Manchester, Manchester University Press.

McCORMICK, R. *et al.* (Eds) (1982) *Calling Education to Account*, London, Heinemann.

McCORMICK, R. and JAMES, M. (1983) *Curriculum Evaluation in Schools*, London, Croom Helm.

MALINOWSKI, B. (1967) *A Diary in the Strict Sense of the Term*, London, Routledge and Kegan Paul.

MORTIMORE, P. and BYFORD, D. (1981) 'Monitoring examination results within a local education authority', in PLEWIS, T. *et al.* (Eds) *Publishing School Examination Results: A Discussion, Bedford Way Papers*, 5, London, University of London Institute of Education.

NIXON, J. (Ed.) (1981) *A Teacher's Guide to Action Research*, London, Grant McIntyre.

POLLARD, A. (1985a) 'Opportunities and difficulties of a teacher-ethnographer', in BURGESS, R.G. (Ed.) *Field Methods in the Study of Education*, Lewes, Falmer Press.

POLLARD, A. (1985b) *The Social World of the Primary School*, Eastbourne, Holt, Rinehart and Winston.

POPKEWITZ, T.S. and TABACHNICK, B.R. (Eds) (1981) *The Study of School-*

ing: Field Based Methodologies in Educational Research and Evaluation, New York, Praeger.

RIST, R. (1984) 'On the application of qualitative research to the policy process: an emergent linkage', in BARTON, L. and WALKER, S. (Eds) *Social Crisis and Educational Research*, London, Croom Helm.

ROBERTS, H. (Ed.) (1981) *Doing Feminist Research*, London, Routledge and Kegan Paul.

ROTHSCHILD, LORD, (1971) 'The organization and management of government R and D', in *A Framework for Government Research and Development* (Cmnd 4184) London, HMSO.

SCHATZMAN, L. and STRAUSS, A.L. (1973) *Field Research: Strategies for a Natural Sociology*, Englewood Cliffs, New Jersey, Prentice Hall.

SHARP, R. and GREEN, A. (1975) *Education and Social Control*, London, Routledge and Kegan Paul.

SHIPMAN, M. (1974) *Inside a Curriculum Project*, London, Methuen.

SHIPMAN, M. (Ed.) (1976) *The Organization and Impact of Social Research*, London, Routledge and Kegan Paul.

SHIPMAN, M. (1985) 'Ethnography and educational policy', in BURGESS, R.G. (Ed.) *Field Methods in the Study of Education*, Lewes, Falmer Press.

SIMONS, H. (Ed.) (1980) *Towards a Science of the Singular*, Norwich, Centre for Applied Research in Education, University of East Anglia, Occasional Publication No. 10.

SMITH, A.G. and ROBBINS, A.E. (1984) 'Multimethod policy research: A case study of structure and flexibility', in FETTERMAN, D. (Ed.) *Ethnography in Educational Evaluation*, Beverley Hills, California, Sage.

SPINDLER, G.D. (Ed.) (1982) *Doing the Ethnography of Schooling: Educational Anthropology in Action*, New York, Holt, Rinehart and Winston.

SPINDLER, G.D. and SPINDLER, L. (1982) 'Roger Harker and Schönhausen: From the familiar to the strange and back again', in SPINDLER, G.D. (Ed.) *Doing the Ethnography of Schooling: Educational Anthropology in Action*, New York, Holt, Rinehart and Winston.

STANLEY, L. and WISE, E. (1983) *Breaking Out*, London, Routledge and Kegan Paul.

STENHOUSE, L. (1975) *An Introduction to Curriculum Research and Development*, London, Heinemann.

STENHOUSE, L. (Ed.) (1980) *Curriculum Research and Development in Action*, London, Heinemann.

STENHOUSE, L., VERMA, G.K., WILD, R.D. and NIXON, J. (1982) *Teaching About Race Relations*, London, Routledge and Kegan Paul.

TAYLOR, W. (Ed.) (1973) *Research Perspectives in Education*, London, Routledge and Kegan Paul.

TROW, M. (1957) 'Comment on "participant observation and interviewing: a comparison"', *Human Organization*, 16, 3, pp. 33–5.

TURNER, G. (1982) *The Social World of the Comprehensive School*, London, Croom Helm.

WAX, R.H. (1971) *Doing Field Work: Warnings and Advice*, Chicago, University of Chicago Press.

WEBB, S. and WEBB, B. (1932) *Methods of Social Study*, London, Longmans.

WOODS, P. (1979) *The Divided School*, London, Routledge and Kegan Paul.

ZELDITCH, M. (1962) 'Some methodological problems of field studies', *American Journal of Sociology*, 67, pp. 566–76, reprinted in BURGESS, R.G. (1982) (Ed.) *Field Research: A Sourcebook and Field Manual*, London, Allen and Unwin.

ZIMMERMAN, D.H. and WIEDER, D.L. (1977) 'The diary: diary-interview method', *Urban Life*, 5, 4, pp. 479–98.

Part One
Issues in Theory
and Method

2 The Micro-Macro Problem in the Sociology of Education

Andy Hargreaves

Organized education is a highly political affair. It shapes and channels life opportunities, it opens up and blocks off careers for those who work within it, it draws heavily on scarce resources from the state budget, and it is subject to a range of competitive pressures from all sectors of society. One does not have to be a sociologist to appreciate this point. Since the late 1970s, cuts in educational expenditure and their effect on the everyday practices of teaching and learning have become a matter of widespread public concern (HMI, 1982). And a whole range of new initiatives to bring about a fundamental restructuring of the educational system, through the provision of assisted places in independent schools, the development of programmes of vocational education and training for less able 14–19 year olds, and the mooting of educational voucher schemes, have all served to heighten public consciousness about the extent to which state provided education is saturated with political significance. For the public at large, education is, in this sense, being subjected to increasing politicization (Hunter, 1983; Dale, 1979; Bush and Kogan, 1982). But for those of us who are fortunate enough to continue earning our living as sociologists of education, these policy changes and their implications for school practice only emphasize in a particularly dramatic way what should perhaps always be at the heart of our professional concern in any case; the explanation of everyday school practices in the context of their wider outcomes and determinants. Among professional sociologists of education the understanding of such connections has come to be known as *the micro-macro problem.*

The micro-macro problem is central to much sociological theorizing of a general kind where it has been taken up in a particularly creative way by such writers as Giddens (1976 and 1979) and Habermas (1976). Nor is it confined to sociology and its derivative sub-disciplines. In the physical sciences, for instance, practitioners have worried for a long time about the troublesome connection between those 'macro' objects given to our sense experience — planets, pendulums and the like — and the sub-atomic micro-particles with which much current theoretical physics is concerned (note here that it is the *micro* objects which cannot be apprehended through immediate sense experience). Our concern here, however, is with the sociology of education, and that is where I shall focus my attention. Here, the micro-macro problem has been the subject of a great deal of theoretical debate, though not much empirical research, since the mid 1970s onwards. Until that point, the sociology of education had been broadly divided into two broad camps — into somewhat insulated small-scale empirical studies of teacher-pupil interaction, pupil sub-cultures and so on on the one hand, and ambitious, speculative, grand theoretical explanations of the relation-ship between schooling and society on the other. The sociology of education, in other words, was segregated into what might be called studies of the schools and studies of 'the system'. Hardly any attempts, it seems, were made to connect the two.

Furthermore, from the relative security of their respective camps, the students of the schools and the scholars of the system made sniping criticisms of each others' work. On the one hand, classroom researchers were strongly criticized for their idealism and 'bourgeois individualism', for the emphasis that writers like Keddie (1973) placed on the possibility that educational change might be brought about through raising individual rather than class conscious-ness. Michael Young and Geoff Whitty, for instance, (1977) in their introduction to a collection of Marxist readings in the sociology of education, complained that 'Many classroom studies, seem to present education as being carried on in a social vacuum.' (p. 7)

But if 'micro' researchers often seemed, like ostriches, to be so preoccupied with the fine-grained detail of school and classroom life, that they rarely took their heads out of the sand to see what was happening in the world outside, theorists of 'the system' appeared all too often to have little contact with the 'real world' at all. As David Hargreaves (1978) put it in his paper with the pleading title 'Whatever happened to symbolic interactionism?'

> Marxist positions appear to offer a new 'paradigm shift' in which sociologists of education in their disturbing flight from the empirical can indulge in polemical pieces which take the format of 'a critique of position X from a Marxist perspective'

through which theoretical kudos is achieved without getting
one's hands dirty with research.

Not everyone was happy with this state of affairs though, and a
number of writers, including myself, began to advocate a synthesis of
'micro' and 'macro' approaches, a binding together of those parts of
the discipline which had hitherto been separate. Their arguments
took many different forms, not least, as I shall go on to show, because
there was a good deal of uncertainty and confusion about what
exactly it was that was being connected. But one general view ran
through all their recommendations — that each approach had something to offer the other, and that together, they might help us
understand a little better how society shapes and is in turn shaped by
the schooling system.

Spirited and impassioned as they were though, the various
appeals were also extremely unclear about what kinds of bridges
needed to be built (Hargreaves, A. 1980). They gave little indication
of what was to be joined together and *how* any synthesis was to be
achieved. At some points, the synthesizers appeared, myself included,
to be proposing links between different levels of reality, between
patterns of educational structure and the texture of daily life. At other
points, the bridge was a theoretical and conceptual one, between
different ways of looking at reality, between 'interpretative' and
'normative' approaches. And David Hargreaves' disdainful remarks
about the unwillingness of macro theorists to venture from their
ivory towers and 'get their hands dirty' with empirical research
suggests yet another kind of connection — between theory and
evidence. In pleas for synthesis, these different possibilities with their
own particular difficulties have typically been run together. What we
have come to know as the micro-macro problem actually subsumes
them all (and more besides). It is not, in that sense, one problem, but
several. Not surprisingly, then, when all the various difficulties have
been compounded together, that problem has often seemed to be
insuperable; just too formidable a challenge to one's time, energy and
imagination as an educational researcher. While I myself sought to
unravel some of these difficulties by developing and giving some
empirical illustrations of the concept of *coping strategy*, and while
indeed Olive Banks (1982) in her review of thirty years of the
sociology of education concluded that such bridging concepts point
to important ways forward for the discipline, it is now clear to me
that I have been just as remiss as my colleagues in specifying with
due precision what the making of 'micro-macro' connections entails

— at some points implying that this involves linking 'structural questions to interactionist concerns' and at others suggesting it as a matter of analyzing how 'classroom matters may relate to the nature of the socioeconomic and political structure' (Hargreaves, A. 1978).

In view of the vagueness of guidelines for synthesis, then, it is not altogether surprising that in recent years, barring a few important exceptions, the sociology of education has become even more strongly characterized by a proliferation of approaches, its proponents becoming ever more firmly entrenched in their own camps, confined to their own 'problematics', blissfully or wilfully ignorant or dismissive of the literature and research findings being produced by their opponents (Hammersley, 1984a). While, in the late 1970s there were at least brief skirmishes between members of the different camps, stereotyped, distorted and hostile as they were, they did at least amount to some kind of communication. What is sadder is that with the cessation of theoretical hostilities, so too has there been an ending to communication. In this sense, perhaps too many of us have settled for the theoretically easier life. By and large, interactionists have gone back to their classrooms and staffrooms, while macro theorists have moved into 'the state' and educational policy. When the current and intensifying educational crisis and its effects on schooling begs decent sociological explanation, this unproductive division of theoretical labour is, in my view, regrettable.

In the rest of the chapter, therefore, I want to try and outline and clarify just three of the different dimensions which make up the micro-macro problem, to outline the problems contained in each, to assess how well these problems have been dealt with in existing studies devoted to making micro-macro connections, and to suggest how these problems might be overcome.

1 Theory and Evidence

The first interpretation of the micro-macro link is that which sees it in terms of the relationship between theory and evidence. It is on this very dimension that much influential Marxist scholarship has 'written off' the possibility of any micro-macro project at all, or interpreted it as involving the subsumption of (usually ethnographic) data within a broadly unquestioned Marxist theory. Since this position is both an influential and controversial one, and since it raises most of the issues concerning the difficulties of relating theory to evidence, I shall concentrate on it here.

One of the most extensive sociological objections to the general worth and possibility of micro-macro work has been advanced by Louis Althusser. Basically, Althusser (1977) indicts those adhering to what he calls an *empiricist* position for advancing *experience* as the ultimate reference point for all knowledge claims about the world. The problem with this, Althusser contends, is that such experience is inescapably suffused with ideological meaning and for that reason cannot provide an adequate discourse of proof (pp. 183–4). Being blind to the ideologically loaded character of their 'evidence', empiricists, Althusser contends, falsely equate the object of their knowledge with the 'real world' object to which it relates. They confuse appearances with reality, that is (for example, Althusser and Balibar, 1970, p. 133). Instead, Althusser proposes, what the social scientist ought to do is purge the 'facts' or 'evidence' with which the theorist is presented of their ideological content, to reveal their inner truth. This, he suggests, can only be achieved by the use of theoretical procedures *alone*, and, much as in mathematics, it is the inner logic of these procedures, not the ideologically-laden world of 'experience', that provides the only acceptable criterion of proof.

Althusser outlines these views in the context of general sociological theory, but interpretations deriving from them have made their mark within the sociology of education too. Rachel Sharp (1980) for instance, has taken issue with the 'retreat into empiricism, the collection of a mass of data and its analysis in terms of low level hypotheses which ultimately do little more than reproduce a more articulated version of common-sense'. And Kevin Harris (1982) in his Marxist analysis of *Teachers and Classes* offers an even more elaborate defence

> All investigations and analyses are made from the perspective of some particular theory or theories: they are theory-dependent or theory laden, and this is so regardless of whether or not the underlying theory is declared, admitted to, or spelt out. There can be no such thing as a neutral examination, or an examination which is objective either in the sense that it is a-theoretic or else sufficiently eclectic so as to encompass all theoretical perspectives ...
>
> The theory-ladenness of investigation gives rise to a large number of methodological issues and problems, and it is hardly our purpose to discuss these here. On the other hand, it is our purpose to undertake an investigation, and this we shall do by ... casting our investigation into the context

of a research programme (or problematic) wherein certain basic or 'hard core' hypotheses and propositions are accepted as being secure and inviolable for the purpose of operating or working with the research programme.

Having laid the philosophical groundwork, Harris then sets out how he proposes to conduct his own research.

The investigation which follows here is carried out within the framework of Marxism or historical materialism, and thus certain 'hard core' propositions of that theory or research programme, propositions regarding the nature of the State, the nature of classes, and the role of class struggle, for example, will form the basis for our investigation: that is, they themselves will not be argued for here (they are being accepted as viable starting points because a wealth of previous argument, along with practical outcomes, has established their value for investigations of social relations).

Now Harris makes a number of appeals here as to why we should accept his claims about the relationship between theory and evidence. Setting aside his exceedingly shaky appeals to 'traditional authority', to the previous, unnamed work of anonymous writers of supposed erudition, I shall concentrate on the other two: the appeal to the irreconcilability of 'problematics' and the appeal to pragmatism.

(a)   *The Irreconcilability of Problematics*

Harris claims that theoretical 'problematics' are irreconcilable, providing different possible starting points for analysis, the soundness of which is to be judged by the logical consistency of the argument that follows. In response to this, it is important to state at the outset that few sociologists would dispute the contention that the adequecy of a theory is dependent upon its logical consistency and internal coherence. Alfred Schutz and Max Weber, for instance, placed great stress on the fact that explanations ought to follow the postulate of adequacy at the level of meaning *and* that of logical consistency.

However, these selfsame sociologists would almost certainly add the rider that logical consistency is only a *necessary*, not a *sufficient* criterion of proof. As E.P. Thompson (1978) states, there are 'other (and equally difficult) procedures of research, experiment and of the intellectual appropriation of the real world, without which the secondary (but important) critical procedures would have neither meaning nor existence' (p. 203). Indeed, without these procedures how would we *know* that capitalist states are *really* as Marxist writers describe them, or if there is any such thing as a 'capitalist state' at all? These should not be resources for analysis but central topics for critical and searching inquiry, not least because if they are not, if state and class struggle remain immune from questioning and justification, it is likely that all but the already converted — the left intelligentsia — will switch off. Empirical research, of one kind or another, then, (though obviously the more rigorous the better), is ultimately indispensable to sustained theoretical advance.

Admittedly it has to be said that a good deal of empirical research is far from rigorous, and if it were brought to Althusser's court of theoretical enquiry, it would quite rightly be found guilty (even if the court were one where 'ignorance of the law' of theory-ladenness did not count as a defence). The highly fashionable and heavily funded tradition of abstracted empiricism, much favoured by certain kinds of psychologist, where masses of data are avidly collected and computed, then generalizations (barely worthy of the designation 'theory') abstracted from them, would certainly be extremely vulnerable to most of the charges that Althusser makes against empiricism — since the very selection of possible variables is based on unexplicated theories of possible causation (for example, Bennett, 1976; Rutter, *et al.*, 1979; Galton, Simon and Croll, 1980). So, as I have argued elsewhere (Hargreaves, 1981) could many ethnographic studies of school life be criticized for adopting a posture of 'splendid isolation', a false claim that their analyses of micro-settings like classrooms and staffrooms are uncontaminated by assumptions about the workings of the wider society when, in fact, they are in many cases based on a loose commitment to pluralist values (for example, Woods, 1979). Furthermore, many of those studies which attempt to link detailed accounts of school processes to 'macro' theories about the operations of social structure would also fare badly against the Althusserian critique. In the details of analysis, they rarely communicate a sense of data having been scrupulously checked, of disconfirming cases having been searched for, and so on (e.g. Sharp and Green, 1975; Willis, 1977; Anyon, 1981). But the real irony in all this, is that those studies which appear to have been *most* susceptible to the selecting and squeezing of data in order to fit a preconceived theory, i.e. those which seem to be most open to the charges of 'empiricism' laid out by Althusser, are not, as Sharp (1980) alleges, 'bourgeois' and 'liberal' at all, but Marxist (Hargreaves, A, 1982).

To be candid, then, educational research, whether Marxist or non-Marxist is often much less rigorous than it ought to be. But this offers no warrant for discarding *all* empirical research as worthless. The best empirical work does *not*, as Althusser contends, use and interpret evidence uncritically, but treats it as constantly problematic. Empirical work of high quality consists of a continuing *dialogue* between theory and evidence where each is continually interrogated against the other *as well as* being tested for its internal consistency and coherence. It is only through such a dialogue that understandings of the social world can ever come to approximate to valid knowledge. Indeed, the greatest impediment to the achievement of such knowledge is the total immersion of the researcher within the worlds of either empirical evidence (empiricism) or 'pure' theory (theoreticism — as in Althusser's work).

Of course, Althusser is correct in saying that evidence is selected, that it is not neutral and self-evident, but produced for particular audiences and purposes. And many ethnographic researchers, it must be said, have too often overlooked the point, failing to note for instance, that what teachers say to researchers during a brief interview may differ from what they say to one another or even from what they puzzle about themselves (Sharp and Green, 1975). Althusser is also right to alert us to the ever-present danger that the theorist's identification and interpretation of data will reflect his or her particular theoretical and value orientations and that the resulting explanations will therefore be prone to ideological contamination. The crucial point, however, is that few empirical researchers would dispute these charges. Moreover, at their best, empirical researchers actually take account of these difficulties in their analyses — they can note the audiences for which documents were produced and deduce the political significance of this fact, they can check out the contaminating influence of their theoretical preferences by actively seeking out disconfirming cases in the data that would challenge their initial prejudices and hunches through cross-referencing (triangulating) different kinds of data on the same topic, or comparing different methods (observation and interview, for instance) in order to check the consistency of what a particular teacher or pupil says between settings, or triangulating the interpretations that different observers make of the same data, and so on (Denzin, 1970; Hammersley, 1979). The processes of analytic induction (Robinson, 1952) or grounded theorizing (Glaser and Strauss, 1967) contain similar procedures for checking the validity of interpretations. And as David Hargreaves (1981) and Pollard (1982) point out, such procedures might be included in forms of ethnographic enquiry directed towards testing theory too, and not just generating it.

Ethnographic practice is, of course, not always, or not even usually, as the handbooks tell us. In a sophisticated defence of the very possibility of Marxist ethnography, for instance, West (1984) criticizes the practice of British educational ethnography in general and of Marxist ethnographies of writers like Willis (1977) in particular on this count. He takes issue with Willis especially for 'spot welding' a Marxist analysis with descriptive ethnographic material. Similarly, one might say that in the case of Woods' (1979) *Divided School*, the author's Weberian claim that the teachers and pupils he studied were trapped within and trying to break free from institutional pressures brought about by increasing bureaucratization and growing disenchantment in society as a whole are also 'bolted on' to the descriptive accounts of subject choice, the typologies of pupil adaptation and teacher survival and so on.

Fortunately there are emerging signs that these weaknesses might now be on the wane as the principal figures involved in the first exploratory phase of British educational ethnography move into a second wave of research, where, aware of their errors and anxious to remedy them, they can produce studies which are more rigorous, tightly focused and theoretically informed than their first efforts (Hammersley, 1980; Woods, 1985; Pollard, 1984). The switch of emphasis is, to be fair, but a glint in the ethnographer's eye at the moment, but it remains to be seen if Marxist ethnographers are willing, at least, to recognize the importance of this challenge too. In this respect, West's (1984) injunctions for greater methodological rigour within Marxist ethnography are both provocative and encouraging. But one would hope here that the interest in testing and therefore in being sceptical about prior theoretical claims will extend not only to the details of analysis, to the characteristics of particular pupil cultures and so on, but will extend to those central concepts and categories, those fundamental domain assumptions, those commitments to a particular view of the social totality, to which West and many of his Marxist colleagues (for example, Wright, 1979) curiously seem to want to attach continued privileged status, to keep immune from and above methodological test, to leave unthreatened by the possibility of incorrectness. If the interrogation of theory with evidence and vice versa is to have any meaning, then, the most basic assumptions of the paradigm (Marxist, Weberian, or otherwise) must be left open to doubt (Hammersley, 1984a), otherwise the supposed validity of our analyses will rest only ignore on the force of our beliefs, in which case we are likely to continue preaching only to the converted.

That such procedures of checking and testing *are* possible rests on the fact that while the interpretations of phenomena can and often do reflect the theoretical predilections of the researcher, the range of possible explanations is not entirely limitless, not completely the product of theoretical/ideological bias; for the object itself as a real object places definite limits on the interpretations that can be made of it (Thompson, 1978, p. 210). Thus, had Althusser set with Willis' lads at Hammertown Secondary School, he might have been able to view their conduct as 'larking about', institutional defiance or class resistance, but I sincerely doubt whether he would have been able to sustain his claims about how working-class pupils conform to the demands of their teachers in preparation for their role in the workplace.

Maintaining a dialogue between theory and evidence therefore demands both theoretical creativity *and* rigorous methodological checking in a context which credits the 'real world' with some potential to impose itself upon the way we think about it. It should be stressed that a great many empirical researchers, whether historians of education of ethnographers of schooling, for instance, would see themselves as contributing to just this sort of enterprise. The major flaw in the Althusserian critique and its derivatives in educational study is that this important tradition of theoretically imaginative and methodologically cautious work which is cast in an *empirical mode*, is confused with a quite narrow *empiricism* (which rests on the view that knowledge claims are valid only if tested against the 'irrefutable' data of our sense experience) (Thompson, 1978, pp. 63–4 and p. 198). Whether this deceit is an innocent or a guilty one is impossible to say, but it is a deceit nonetheless, and one which has constituted a sizeable barrier to the advancement of sociological understanding in all fields of enquiry including education. It is perhaps salutary to note that Marx himself was, at one point in his writings at least, much less confused by this distinction. He drew a clear dividing line between shallow *empiricism* and well-conducted *empirical research*. In the *German Ideology*, he argued that ...

> Empirical observation must in each separate instance bring out empirically, and without any mystification and speculation, the connection of the social and political structure with production. The social structure and the state are continually evolving out of the life process of definite individuals, how-

ever, of these individuals, not as they may appear in their own or other people's imagination, but as they *actually* are, i.e. as they act, produce materially, and hence as they work under definite material limits, presuppositions and conditions in-dependent of their will ... This manner of approach is not devoid of premises. It starts out from the premises and does not abandon them for a moment. Its premises are men, not in any fantastic isolation and fixity, but in their actual, empirically perceptible process of development under definite conditions. As soon as this active life process is described history ceases to be a collection of dead facts, as it is with the empiricists, or an imagined activity of imagined subjects, as with the idealists. Where speculation ends, where real life starts, there consequently begins real positive science, the expounding of the practical activity, of the practical process of the development of men ... (Marx and Engels, 1976, pp. 35–7)

What is interesting about the comments of Marx and Engels here is that their defence of the role of empirical observation is made not just against a quite narrow empiricism, but also against 'speculation' and 'mystification' which, at the time Marx was writing, were characteristic defects of German Idealism. The irony of this second part of their argument, though, is that as well as being an effective attack on German Idealism, it now amounts to a trenchant critique of the speculative character of much contemporary neo-Marxist writing, and its refusal to acknowledge the admissability of empirical evidence.

Paradoxically, the theoreticist position with its refusal to take account of empirical evidence actually allows the most iniquitous kind of empiricism of all to creep in, in the shape of unacknowleged, unexamined, and unchecked assumptions of what, as a result of the capitalist system, 'really' happens in schools and elsewhere. Althusser and his followers, that is, have indulged in some of the worst empiricist excesses of all — erecting whole theoretical edifices on the basis of unacknowledged and unchecked assumptions — leading to what some have rightly called an 'indefensible dogmatism' (Culter *et al.*, 1977, p. 211). Indeed, in one of the more extreme instances of this, a scathing critique of 'uncontexted' ethnography, by Rachel Sharp (1982), not a single example of the kind of work she is taking issue with is cited. Instead, she presents us merely with her own *imaginary* ethnographic account of a Facist school in Nazi Germany, and the political context of that school which the account would allegedly ignore. If uncontexted ethnography really is as defective as Sharp claims, could she not have found a single example of 'bad' practice to support her case? Why should she feel the need to fall back on an (albeit dramatic) fictional case rather than a real one to provide her burden of proof? And if such neglect and fictionalized critiques run through her assessments of alternative research traditions whose texts and arguments are tangible and easily accessible, what faith can we reasonably have in her similarly unsupported claims about the nature and functions of schooling?

Judging by the work of both Sharp and Althusser, then, it seems that unbridled theoretical speculation and assertion offers a most suitable environment for crude empiricism to flourish[1].

(b) Pragmatic Necessity

If the objections in principle to incoherent theoreticism and vulgar empiricism seem well founded, if the ideal case for a carefully nurtured *rapprochement* between theory and evidence seems well made, that task may still be impeded by strong and perhaps insurmountable practical difficulties. In this sense, one might say, with Harris (1982), that while a rigorous dialogue between theory and evidence, a dialogue which involves adjudicating between competing theories as well as modifying existing ones, is desirable in an ideal world where researchers have unlimited resources of time, money and energy, in practice, a choice has to be made between one seemingly arbitrary set of concepts and categories and another on *pragmatic* grounds.

There is something in this. For one thing, at the 'micro' end of the research scale in studies of face-to-face interaction and so on, it is not possible, as ethnomethodologists discovered to their cost, to deal with all data literally and exhaustively, to notice and interpret every word, every gesture, every glance that passes between participants. Nor are these difficulties resolved by adopting increasingly sophisticated techniques of recording, such as videotape, for while such techniques may increase the amount of data we have available, this in turn only magnifies the problem of selecting which data we should attend to, and of how those data, those forms of talk and gesture, should then be interpreted. Attempts at providing entirely presuppositionless accounts of such phenomena have not been promising, and while a certain degree of reflexivity in our accounts, while deep awareness of why we interpret the data this way and not that, is to be applauded, there does come a point when the reflexivity has to stop, when some working assumptions, however provisional, have to be made in order to organize the data into some coherent, intelligible form. This is what David Hargreaves and his colleagues (1975) discovered, for instance, when they tried to provide an assumption-free account of classroom rules. In the end, they found it necessary, on practical grounds, to construct what they called a 'working platform', a theoretical model of the rule system, against which their observations could then be compared. At the 'micro' end, then, there *are* times, even in the most methodologically rigorous research, when the reflexivity has to stop; when working assumptions must be *made*, however provisionally.

Similarly, it is also expedient, indeed necessary, to make arbitrary cut-off points at the 'macro' end of the scale too. Many writers have spoken of the importance of situating small-scale ethnographic accounts of particular aspects of school life in a larger context that takes account of the structural pressures that move the school and its participants one way and not another (Sharp, 1980; Apple, 1979 and 1982; Harris, 1982; Pollard, 1984). And elsewhere I have rekindled Mills' (1959) conception of the sociological imagination as a way of encouraging sociologists of education to 'grasp the richness of personal and interpersonal experience', while also noting the ways in which social structures impinge upon and partially shape the organization of peoples' everyday lives' (Hargreaves, A., 1981, p. 162). However, persuasive as they might sound, these appeals leave unanswered the vital question of just how far this process of situating should go. Should the internal processes of schooling be placed in the context of the local community, the demands and pressures of the local education authority, changes in the local economy and so on? And should these local patterns in turn be related to changes at the national level — to the nature of class struggle, the requirements of the economic mode of production, the nature and demands of the capitalist state and the extent of its dependence on and independence from the capitalist economy? But why stop there? For states, economies and politics are not insulated systems, but part of a vast and complexly interconnected global pattern — in which case, it might be argued, studies of pupil peer groups, staffroom cultures, teaching methods, subject subcultures and so on, should perhaps be related not just to the local and national context, but to the whole social totality (Sharp, 1980), to the entire world system, no less (Wallerstein 1974).

For researchers whose immediate concern (and the thing for

which they have been funded) might be something as specific as 'gifted children', the establishment of tertiary colleges, pupil profiles or whatever, this is clearly a daunting prospect. For one thing, data on some parts of the 'world system', on some non-capitalist modes of production, for instance, may be severely restricted. Nor, given the shortness of our lives and the finite nature of human effort, would it be feasible, even if such data were available, to show the extent to which and ways in which schools in all known societies produced patterns of reproduction and/or resistance to the social, political and economic orders in which they were located. And again, from a practical perspective, there are clear limits to just how many concepts can be rigorously interrogated for their validity in any particular study, just as there are to the exhaustiveness of that interrogation. Moreover, as cartographers of the social world, we must also be mindful of the mapmaker's dilemma — that the more complex and comprehensive our maps become, the more closely they resemble the actual territories they represent, the less useful they serve as guides through it.

For a host of sound practical reasons then, some things must be left out. Neither the world system, nor the smallest interactional encounter can be described in their entire complexity, nor is it obvious that they should be. Life, as they say, is simply too short.

Faced with such awesome tasks of macro-micro integration, of interrogating theory with evidence and vice versa, a solution recommended by Hammersley (1980) begins to sound extremely attractive. What Hammersley suggests is that 'any piece of research should be explicity directed predominantly towards' one of four different areas — *micro-formal* (for example, the rules of conversation), *micro-substantive* (for example, differentiation and polarization of pupils), *macro-formal* (for example, the division of labour) and *macro-substantive* (for example, the history of education in France). Turner (1983) seems to interpret this as implying a policy of 'live and let live' — 'you do your research and I'll do mine!' — a policy which would allow us all to sleep more soundly in our beds (or under them!). Turner argues:

> It is surely quite legitimate to pursue a particular project from a particular standpoint, such as interactionism, whilst accepting that this work will have deficiencies which can be compensated for by other researchers perhaps from a different theoretical standpoint... Indeed it seems naive to assume that any research project could achieve anything other than a

partial explanation of the workings of society. Thus what is important about a piece of research is not so much its scope, but its validity. (pp. 4–5)

This, it seems to me, is a naive solution. It promotes the misleading idea that work located in different traditions will somehow 'add up' to produce a more rounded picture of schooling or whatever. And it implies, as a characteristic piece of 'splendid isolation' that matters of scope are unrelated to matters of validity when, as I have noted, and as Turner's own study of 'conformist' pupils illustrates, interactionist studies of schools and classrooms, by ignoring the context in which their 'cases' are situated, often exaggerate the moment by moment fluidity and variability, the pluralistic diversity of pupil conduct. Moreover, having recognized the impossibility of achieving total integration of theories, Turner's solution, his policy of 'separate development' is of dubious virtue for it is likely to lead not to greater understanding between the adherents of different perspectives, but to a reinforcement of theoretical prejudice and intolerance.

Actually, what Hammersley proposes is more subtle than Turner suggests. Hammersley's argument is for work focused *predominantly* at one level, but sensitive to work in other traditions pitched at other levels, too (see also, Hammersley, 1984b). In this sense it would not be unreasonable to expect interactionist researchers who are studying deviance and disruption to take account of Marxist work on pupil resistance, for instance (and vice versa), and to make some attempt to argue through the continuities and discontinuities that arise from such a comparison. Similarly, it is fair to ask that the validity and utility of some of the most contestable concepts that sociologists of education use, like 'state', should be justified against competing ones. Clearly, it is not possible to explain everything, but we should not use this as an excuse to bury our heads in small-scale empirical studies, or to become exclusively preoccupied with speculation about the nature of 'the social totality'. Though we cannot say everything, the solution is not to say almost nothing. There may be disagreements about just how far we should be sensitive to one another's work, about the number of competing perspectives and concepts we should take on board when justifying our own and so on, but the case for heightening that sensitivity, for leaving at least some of our concepts open to question and to empirical test is clearly very strong. Theory and evidence, that is, do have something to say to one another. They should be allowed to do so.

Some time ago, in his essay on 'The bearing of sociological theory on empirical research', Robert Merton (1968) 'pointed to the need for a closer connection between theory and empirical research'. 'The prevailing division of the two', he argued

> ... is manifested in marked *discontinuities* of empirical research, on the one hand, and systematic theorizing un-sustained by empirical test on the other. There are conspicu-ously few instances of consecutive research which have cumulatively investigated a succession of hypotheses derived from a given theory. (pp. 153–4)

'It is a commonplace', Merton concluded, 'that continuity can be achieved only if empirical studies are theory-oriented and if theory is empirically confirmable'. How sad it is, then, *pace* Althusser, Sharp and Harris, that this commonplace still needs to be reasserted.

2 Micro Theory — Macro Theory

In educational research, as in other forms of social enquiry, then, it is important to connect theory with evidence and to modify each accordingly if they do not fit. It would be a mistake to infer from this, however, that evidence is necessarily 'micro' and provides a testing ground for theory which is necessarily 'macro'. Statistical generali-zations which point to the tendential characteristics of whole collect-ivities, to the social origins of university students, or to the destina-tions of secondary modern as against grammar school pupils (Halsey, Heath and Ridge, 1980), for instance, are not at all 'micro' in character. Similarly, not all theory is what Mills (1959) called Grand theory: interrelated propositions on a vast scale about whole socie-ties, their forms of economic organization and so on. Many theories are, in fact, directed to 'micro' concerns — to aspects of interpersonal relations, peer group dynamics and the like.

In clearing up this possible muddle, I am, of course, now raising a further distinction between micro and macro, one which lies within theory itself. The contrast between micro and macro in this sense is between explanations of social behaviour and interaction in particular settings like classrooms or staffrooms on the one hand, and explana-tions of supra-individual forces like social classes and the state which are more than aggregates of the individuals which make them up, and which transcend particular settings on the other. Some might see this as the difference between interaction and structure, but that would be a misleading distinction, for it is not only things like classes and economies that have structures, but forms of interaction too, as in structures of conversational turn taking or of classroom discourse.

How, then, do micro and macro theory interconnect? Can they be so connected? And if so, by what mechanisms? These are surely important questions for anyone who is attempting to deal with the problem of micro-macro integration. But before they can be treated properly, there is a more fundamental issue still that must be tackled — the serious allegation that macro theory may be of no worth at all, that it is just an assemblage of unverifiable speculation which ought not to be treated seriously. According to this view, the objects of macro theory are not real but simply fictionalized products of the fertile imaginations of those sociologists who, as Merton (1968, p. 139) puts it 'seek the grandeur of global summaries'. Thus, Paul Rock argues that:

> In a rigorous scheme, it is impossible to derive a totality from the partial and ambiguous fragments which are alone available to observational science... Interactionism discards most macro-sociological thought as an unsure and over-ambitious metaphysics. It claims that the realm described by macro sociology is not open to intelligent examination.

Macro sociology, then, allegedly refers to a realm which lies outside of, or beyond, direct observation, and is, therefore, either unknowable or non-existent. This view has been echoed by a number of ethnomethodologists who have likewise discarded the idea that macro theories refer to anything of substance in the real world, and instead have used these theories only as an occasion for investigating the peculiar practices in which social scientists engage when they go about the business of theorising (Philippson, 1972). But one of the clearest and most forceful attacks on the very possibility of macro-sociology has been mounted by Rom Harré (1982).

Macro concepts, Harré argues, are nothing more than rhetorical devices which social scientists employ to score points off one another in seminar debates. At the very best, Harré concedes, concepts like class refer only to what he calls taxonomic collectivities — to groups who might happen to have some attribute in common, but have no collective agency or causal powers. In that sense, the working class, for instance, is no more interesting, real and effective than the group of British passport holders. For it to be any more than this, for it to be a real entity, Harré argues, the existence of the working class would need to be demonstrated through evidence concerning real relations among its members. The working class, that is, would presumably have to be seen picketing the gates of factories in their thousands, or storming through the streets waving red banners. The fact is, Harré claims, that no such relations exist. 'In consequence, the status of alleged large scale macro groupings must be equivocal. At the very best, they might be conceived as theoretical entities whose existence ... must be hypothetical' (pp. 148–9). According to this view, the only things that do exist in the social sense are phenomena which are bounded in space and time and which have causal powers — classroom groups, not class groups; interpersonal relations not relations of production. This, therefore, is where research should be focused.

This is a powerful argument. Unlike the debate about the relationship between theory and evidence, it does not suggest that macro theory *happens to be* speculative, that it is neglectful of evidence; but that it is *necessarily* and *unavoidably* speculative, since the objects to which it refers do not, as such, exist. Macro theorizing is, in that sense, not just a flawed venture but a futile one. No good can come of it. These objections are persuasive, not least because they cohere with a good deal of common sense prejudice — if we cannot *see* the logic of the capital accumulation process, or the new middle class, or the *conscience collective*, or the reproduction of cultural capital, why should we believe that these things exist other than as pretentious bits of sociological mystification? Running against the grain of such prejudice, there are, I want to propose, at least two good reasons why these objections should be reconsidered.

First, members of social groups often belong not only to the same social category (like passport holders) but also share the same experiences. Nor does that sharing have to be self-conscious, or expressed in one time and place either on the miners' picket lines or in the Gdansk shipyards, for that group to be real. This, in a sense, is the classic difference that Marx drew between class-in-itself and class-for-itself. Many people will be familiar with Aldous Huxley's (1959) account of *Brave New World* where, through hypnopaedia and other techniques, the four different caste groupings — the alphas, the betas, the gammas and the epsilons — were made aware of their group identity and of the advantages of their own group compared to the others. Presumably not even Harré would question the existence, the reality of these four different groups. But supposing that hypnopaedia and all the other techniques of socialization in Huxley's *Brave New World*, had been directed towards softening senses of group identity, to instilling powerful if false ideologies of individual opportunity and mobility, meritocracy and so on. Would their resulting lack of sense of group belonging have made the common experiences of these groups any less real? Would it have made the differences between the conditions and lifestyle of the alphas, betas, gammas and epsilons, any less marked or causally significant? I doubt it. And so it is with such things as social class. It may be that the clear community basis of working class groups has been eroded by the decline of heavy manufacturing industries and the movement of council housing to the estates of the city periphery, and that if anything, this weakening of class identity has been reinforced by the mass media, the schooling system, and the very organization of production itself with its growing tendency to individualize the labour process. But this does not detract one bit from the fact that experiences of working are often similar from assembly to assembly line, factory to factory, or office to office, where people are caught up in similar relations to their product and to those who exercise authority over them; and that the effects of these relations carry over into family life, leisure, voting behaviour and so on.

Classes, in this sense, are very real things, even if their members are not fully aware of the fact. How exactly such groups should be defined is, of course, properly a matter of vigorous debate. And some definitions — especially those which help us to make sense of peoples' experience — are clearly more useful than others. Here, I am thinking in particular of the rather sterile exercise some theorists engage in of trying to assign occupational groups like teachers to one class or another according to whether they are engaged in productive or unproductive labour, a distinction which seems to have virtually no implications for teachers working or life experience at all (Ozga and Lawn, 1981; Ginsburg *et al*, 1980; Poulantzas, 1973; Cardechi, 1975). But while particular definitions at the macro level may be subject to dispute, it does seem unduly restrictive to suggest that only those social collectivities which are bounded in time and space are worthy of our serious sociological attention.

This leads to a second point. It is not the case that only those things which can be observed are the ones which have any real existence. Theoretical physicists deal all the time with sub-atomic particles whose existence they posit by mathematical inference rather than direct observation. Likewise, in astronomy, the existence and location of the planets Neptune and Pluto was established mathematically as a way of explaining observable disturbances in the motions of Uranus. The existence of Neptune and Pluto, that is, was inferred through empirical observation of their effects. Bearing in mind the analogy with such things as social class and similar constructs, it makes no difference that Neptune and Pluto were at the time of their discovery still observable in principle and that indeed they did become visible later through the use of powerful telescopes in one case, and sophisticated photography in the other. The point is that at the time of their discovery, these sources of tangible empirical confirmation were not available, nor, for all their discoverers knew, might they ever be. Sometimes, then, if only as a starting point for further investigation and testing, it is useful to see a range of disparate phenomena as the effects of some common, yet unseen, cause. Thus, one might propose, for instance, that the growth of pupil disruption in school, and the declining rate of student applications to university (even at a time when places are more scarce), coupled with a massive rise in youth unemployment are all effects of a growing crisis of pupil and student motivation (why bother subscribing to a system which offers you no rewards), which is in turn linked to an intensifying crisis in the economic system. This hypothesis would require further test, of course — other effects would need to be predicted then tested for (the growth of girls' interest in marriage rather than job or career might be one). But the principle of inferring systems and structures at the macro level through their effects, remains a sound one. Theories of what is unobservable can, therefore, stand up, if, that is, they are made to work in relation to available evidence of what *is* observable.

It seems reasonable to suggest, then, that we need theories of what occurs in particular settings bounded in time and space, *and* of the supraindividual entities which provide a context for what goes on in those particular settings. But this still begs the question of how exactly these theories at the micro and macro level are to be combined. Some solutions to this problem are impressive in their elegance and sophistication, most notably in the highly acclaimed work of Giddens (1976 and 1979). Giddens speaks with teasing persuasiveness about what he calls the *duality of structure*, about how 'structure is both the medium and the outcome of the social practices it recursively organizes' (Giddens, 1981; p. 171). Structures, he points out, are not only constraining but enabling too. And given that they are reproduced through interaction, every act is therefore a moment of possible change, an act of production as well as reproduction, containing within itself both the likelihood of continuity and the seeds of change. What Giddens achieves with great skill here, is a subtle resolution of the conventional dualism between action and structure. He demonstrates their mutual dependence, their logical entailment. However, while Giddens' writings are peppered with a most attractive collection of phrases and arguments which affirm the interdependence of action and structure, micro and macro, they are also largely devoid of empirical examples. There are no suggestions as to what implications his observations on social theory might have for any particular programme of empirical research.

I suspect the reason for this is not just Giddens' personal preference for 'Grand' theory of the classical kind, but that the gap between the elements he seeks to draw together is too great — a gap between the world of small scale face-to-face interaction, on the one hand, and vast social structures of immense proportions on the other. Such a gap is unbridgeable without the provision of some additional support. That kind of support, I want to propose, might well be found in the form of what Merton (1968) calls *theories of the middle range*. These theories, Merton argues

> lie between the minor but necessary working hypotheses that evolve in abundance during day to day research and the all-inclusive systematic efforts to develop a unified theory that will explain all the observed uniformities of social behaviour, social organization and social change... Middle range theory is ... intermediate to general theories of social systems which are too remote from particular classes of social behaviour, organization and change to account for what is observed and to those detailed orderly descriptions of particulars that are not generalized at all. Middle range theory involves abstractions, of course, but they are close enough to observed data to be incorporated in propositions that permit empirical testing. (p. 39)

In this sense, between the rules, negotiations and bargainings of classroom interaction, and the dynamics of the capitalist economy, or the relative autonomy of the state, lie a whole range of intermediary processes and structures which have been largely neglected in sociological accounts of education; such things as school ethos, or institutional bias (Rutter *et al*, 1979; Pollard, 1982), teacher cultures (Hargreaves, D., 1982), teacher coping strategies, (Hargreaves, A., 1978), and so on. Were more attention paid to structures and processes at this middle or 'meso' level of analysis, then researchers like Anyon (1981) and Sharp and Green (1975) would not find themselves forced, in their wish to make micro-macro links, to leap from highly localized observations of teacher-pupil interaction in a small number of classrooms, to speculative assertions about how far these processes are determined by class struggle and other forces within capitalism. The existence of such leaps between classroom and society, as it were, in sociological accounts of schooling brings me on to my third and final interpretation of the micro-macro distinction — the difference between school and society.

3   School and Society

Of the many interpretations of the micro-macro relationship, one of the most dominant has entailed a usually implicit but nonetheless powerful distinction between schools and society. In particular, in case study work which attempts to make macro linkages, there is a tendency to bolt on observations of what goes on in schools, to speculative understandings and assertions about the very nature of society. This, in turn, tends to reinforce the divisions I have already discussed: between theory and evidence, between what come across as unsubstantiated assertions about the requirements of capitalism, for instance, and detailed observations of school life. Moreover, when vast generalizations are made about the whole of society, about the needs of the capitalist economy, the effects of class struggle and so on, and these are then set alongside data on three teachers in one infants' school (Sharp and Green), or twelve working class lads (Willis), or five US elementary schools (Anyon), we, as sociologists of education, start to look as if we have badly overreached ourselves, as if we have seriously overstated our case. Worse still, when the case study analysis is presented as describing educational appearances, and the grand scale theorizing about 'society' is said to document some underlying fundamental 'reality', claims about that reality, given the shaky empirical foundations on which they rest, start to look at best like acts of sociological arrogance, and at worst like downright bias. None of this, as Nisbet and Broadfoot (1980) point out, impresses those teachers or administrators who might otherwise be in a position to make use of the findings of educational research.

Fortunately, these difficulties are to some extent, avoidable. There is no necessary reason, for instance, why 'society' must be dealt with or explained as an undifferentiated unit. It is true that those who have tried to bring off some kind of micro-macro integration in their work, have in fact tended to focus their empirical energies on the classroom, and to bracket off everything else that happens outside those walls as belonging to 'society', but this weakness need not continue. For instance, many of the so-called macro constraints which teachers face that are usually attributed to the operation of vast social structures could actually be analysed by studying interactions *outside* the classroom — in the headteacher's office, County Hall, the Department of Education and Science, and so on. Admittedly, it is not so easy gaining access to the office of a senior administrator as it is to the classroom of a low status teacher. But the barriers are not insuperable and even if direct observation is not possible much can still be gleaned from interviews or from the careful scrutiny of historical documents such as LEA memoranda (Hargreaves, A. 1983).

One very fruitful way of clarifying the micro-macro relation-ship, then, would involve undertaking a number of studies of different educational settings and spelling out the links between them. My own work on middle schools is an attempt to do this, to show how the constraints that middle school teachers and heads faced in the mid 1970s, could in many cases be traced to accumulated decisions that policy makers made about the establishment of middle schools during the late 1960s (Hargreaves, A., 1985). It is a mistake, then, to regard educational policy as belonging exclusively to the world of macro theory (as in Ahier and Flude 1983; Dale, 1981) not just because classroom teachers have policies too (Pollard, 1984), but also because even outside the school, policy still has to be negotiated and implemented through interaction, be this face to face, on the telephone or via correspondence.

The growth of linked micro studies could be one of the most significant future developments in the sociology of education, not only for micro-macro integration as an interesting if esoteric theoret-ical project, but also for the much needed attempt to understand the schooling process in the context of policy changes, economic pres-sures and so on, and not in isolation from them. One might, in this sense, reasonably hope to see future research projects which are based not just on a single school or classroom, nor even on a number of schools or classrooms, but on processes in two or more linked settings, drawn from such places as classrooms, staff meetings, LEA offices, teacher union branches and so on. Given such research programmes we might just begin to gain a serious, well grounded understanding of the complicated mechanisms by which economic, political and social constraints on teaching and learning are filtered down to school level. Of course, these linked micro-studies would still not remove the need and relevance for concepts like state, class and economy which transcend space and time, but they *would* prevent us relegating much of our analyses to that level by default simply because we *chose* not to study them empirically. And in broadening the areas of empirical enquiry beyond the classroom, we would also be widening the base of evidence according to which our theories could be tested and modified. If linked empirical studies can sharpen our procedures and heighten our awareness on all these fronts, then they are to be recommended strongly, not only for those with lofty theoretical ambitions but also for those who have a strong sense of political urgency too.

Note

1 This perhaps explains why, on those occasions when Althusser drops his vague and bewildering formulations of the complicated relationships between the economic, political and ideological 'levels' of the capitalist social formation, and tries instead to outline the processes that occur in one particular sphere — in the educational system, say — his argument, shot through with unchecked assumptions, then degenerates into an exceedingly deterministic account of schools as efficient servants of capitalism. Beneath the vagueness of Althusser's general social theory, then, lies a deep-seated empiricism which comes to light in his analyses of more specific issues. Contrary to initial appearances, there are not, in that case two Althussers, as it were — an Althusser of vulgar reproduction theory (the ISA's Althusser), and an Althusser of indeterminate relative autonomy theory (the Althusser of *For Marx*) — but one, whose theoretical scheme is at once a speculative theoreticism (leading to relative autonomy theory) and a most pernicious kind of empiricism (leading to direct reproduction theory), each of which supports the other in a mutually self-confirming scheme of dogmatic explanation.

References

AHIER, J. and FLUDE, M. (Eds) (1983) *Contemporary Education Policy*, London, Croom Helm.

ALTHUSSER, L. (1971) 'Ideology and ideological state apparatus', in COSIN, B. (Ed.) *Education, Structure and Society*, Harmondsworth, Penguin.

ALTHUSSER, L. (1977) *For Marx*, London, New Left Books.

ALTHUSSER, L. and BALIBAR, E. (1970) *Reading Capital*, London, New Left Books.

ANYON, J. (1981) 'Social class and school knowledge', *Curriculum Inquiry*, 11, 1, pp. 3–41.

APPLE, M. (1979) *Ideology and Curriculum*, London, Routledge and Kegan Paul.

APPLE, M. (1982) *Education and Power*, London, Routledge and Kegan Paul.

BANKS, O. (1982) 'The sociology of education 1952–1982', *British Journal of Educational Studies*, 30, 1, pp. 18–31.

BENNETT, N. (1976) *Teaching Styles and Pupil Progress*, London, Open Books.

BUSH, T. and KOGAN, M. (1982) *Directors of Education*, London, Allen and Unwin.

CARCHEDI, G. (1975) 'On the economic identification of the new middle class', *Economy and Society*, 4, 1.

CUTLER, A. *et al.* (1977) *Marx's Capital and Capitalism Today Volume 1*, London, Routledge and Kegan Paul.

DALE, R. (1979) 'The politicisation of school deviance: reactions to William Tyndale', in BARTON, L. and MEIGHAN, R. (Eds) *Schools, Pupils and Deviance*, Driffield, Nafferton Books.

DALE, R. (1981) 'The state and education: Some theoretical approaches', Unit 3, E353, *Society, Education and the State*, Milton Keynes, Open University Press.

DENZIN, N. (1970) *The Research Act*, Chicago, Aldine.

GALTON, M., SIMON, B. and CROLL, P. (1980) *Inside the Primary Classroom*, London, Routledge and Kegan Paul.

GIDDENS, A. (1976) *New Rules of Sociological Method*, London, Hutchinson.

GIDDENS, A. (1979) *Central Problems in Social Theory*, London, Macmillan.

GIDDENS, A. (1981) 'Agency, institution and time-space analysis', in KNORR-CETINA, K. and CICOUREL, A.V. (Eds) *Advances in Social Theory and Methodology: Toward an Integration of Micro and Macro Sociologies*, London, Routledge and Kegan Paul.

GINSBURG, M.B., MEYENN, R.J. and MILLER, H.D. (1980) 'Teachers' conceptions of professionalism and trades unionism; an ideological analysis', in WOODS, P. (Ed.) *Teacher Strategies*, London, Croom Helm.

GLASER, B. and STRAUSS, A. (1967) *The Discovery of Grounded Theory*, Chicago, Aldine.

HABERMAS, J. (1976) *Legitimation Crisis*, London, Heinemann.

HALSEY, A.H., HEATH, A.F. and RIDGE, J.M. (1980) *Origins and Destinations: Family Class and Education in Modern Britain*, Oxford, Clarendon Press.

HAMMERSLEY, M. (1979) 'Analysing ethnographic data', Part 1, Block 6, DE304, *Research Methods*, Milton Keynes, Open University Press.

HAMMERSLEY, M. (1980) 'On interactionist empiricism', in WOODS, P. (Ed.) *Pupil Strategies*, London, Croom Helm.

HAMMERSLEY, M. (1984a) 'The paradigmatic mentality: a diagnosis', in BARTON, L. and WALKER, S. (Eds) *Social Crisis and Educational Research*, London, Croom Helm.

HAMMERSLEY, M. (1984b) 'Some reflections upon the micro-macro problem in the sociology of education', *Sociological Review*, 32, 2, pp. 316–324.

HARGREAVES, A. (1978) 'The significance of classroom coping strategies', in BARTON, L. and MEIGHAN, R. (Eds) *Sociological Interpretations of Schooling and Classrooms: A Reappraisal*, Driffield, Nafferton Books.

HARGREAVES, A. (1980) 'Synthesis and the study of strategies: A project for the sociological imagination', in WOODS, P. (Ed.) *Pupil Strategies*, London, Croom Helm.

HARGREAVES, A. (1982) 'Resistance and relative autonomy theories: Problems of distortion and incoherence in recent Marxist sociology of education', *British Journal of Sociology of Education*, 3, 2, pp. 107–26.

HARGREAVES, A. (1983) 'The politics of administrative convenience', in AHIER, J. and FLUDE, M. (Eds) *Contemporary Education Policy*, London, Croom Helm.

HARGREAVES, A. (1985) English Middle Schools: An historical and ethnographic study, unpublished Ph.D thesis, University of Leeds.

HARGREAVES, D. (1978) 'Whatever happened to symbolic interactionism?', in BARTON, L. and MEIGHAN, R. (Eds) *Sociological Interpretations of Schooling and Classrooms: A Reappraisal*, Driffield, Nafferton Books.

HARGREAVES, D. (1981) 'Schooling for delinquency', in BARTON, L. and WALKER, S. (Eds) *Schools, Teachers and Teaching*, Lewes, Falmer Press.

HARGREAVES, D. (1982) *The Challenge for the Comprehensive School*, London, Routledge and Kegan Paul.

HARGREAVES, D., HESTER, S. and MELLOR, F. (1975) *Deviance in Classrooms*, London, Routledge and Kegan Paul.

HARRÉ, R. (1982) 'Philosophical aspects of the micro-macro problem', in KNORR-CETINA, K. and CICOUREL, A.V. (Eds) *Advances in Social Theory and Methodology: Towards an Integration of the Micro-Macro Problem*, London, Routledge and Kegan Paul.

HARRIS, K. (1982) *Teachers and Classes: A Marxist Analysis*, London, Routledge and Kegan Paul.

HER MAJESTY'S INSPECTORATE (1982) *Report by Her Majesty's Inspectorate on the Effects of Local Authority Expenditure Policies on the Education Service in England, 1981*, London, HMSO.

HUNTER, C. (1983) 'Education and local government in the light of central government policy', in AHIER, J. and FLUDE, M. (Eds) *Contemporary Education Policy*, London, Croom Helm.

HUXLEY, A. (1959) *Brave New World*, London, Chatto.

KEDDIE, N. (1973) *Tinker, Tailor ...*, Harmondsworth, Penguin.

MARX, K. and ENGELS, F. (1976) *Collected Works*, 5, London, Lawrence and Wishart.

MERTON, R. (1968) *Social Theory and Social Structure*, New York, Free Press.

MILLS, C.W. (1959) *The Sociological Imagination*, New York, Oxford University Press.

NISBET, J. and BROADFOOT, P. (1980) *The Impact of Research on Policy and Practice in Education*, Aberdeen, Aberdeen University Press.

OZGA, J. and LAWN, M. (1981) *Teachers, Professionalism and Class: A Study of Organized Teachers*, Lewes, Falmer Press.

PHILLIPSON, M. (1972) 'Theory, methodology and conceptualisation', in FILMER, P., PHILLIPPSON, M., SILVERMAN, D. and WALSH, D., *New Directions in Sociological Theory*, London, Collier-Macmillan.

POLLARD, A. (1982) 'A model of classroom coping strategies', *British Journal of Sociology of Education*, 3, 1, pp. 19–37.

POLLARD, A. (1984) 'Ethnography and social policy for classroom practice', in BARTON, L. and WALKER, S. (Eds) *Social Crisis and Educational Research*, London, Croom Helm.

POULANTZAS, N. (1973) *Political Power and Social Classes*, London, New Left Books.

ROBINSON, W.S. (1952) 'The logical structure of analytic induction', in McCALL, G. and SIMMONS, J. (Eds) (1969) *Issues in Participant Observation*, Reading, Mass., Addison Wesley.

ROCK, P. (1979) *The Making of Symbolic Interactionism*, London, Macmillan.

RUTTER, M., MAUGHAN, B., MORTIMORE, P., OUSTON, J. and SMITH, A. (1979) *Fifteen Thousand Hours: Secondary Schools and Their Effects on Children*, London, Open Books.

SHARP, R. (1980) *Knowledge, Ideology and the Politics of Schooling*, London, Routledge and Kegan Paul.

SHARP, R. (1982) 'Self-contained ethnography or a science of phenomenal forms and inner relations', *Boston University Journal of Education*, 164, 1.

SHARP, R. and GREEN, A. (1975) *Education and Social Control*, London, Routledge and Kegan Paul.

THOMPSON, E.P. (1978) *The Poverty of Theory*, London, Merton Press.

TURNER, G. (1983) *The Social World of the Comprehensive School*, London, Croom Helm.

WALLERSTEIN, I. (1974) *The Modern World System: Capitalist Agriculture and the Origins of the European World-Economy in the Sixteenth Century*, London, Academic Press.

WEST, G. (1984) 'Phenomenon and form in the interactionist and neo-Marxist qualitative educational research', in BARTON, L. and WALKER, S. (Eds) *Social Crisis and Educational Research*, London, Croom Helm.

WILLIS, P. (1977) *Learning to Labour*, Farnborough, Saxon House.

WOODS, P. (1979) *The Divided School*, London, Routledge and Kegan Paul.

WOODS, P. (1985) 'Ethnography and theory construction in educational research', in BURGESS, R.G. (Ed.) *Field Methods in the Study of Education*, Lewes, Falmer Press.

WRIGHT, E. (1979) *Class, Crisis and the State*, London, New Left Books.

YOUNG, M. and WHITTY, G. (Eds) (1977) *Society, State and Schooling*, Lewes, Falmer Press.

3 Developing and Testing Theory: The Case of Research on Pupil Learning and Examinations

Martyn Hammersley, John Scarth and Sue Webb

Ethnographers often seem ambivalent about theory. There are all kinds of reasons for this, but perhaps the most crucial is that 'theory' has positivist and system theory connotations. Given the weighty influence of interactionism and ethnomethodology upon much ethnography, distaste for theory is thus not very surprising. There are at least two aspects to this. On the one hand, the pursuit of theory is often taken to imply the belief that social processes can be explained in causal terms. A central feature of interactionist meta-theory is, of course, a rejection of 'over-deterministic' sociological approaches which ignore the creativity of social interaction:

> It would seem that few scholars would see anything wrong with the premise that human beings act toward things on the basis of the meanings which these things have for them. Yet, oddly enough, this simple view is ignored or played down in practically all of the thought and work in contemporary social science and psychological science. Meaning is either taken for granted and thus pushed aside as unimportant or it is regarded as a mere neutral link between the factors responsible for human behavior and this behavior as the product of such factors. We can see this clearly in the predominant posture of psychological and social science today. Common to both of these fields is the tendency to treat human behavior as the product of various factors that play upon human beings; concern is with the behavior and with the factors regarded as producing them. Thus, psychologists turn to such factors as stimuli, attitudes, conscious or unconscious motives, various kinds of psychological inputs, perception and cognition, and

various features of personal organization to account for given forms or instances of human conduct. In a similar fashion sociologists rely on such factors as social position, status demands, social roles, cultural prescriptions, norms and values, social pressures, and group affiliation to provide such explanations. In both such typical psychological and socio- logical explanations the meanings of things for the human beings who are acting are either bypassed or swallowed up in the factors used to account for their behavior. If one declares that the given kinds of behavior are the result of the particular factors regarded as producing them, there is no need to concern oneself with the meaning of the things toward which human beings act, one merely identifies the initiating factors and the resulting behavior. (Blumer, 1969; pp. 2–3)

The other component of interpretive approaches which leads to ambivalence towards theory on the part of ethnographers is the treatment of participant perspectives as 'rational and valid' in their own terms. Interactionists generally take the view not only that the understanding of participants' own accounts is an essential first step in any attempt to explain their behaviour, but also that these accounts must in some sense form the key element or foundation of any explanation:

To understand why someone behaves as he does you must understand how it looked to him, what he thought he had to contend with, what alternatives he saw open to him; you can understand the effects of opportunity structures, delinquent subcultures, social norms, and other commonly invoked explanations of behavior only by seeing them from the actor's point of view. (Becker, 1970, p. 64)

Furthermore, ethnographers often show great reluctance to question the validity of participants' accounts. Indeed, the latter may be treated as beyond question, as simply *constituting* particular 'forms of life' whose validity must be taken as given, the task being to describe the culture as faithfully as possible (Hammersley and Atkinson, 1983). Some writers go even further, drawing upon ethnomethodol- ogy, to argue that the goal of ethnography must be limited to description of the methods by which accounts are produced (Shar- rock and Anderson, 1980). From this point of view one must not 'argue with the data' (Coulter, 1971), and so theory, at least under most definitions, is ruled out.

Theory and Cumulative Knowledge

Despite ambivalence, there are few ethnographers who deny the role of theory altogether. After all, this would be to adopt the implausible and, ironically, once again positivist claim that there can be theory-free description. (Some do come very close to this position: see for example, Hammersley, 1974!) Rather, the response is generally to try to fuse description and the generation of theory (Woods, this volume). The goal of ethnography is often portrayed as 'presenting a theoretical account' of an institution or culture. Both this merging of description and theorizing, and the ambivalence which underlies it, are nicely captured in the following quotation:

> The analysis of case-study data is essentially concerned with the process of interpretation. That is, the translation of raw data into a coherent portrayal of an institution and of institutional processes. The process of interpretation involves the data coming to stand for and represent a field of reality as the basis for a 'theoretical' (or some other kind of) account of the setting. (Ball, 1983a, p. 96)

This approach reflects a particular view of theory as constituting a picture of reality. On this view, studies complement one another in much the same way as pieces of a mosaic fit together:

> The group that got its start under Park during the twenties in Chicago saw connections among all the various problems they were working on. Above all, they saw that the things they were studying had close and intimate connections with the city, considered in the abstract, and with Chicago itself, the particular city they were working in. For the Chicago group, whatever the particular subject matter under study, the researcher assumed that it took its character in part from the unique character and form of the city it occurred in. He relied, implicitly and explicitly, on the knowledge that had already been gathered, as he contributed his own small piece to the mosaic of the theory of the city and knowledge of Chicago that Park was building.
> The image of the mosaic is useful in thinking about such a scientific enterprise. Each piece added to a mosaic adds a little to our understanding of the total picture. When many pieces have been placed we can see, more or less clearly, the objects and the people in the picture and their relation to one

another. Different pieces contribute different things to our understanding: some are useful because of their color, others because they make clear the outline of an object. No one piece has any great job to do; if we do not have its contribution, there are still other ways to come to an understanding of the whole.

Individual studies can be like pieces of mosaic and were so in Park's day. Since the picture in the mosaic was Chicago, the research had an ethnographic, 'case history' flavor, even though Chicago itself was seen as somehow representative of all cities. Whether its data were census figures or interviews, questionnaire results or life histories, the research took into account local peculiarities, exploring those things that were distinctively true of Chicago in the 1920s. In so doing, they partially completed a mosaic of great complexity and detail, with the city itself the subject, a 'case' which could be used to test a great variety of theories and in which the interconnections of a host of seemingly unrelated phenomena could be seen, however imperfectly. (Becker, 1970, pp. 65–6)

This is an influential model. Here the relationship between studies is that each provides a bit of the total picture (the jigsaw puzzle and the map are the other analogies which come to mind). Each study provides a description of one part of the city, education system, or society. Added together, they give a panoramic view.

Very much in line with this model have been some proposals for the linking of macro and micro levels of analysis. For example, in promoting the concept of teachers' 'coping strategies' as a macro-micro link, Hargreaves (1980, pp. 186–8) identifies the following areas as requiring further research before the theoretical synthesis he recommends can be achieved:

1 Studies of the dimensions of and variations in the commonsense thinking of teachers; of the assumptions which underlie not only their actions but also their accounts of such actions; of the historical and experiential origins of those assumptions.
2 Studies of the constraints which teachers experience; like class sizes, school buildings, shortage of materials, the incompatible goals of schooling (of discovery versus direction for example), and current definitions of desirable educational practice held by influential personnel like

headteachers and advisers. What would also be required here are studies of the extent to which the election of particular strategies and the construction of appropriate repertoires of strategies are based upon the assumptions mentioned in 1, and of the extent to which they bring about modifications of those assumptions.

3   Studies of the constraints which teachers have faced *in the past* and the strategies which they *then* developed to cope with these. Thus we may begin to discover how the accepted, legitimate pedagogic repertoires of the present are rooted in conflicts fought out in the past, along with the consciously developed but now taken-for-granted strategies which those conflicts produced.

4   Studies of the origins of the constraints experienced by teachers which they attempt, constructively, to resolve. These origins need to be located beyond the immediate, apparent and relatively obvious institutional level. For example, it is not enough simply to point to the problem of class sizes as one constraint with which teachers have to deal — more difficult questions also need to be asked about why, even at a time of high rates of unemployment amongst teachers, the opportunity has not been taken to reduce the teacher-pupil ratio.

Hargreaves goes on to itemize five further areas which need to be covered by a theory of coping strategies. And indeed, Pollard (1982) has taken this a step further, arguing that Hargreaves underplays the role of teacher biography. He provides the following diagrammatic account of a theory of coping strategies as shown in figure 1. These proposals are in effect maps of the wide range of factors which probably play a role in shaping the character of teacher-pupil interaction in schools. However, while such maps are useful in laying out an agenda for future research, in our view they are not, nor do they promise to turn into, effective social theories.

   We believe that to conceptualize theories as describing the world, so that each study adds another bit of the picture, is fundamentally misleading. Description is certainly a worthwhile activity, and there is no clear division between description and explanation, descriptions frequently involve claims about causal relationships between different events. But the provision of a descriptive/explanatory account of a particular setting or sequence of events is very different from the development and testing of a theory about

Figure 1: Coping strategies

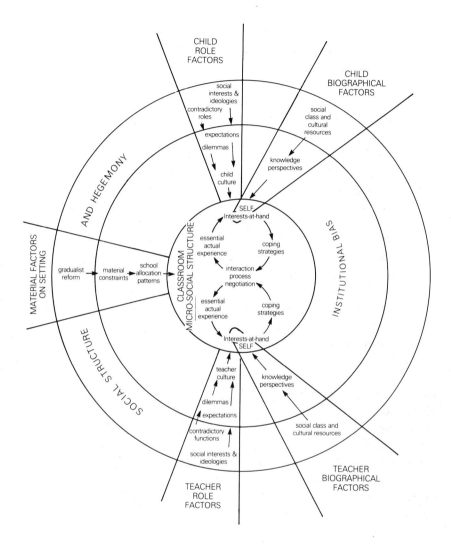

some aspect of that setting or sequence (Hammersley, 1984). Moreover, the former relies upon the latter. As is well known one cannot exhaust the description of a setting, there must always be selection criteria and these are derived, in part at least, from theoretical assumptions, from ideas about what produces what. Where those assumptions have been systematically tested, and have survived the test, their use is perfectly acceptable. In sociology, though, few theories fall into this category, for the most part we rely on theories which seem plausible, given the facts available to us, but which have been subjected to minimal, if any, checks. The result is that the 'pictures' we produce are of limited validity. To conflate the application of theories in the production of descriptions and explanations with the testing of theories discourages theory-testing, and thereby forces us to continue to rely on highly questionable theoretical ideas in explaining social events.

The logic of developing and testing theory is quite different from that of adding further pieces to a mosaic. Rather than simply finding plausible theories for the events observed the task is also to check which of the variety of possible theories available is the correct one. This is not a simple matter, and can rarely be completed within the scope of a single study (here Becker (1970) is correct in his criticism of the 'single study' paradigm). More than one case, and perhaps a large number of cases, must be investigated. Moreover, the development and testing of theory requires a narrow focus since even to test a single relationship between two variables involves the collection and analysis of a considerable amount of data; and the more complex the theory, the more variables and relationships involved, the more difficult it is to assess its validity (Lijphart, 1971). To attempt to test a theory of the scope outlined in Pollard's diagram (p. 53) would be futile, even for a large research team over a lengthy period of time. The number of variables is far too great.

There are very few examples of the systematic development and testing of theory in the sociology of education (or in sociology generally for that matter), and in this respect the work of Hargreaves (1967), Lacey (1970) and Ball (1981) provides a model. The work of each of these researchers focuses upon differentiation-polarization theory. Stated in abstract terms, this theory claims that where pupils are differentiated according to a set of academic and behavioural values, pupils will become polarized in their attitude to those values, with those pupils given a low rating rejecting the values and behaving accordingly. The studies by Hargreaves, Lacey and Ball also provide a good exemplar, in the Kuhnian sense (Masterman, 1970; Barnes,

1982), of the kind of research strategies necessary for the development and testing of theory (Hammersley, 1985).

Interestingly, even in the case of these studies, the mosaic model of complementarity seems to have played a role. The original Manchester studies were designed to cover three of the main types of secondary school in the English educational system: boys' grammar school (Lacey), girls' grammar school (Lambart), boys' secondary modern (Hargreaves). Moreover, Hargreaves and Lacey seem to have thought of themselves, at least in part, as doing a kind of community study of their schools. Signs of this are to be found in the titles of their books. Hargreaves refers to 'social relations in the secondary school', Lacey uses the sub-title 'the school as a social system'. The implication is that what is offered are studies of different types of school which could be complemented by descriptions of further types of school so as to produce a model of the education system as a whole.

Ball too seems to have operated in part upon the mosaic model. He sees the primary importance of his study lying in its provision of the first major ethnographic account of a comprehensive school. Thus, he sub-titles his book 'a case-study of secondary schooling', and while he takes differentiation/polarization as his central theme, he does not limit himself to this. He also studies, for example, the process of innovation in the school. Moreover, in commenting on the weaknesses of Beachside Comprehensive, he highlights the problem of 'coverage':

> There are areas of the school which one inevitably neglects. And I think it would be quite valid for people to criticize the Beachside study for neglecting things like pastoral care, for not saying much about the extra-curricular activities within the school, for not having much to say about subjects other than those within the academic core. (Ball, 1983b)

Like Hargreaves and Lacey before him, Ball was clearly concerned with providing a 'coherent portrayal' of the school he studied.

Nevertheless, while these three studies fit together as pieces of a mosaic, there is a much more important respect in which they are complementary, stemming from an underlying concern with the social causes of variations in pupil achievement and behaviour. Each study develops and tests differentiation-polarization theory under different conditions. Lacey's and Ball's work is particularly significant for the nature of the cases they investigated. Rather than simply representing other types of educational institution to Hargreaves' secondary modern, these provide variations in conditions which allow the theory's explanatory force to be tested.

Lacey (1970, p. 50) points out that the pupils entering Hightown Grammar were generally those who had been academically successful and committed to school values in their junior schools. As a result, this school represents a case in which one set of factors which we might suspect to be a possible alternative source of polarization — factors outside the school — is partially controlled. Whereas in response to Hargreaves' study we might well be inclined to argue that perhaps the polarization he documents has little to do with streaming and can be wholly explained in terms of the social class backgrounds of pupils, this criticism of the theory is rendered somewhat weaker (though not entirely eliminated) by Lacey's study.

Ball's work provides another variation in conditions and thereby facilitates further assessment of the plausibility of the theory. He investigates the effects of a reduction in differentiation, the shift at Beachside Comprehensive from banding to mixed ability grouping. What we have here is a kind of natural experiment. The theory predicts that, given such a change, polarization would be reduced, and the fact that this seems to have been the case at Beachside increases our confidence in the theory.

In short, then, there are relationships among these studies which are quite different from those among pieces of a mosaic. Lacey and Ball investigate critical cases in which the implications of the theory are tested out. The underlying logic is that of the comparative method, and in our view comparative analysis is the key to the development and testing of theory.

The Comparative Method

Despite the influence of more descriptive conceptions of ethnography, the comparative method is quite well-represented in the methodological literature, notably in the form of Glaser and Strauss' grounded theorizing (Glaser and Strauss, 1967; Glaser, 1978) and in the concept of analytic induction (Znaniecki, 1934; Lindesmith, 1947; Cressey, 1950; Bloor, 1978). While grounded theorizing is primarily concerned with the *development* and analytic induction the *testing* of theory, both recommend the analysis of cases related to one another in theoretical terms, *not* as separate bits of a larger picture.

Of course, there is some conflict between these two versions of the comparative method, and neither is entirely satisfactory in our view. The model of ethnographic research provided by Glaser and Strauss, valuable as it is, suffers from the fact that it takes over the positivist distinction between the context of discovery and the context of justification (Reichenbach, 1938). Glaser and Strauss seem to be unsure whether grounded theorizing includes theory *testing*; but their dominant message seems to be that it develops but does not test theory. Such a separation of theory development and testing is surely unproductive, however. Do we not need to make assessments of the likely validity of a theory in the process of developing it? Otherwise, might we not end up with a highly developed but invalid theory, given that any set of theoretical ideas can be developed in many directions? Of course, the practices Glaser and Strauss recommend *do* involve an element of testing, but this is minimal and needs to be extended if we are to be able to have much confidence in the validity of the theories we produce.

Analytic induction suffers from rather different problems. Its great strength is the way in which analysis of cases facilitates testing of the theory, including modification of the conditions under which the relationships specified by the theory are held to apply. But, as currently developed, analytic induction gives no advice as to how cases are to be selected. Yet, as we saw in the discussion of the work of Hargreaves, Lacey and Ball, the selection of critical cases is a particularly fruitful, indeed we would say essential, strategy for the development and testing of theory.

There is an even more powerful, and not unrelated, criticism of analytic induction: that it identifies only necessary and not sufficient conditions for the occurrence of phenomena (Robinson, 1951). This is because the cases selected for study are those in which the phenomenon to be explained is known to be present, rather than cases where the theory would predict the phenomenon to occur. Thus Cressey (1950 and 1953) takes as his subjects prisoners whose offences fall into his category of 'financial trust violation; Lindesmith (1947), in his study of opiate addiction, only interviews known addicts.[1] Robinson (1951) argues that contrary to the claims of its proponents (see especially Znaniecki, 1934), the logic of analytic induction is the same as that underlying the exercise of physical and statistical control. This is a convincing argument. While much of the power of experiments stems from the physical manipulation of variables, their logic is that of the comparative method. Experiments are, after all, critical cases 'par excellence'.

In our view, then, the comparative method is the essential foundation for the development and testing of theory. Our conception of that method is constructed from several sources. We take the importance of finding strategies to generate and develop theory from Glaser and Strauss. From analytic induction we derive the insight that the development and testing of theory are closely interrelated. From the work of Hargreaves, Lacey and Ball, and experimental methodology, we note the importance of the selection of critical cases for study.

The Comparative Method Applied

Discussing the comparative method in abstract is all very well, but in this as in most other activities there is some distance between theory and practice. In the remainder of our chapter we examine our own attempt to put the comparative method into practice in our current research into the effects of external assessment on teaching and learning in secondary schools.

Our starting point in the research was the idea that external examinations lead to lecturing and note-giving on the part of secondary school teachers, and to rote learning and instrumental attitudes among their pupils (Board of Education, 1911; HMI, 1979; Turner, 1982). One of our major concerns was to find out whether this relationship held, and if so why.

Our initial research design took the form of a longitudinal study following a sample of pupils from their third to their fifth year. The idea was that, if the conventional view about the effects of examinations was correct, we would be able to see how the kinds of teaching the pupils experienced, and their own orientation towards school and school work, changed as they got closer to the point of assessment. We selected two schools of contrasting kinds in order to get some sense of the parameters of pupils' experience and orientations. One of the schools was of a fairly traditional, exam-oriented character, the other was a 'progressive' community school offering predominantly mode 3 courses involving a large element of course work assessment, and taught in mixed ability groups.

From the start we realized that we would have to adopt a relatively narrow focus, though we did not realize just how narrow it would eventually have to be. At first sight the problem of what was and was not relevant seemed straightforward: we had to select a sample of third-year pupils in each school whom we would follow through to the end of compulsory schooling. In one of the two schools this proved relatively straightforward since the mixed ability tutor group was the major unit in terms of which the timetable was organized in the third year, and to a considerable extent in the fourth and fifth years too. The other school proved much more of a problem since it adopted the more conventional practice of banding and setting, with pupils being allocated to fourth/fifth-year courses on the basis of an option choice system towards the end of the third year. Here it was not practicable to follow through a sample of pupils since any sample of third-year pupils was likely to be widely distributed across many fourth and fifth-year sets. We reconciled ourselves to having to study some pupils at the later stage of schooling who were not studied in the third year, in at least one of the schools.

In both schools, though, we were also faced with the problem of deciding which subjects to focus on; studying all of them was out of the question given our resources (one researcher per school). Of course in deciding what subjects to select we had to bear in mind the different kinds of external assessment to be found in the fourth and fifth year in each subject area. In order to make the selection in the most effective manner possible, we sought to clarify the different dimensions of variation which seemed relevant to our research problem. We identified three aspects of variation in external assessment which we needed to take account of:

(I)   GCE/CSE/other;
(II) mode 1, 2 or 3;
(III) external examination alone/external examination plus continuous assessment/continuous assessment alone.

It seemed to us that we ought to select courses for study which provided us with comparisons in each of these respects.

However, there were other aspects of courses which we felt we had to allow for as extraneous variables. One of the most important concerned the nature or status of different subjects themselves. Two dimensions seemed important here. One was the contrast between 'literate' and 'practical' subjects. We hypothesized that in some respects the effects of external written examinations might be greater, or more obvious, in 'practical' than 'literate' subjects. Equally, though, we had to try to make sure that any relationship we found held for both types of subject. The same applied to our other dimension: we needed to cover both 'high status' and 'low status' subjects.

We set out to choose courses for study in such a way as to maximize variation on these dimensions. Initially we selected English, maths, physics/integrated science and history/integrated humanities. Later we added drama, art and technology.

Even having selected particular courses for study, we were still faced with sampling problems. We could not cover all tutor groups (eight in all) and certainly not all sets (fourteen in many subjects) in the schools. In one of the schools, where pupils were organized into mixed ability groups, we sought to resolve this problem by seeking the advice of teachers as to the 'least untypical' tutor group. In the other school we selected the top and bottom sets on each course on the grounds that this would maximize the effects of setting and allow us to control for these.

We also faced the problem of sampling over time. We did not plan to spend every day in the classrooms collecting data. After all, one of the key features of both grounded theorizing and analytic induction is that much of the analysis occurs in the process of data collection, providing guidelines as to what further data is needed. Moreover, we did not want to restrict our focus to classroom processes. It seemed likely that the effects of external examinations might be mediated by the ways in which the schools were organized (Scarth, 1985). On these grounds we sought to collect data on decision-making processes in the two schools, where these had some bearing on external assessment. We began to collect data on a wide range of meetings in each school and discovered, of course, that external examinations and exam results were not only an issue for discussion in their own right, but were often invoked in support of arguments about many different issues, from changes in the timetable to the relationship between the two sites making up one of the schools.

This, then, was our first research design. We soon realized, however, that it needed modification. It is all very well collecting data in third-year classrooms watching out for changes, but of course even if changes do occur they are often so gradual as to go unnoticed. Indeed, it proved impossible to distinguish change from flux. As a result, we decided that it was essential that we introduce a cross-sectional element into our research design, collecting some data on fourth and fifth-year lessons right at the beginning so as to give us some idea of what kinds of change we could expect.

At this time we were resisting the idea that our task was to test the hypotheses implicit in the traditional criticisms of exams. While we had these in the back of our minds as foreshadowed problems, we adopted a more inductivist approach — reading through fieldnotes (and the occasional transcript when we could get these typed) — and developing a set of categories in much the manner of Glaser and

Strauss. Quite what made us rethink this approach we can no longer remember. Perhaps it was the persistence of the problem of adopting a focus narrow enough to be practical and yet wide enough to collect all the data we thought we needed. Certainly, the attempt to combine a longitudinal and cross-sectional design placed a great strain on us. The two of us (Sue Webb and John Scarth) who were at that time doing the data collection spent virtually the whole time in school and very little on processing, let alone analyzing, the data. (Martyn Hammersley struggling with a voracious Open University course also had difficulty finding time to do much analysis, for him keeping track of how the research was going and discussing fieldwork problems took up all the available time).

In the face of a mounting pile of data and the feeling that more data collection on an even wider front was necessary, we decided to adopt a more hypothetico-deductive approach. We looked more closely at the criticisms that had been made of exams in the literature, hoping that these would provide a basis for narrowing our focus. Unfortunately, we found that these were vague at crucial points. It was not at all clear exactly what concrete effects exams were thought to have or why they had these effects. We set about clarifying this by means of the concept of 'transmission teaching', borrowed from the general literature on teaching (Barnes, 1976). We defined it as the presentation of facts to be memorized and reproduced, and we attempted to specify what kinds of teacher behaviour could be taken to indicate its operation. We also started to do the same thing for 'transmission learning', the pupil orientation which the critique of exams postulated.

At the same time we began to consider what it was about different types of assessment that might be expected to cause trans-mission teaching and learning. We came to the conclusion that both variations in the extent to which teaching was transmission-oriented *and* differences between assessment regimes likely to cause such variation could be conceptualized in terms of the openness or closedness of the tasks set pupils and examination candidates. Our (rather banal) argument was that external assessment involving pre-dominantly closed tasks (i.e. simply requiring recall) would en-courage teachers to set classroom tasks of a 'closed' character.

At around this time we also began to worry that in effect we were developing a theory for a phenomenon we did not know existed. Not only was there no sound documentation of variations in teacher practice and pupil orientation in the literature on the effects of examinations, but in our preliminary analyses of lesson transcripts we could find no clear inter-course variation, while there was considerable intra-course variation even among different lessons involving the same teacher and class.

This, along with the continuing strain of data collection, forced the next major change in our research design. We decided to abandon the longitudinal strategy altogether and resolved to focus our data collection on the comparison of a few courses among which would be those which on theoretical grounds we would expect to find the sharpest differences in teacher and pupil orientations. One of the fourth and fifth-form courses we were studying was an integrated humanities course which at GCE level was assessed entirely in terms of course work (at CSE there was an exam counting for 20 per cent). We decided to compare this with more traditional exam-assessed courses in geography and history, as well as with a Schools Council history course which combined examination and course work. We felt that if the differences in teaching and learning we were interested in would turn up anywhere they should arise in the comparison of these courses.

Initially we planned to collect data on these courses for half a term and then spend time analyzing the data before returning to the schools for the rest of the term to test out whether the relationship we had discovered held in other subjects too. However, we found that, once again, no clear inter-course differences emerged. We decided that this might be because we had not observed enough lessons. We therefore pressed on to collect more data on the same courses. However, even towards the end of the term we still found no clear differences between the exam and non-exam courses. The least transmission oriented course was the Schools Council history course. The integrated humanities course seemed to display much the same level of transmission-oriented pedagogy as the traditional exam courses.

At this point we had what we thought at the time was a stroke of luck. We realized that we could make sense of our data if we assumed that form of external assessment was not the only variable producing transmission orientation. If we also took account of the ability level of the pupils, as defined by the schools (in terms of whether the course was taught to top set, bottom set, intermediate or mixed ability groups) a pattern did emerge. Thus the Schools Council history course was the least transmission-oriented because it set relatively open assessment tasks *and* was taught to a top set group. The most transmission-oriented course, by contrast, was an exam-based CSE history course involving predominantly closed exam questions and taught to a lower set. The integrated humanities course was in the middle, we hypothesized, because while it was relatively open in character it was taught to mixed ability groups (i.e. having fairly low average ability). The pattern is captured in the following diagram, in which the arrows indicate the direction in which each factor was thought to be pushing teaching on the courses:

Figure 2:   An Outline of the Theory

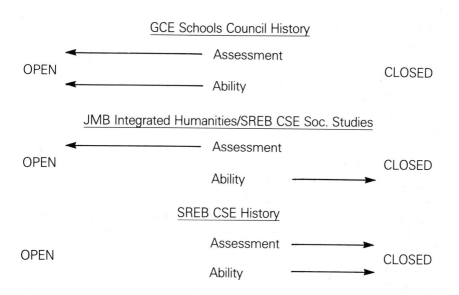

On the basis of this pattern we resolved both to try to specify why 'ability level' of pupils seemed to have this effect, and to collect data on Schools Council history taught to a lower set, as well as integrated humanities taught to top and bottom sets, which would allow us to check the emerging theory.

While this rethinking of our research design was going on, the number of lesson transcripts available to us began to increase as a result of an input of secretarial assistance. Our initial pattern among the courses had been based on a relatively small number of lessons, sometimes only two or three on a course. As we coded these newly available transcripts (and revised our coding scheme) we found, to our disappointment, that the pattern no longer held. While the Schools Council course remained the least transmission-oriented, now it seemed that the *most* transmission-oriented course was one of

Martyn Hammersley, John Scarth and Sue Webb

the GCE geography courses taught to a top set. Our hypothesis about the effects of 'ability level' no longer seemed to work.

The research is still in progress and this brings us close to its current state[2]. In the face of the evidence no longer fitting our theory we have concluded (reluctantly since it makes the task of theory-testing more difficult) that transmission orientation may be produced by a large number of factors besides assessment, and that only if we can control for these factors will we detect the influence of different types of assessment on teaching. What this implies is that we should focus on the same teacher teaching different courses. If we find consistent differences between courses taught by the same teacher in line with the predicted effects of contrasting types of assessment, then we will have a new basis for theory development and testing.

Conclusion

In this chapter we have sketched the attitudes of ethnographers to theorizing and outlined what we think is the most productive strategy for developing and testing theory: the comparative method. In recounting our own research experience we hope to have shown what this strategy amounts to in practice. It should be clear that it does not provide some standardized procedure for producing theoretical goods. It requires continual reflection on purposes, theory, methodology and data; and there is no guarantee of a worthwhile outcome. Nevertheless, for us it remains the best hope for the cumulative development of sociological knowledge.

Note

1 It should be noted, however, that both authors do use as evidence previous occasions in their informants' lives when some but not all of the causal factors were present and addiction/trust violation did not occur.
2 This Chapter was first drafted in January 1983. A move up-to-date report on the research us available from the authors.

References

BALL, S.J. (1981) *Beachside Comprehensive: A Case Study of Secondary Schooling*, Cambridge, Cambridge University Press.
BALL, S.J. (1983a) 'Case study research in education', in HAMMERSLEY, M.

(Ed.) *The Ethnography of Schooling*, Driffield, Nafferton.

BALL, S.J. (1983b) Personal Communication.

BARNES, B. (1982) *T.S. Kuhn and Social Science*, London, Macmillan.

BARNES, D. (1976) *From Communication to Curriculum*, Harmondsworth, Penguin.

BECKER, H.S. (1970) *Sociological Work*, Chicago, Aldine.

BLOOR, M. (1978) 'On the analysis of observational data: A discussion of the worth and uses of inductive techniques and respondent validation', *Sociology*, 12, 3.

BLUMER, H. (1969) *Symbolic Interactionism: Perspective and Method*, Englewood Cliffs, New Jersey, Prentice Hall.

BOARD OF EDUCATION (1911) *Report of the Consultative Committee on Examinations in Secondary Schools*, London, HMSO.

CRESSEY, D. (1950) 'The criminal violation of financial trust', *American Sociological Review*, 15.

CRESSEY, D. (1953) *Other People's Money*, Glencoe, Illinois, Free Press.

COULTER, J. (1971) 'Decontextualised meaning: Current approaches to verstehende investigations', *Sociological Review*, 19, 3.

GLASER, B. (1978) *Theoretical Sensitivity*, Mill Valley, California, The Sociology Press.

GLASER, B.G. and STRAUSS, A. (1967) *The Discovery of Grounded Theory*, Chicago, Aldine.

HAMMERSLEY, M. (1974) 'The organisation of pupil participation', *Sociological Review*, 22, 3.

HAMMERSLEY, M. (1984) 'Making a vice of our virtues: some notes on theory in ethnography and history', in GOODSON, I.F. and BALL, S.J. (Eds) *Defining the Curriculum*, Lewes, Falmer Press.

HAMMERSLEY, M. (1985) From 'Ethnography to Theory' *Sociology* 19, 2, pp. 244–259

HAMMERSLEY, M. and ATKINSON, P. (1983) *Ethnography: Principles in Practice*, London, Tavistock.

HARGREAVES, A. (1980) 'Synthesis and the study of strategies: a project for the sociological imagination', in WOODS, P. (Ed.) *Pupil Strategies*, London, Croom Helm.

HARGREAVES, D.H. (1967) *Social Relations in a Secondary School*, London, Routledge and Kegan Paul.

HER MAJESTY'S INSPECTORATE (1979) *Aspects of Secondary Education in England*, London, HMSO.

JOHNSON, J. (1975) *Doing Field Research*, New York, Free Press.

LACEY, C. (1970) *Hightown Grammar: The School as a Social System*, Manchester, Manchester University Press.

LIJPHART, A. (1971) 'Comparative politics and the comparative method', *American Political Science Review*, 65.

LINDESMITH, A. (1947) *Opiate Addiction*, Principia Press, republished (1968) as *Addiction and Opiates*, Chicago, Aldine.

MASTERMAN, M. (1970) 'The nature of a paradigm', in LAKATOS, I. and MUSGRAVE, A. (Eds) *Criticism and the Growth of Knowledge*, Cambridge, Cambridge University Press.

POLLARD, A. (1982) 'A model of classroom coping strategies', *British*

Journal of Sociology of Education, 3, 1.

REICHENBACH, H. (1938) *Experience and Prediction*, Chicago, Illinois, University of Chicago Press.

ROBINSON, W.S. (1951) 'The logical structure of analytic induction', *American Sociological Review*, 16, reprinted in MCCALL, G.J. and SIMMONS, J.L. (Eds) *Issues in Participant Observation, A Text and Reader*, Reading, Massachusetts, Addison-Wesley.

SCARTH, J. (1985) The Influence of Examinations on Curriculum Decision-Making. Unpublished Ph.D. Thesis, University of Lancaster.

SHARROCK, W.W. and ANDERSON, R.J. (1980) 'On the demise of the native: Some observations on and a proposal for ethnography', Occasional paper No. 5, Department of Sociology, University of Manchester.

TURNER, G. (1982) *The Social World of the Comprehensive School*, London, Croom Helm.

ZNANIECKI, F. (1934) *The Method of Sociology*, New York, Farrar and Rinehart.

4 Feminist Research and Qualitative Methods: A Discussion of Some of the Issues

Sue Scott

In this chapter I want to address a problem which appears only to be partially resolved when it is addressed at all; that is the relationship between personal experience and the research process. For me this problem is most significant in the relationship between my feminism and my work in sociological research, and includes the question of what can be said to constitute feminist research, and in particular, whether such an enterprise consists or is dependent on certain methodologies.

Specifically I want to question two assumptions which I feel may be in danger of generating an orthodoxy in feminist research. These assumptions, which I have accepted rather uncritically at times, are first, that feminist research is necessarily research by women *on women*, and secondly, that qualitative methodologies are essentially and unproblematically better suited to doing feminist research. I hope that by describing some of my experiences to analyze some of the ways in which these assumptions may have been generated and what might be problematic about them.

Learning about Feminist Research

Although I do not want to suggest a necessarily linear progression of ideas or understanding (and for many feminists the line of development which I can see in my own history will not correspond directly to their own) I do think that the development of my thinking on feminist research has been paralleled by many women, particularly those involved in sociology.

My involvement in sociological research predates slightly my public involvement in the Women's Liberation Movement. At the time when I first became aware of the possibility of carrying over my feminism into my work, I was also employed by the Health Education Council to do research into attitudes of patients and staff towards smoking in hospitals. Another aspect of this research was to assess the level of knowledge which patients had about smoking related diseases so that educational interventions could be designed more effectively. Although the research officially involved a small amount of participant observation, the bulk of the work was done by using a pre-coded questionnaire, and the data rendered in statistical terms. My principal dissatisfaction was with the narrow scope of the study which was reinforced by the use of survey methods. In sociological terms, I was increasingly becoming convinced of the value of qualitative methods as a means of explaining the interface between personal life and social structure, while in terms of my feminism, I wanted to do research which had meaning, for me personally, and for other women including the respondents.

I could see no way at the time in which a feminist analysis could be introduced into the research without completely restructuring it, as the research design took no account of gender differences. In retrospect I see that my critique of the research was the beginning of a feminist analysis and should have been written up as such, had I had the confidence to do so, but at the time I did not see that as a valid research activity. It was still a personal problem. These dissatis-factions became meshed together through my experience of the research process to produce a felt link between feminist research and qualitative methods, and although this process was highlighted by many incidents during the research, one in particular stands out.

I was interviewing a woman patient, newly admitted to the hospital in which I was working. She was in a side ward on her own, but I had checked with the ward sister and was told it was all right to talk to her. No mention was made of her condition. There I sat ticking off questions on my questionnaire, and when I reached the question about the reason for her admission to hospital she burst into tears and told me that she had attempted suicide the day before because her dog had died. She had spent all her time caring for her crippled husband and the dog was her only friend and her only excuse for going out. I was the first person she had talked to since coming into hospital and the only person she had seen since breakfast. She was racked with guilt about what would have happened to her husband had her attempted suicide been successful. The staff, she felt, were treating her like a 'damned nuisance' and there I was asking her

silly questions about how she perceived the hospital smoking regula-
tions. I scrapped my interview schedule and stayed to talk to her for a
couple of hours. The incident focused my mind wonderfully on some
of the contradictions inherent in doing research in general, and doing
survey research in particular.

I left that research with an implicit linking in my mind of
feminism and qualitative methods, this stemmed from a desire to say
something meaningful about women's lives and also about my own,
and to attempt to fill the enormous gap in sociology on the subject of
women's experience. My experience of survey research had enabled
me to see the dangers of merely reproducing stereotypes. I had no
clear idea at this stage, however, of how to do feminist research or
qualitative research. At that time for me feminist research was
qualitative research by women 'on' women. It is not really surprising
that this was how I understood feminist research as the bulk of
feminist work then and now falls roughly into this category and for
good reason some of which I will discuss later. (For discussions of the
relationship between feminism and sociology see Bernard, 1973;
Daniels, 1975; Eichler, 1980; Scott, 1984; and Smith, 1974).

Following this research I registered as a part-time postgraduate
student with a view to working out some of these ideas and
contradictions in a piece of research of my own. However, the
pressure of several part-time teaching jobs, and very little money led
me back into a full-time research post within fifteen months.

Qualitative Methods, Feminist Research and an Educational Research Project

In January 1979 I took up a post as Research Associate in the
'Postgraduate Research Project' which was based in the Sociology
Department at the University of Lancaster. The Project was funded
by the then Social Science Research Council (SSRC) for three years
and directed by John Wakeford. The Project stemmed originally
from discussions between the SSRC and the British Sociological
Association (BSA) about the particular problems facing part-time
postgraduate students. The 'Project' set out to examine the context
and process of postgraduate research in sociology and social administration with special reference to part-time students, and was to take a
grounded theory approach (see Glaser and Strauss, 1967). Mary
Porter and I were appointed as the research workers, and soon
afterwards we appointed Jackie Covill as Project Secretary. John

Sue Scott

Wakeford made it clear from the outset that he saw his role as one of giving advice and support rather than close direction and that the development of the 'Project' and any publications stemming from it would, in the main, be our responsibility. I was pleased to have a research post, and although I had doubts about whether the face of British sociology would be changed by this particular piece of research, I was keen to develop my skills in qualitative methods, especially as an interviewer. I also felt that the 'Project' would allow me scope to interview a number of women and to contribute to a feminist account of the position of women in academia. Although we did modify the research in various ways (see Porter, 1984) we did not stray very far from John Wakeford's original conception, and at least not as far as the fieldwork was concerned. We conducted in-depth interviews with postgraduate students and their supervisors in twelve sociology and social administration departments as well as six chemistry departments for comparison. Most of these interviews were repeated twice within the three-year period. Although there were rather more men than women registered as postgraduates in our chosen departments, we deliberately interviewed a disproportionate number of women in order to be able to present a broad view of women's experience.

In the early stages of the project I felt that as I was a feminist, (as was Mary Porter) and because we were to be using qualitative methodology then what we produced would be feminist research. This, I feel now, was rather a simple view and took little account of the need to ask feminist questions from the outset. I think I expected the feminist content to relate primarily to the interviews with women as I had no clear framework at that time for doing feminist research on men. Now that the research is over I still feel that what I did was feminist research but for rather different reasons. I found that qualitative methods and specifically the 'ethnographic interview' are not without their problems. I also found that while interviewing women as a feminist is highly satisfying, it is not without its ethical and political problems (see Finch, 1984), and that while interviewing men is often problematic, it can be very stimulating for ideas and analysis. Finally, and perhaps most importantly, I discovered the necessity of researching my own position and the effects which the research had on the development of my ideas.

The postgraduate research project had some notable effects on my understanding of research in general and feminist research in particular and it is this material on which I will draw during the course of this chapter. (For further discussion of the Postgraduate

Research Project see Scott and Porter, 1980, 1983 and 1984; Scott, 1984 and 1985; Porter, 1984; and Wakeford, 1985).

Why Qualitative Methods?

The common view of feminist research is that it is qualitative methodology and more precisely in-depth interviews with women respondents. This tendency can be seen, for example in the work of Anne Oakley (1981), Janet Finch (1984), and many others. There has, in fact, been a proliferation of studies of 'Women and everything'; these have been in largely ethnographic studies of women in schools and colleges, and in a range of workplaces, as housewives, as mothers, as daughters, and so on. This is not, of course, to suggest that all feminist social scientists use qualitative methods, some produce largely theoretical writings without engaging in fieldwork, while others work solely with secondary sources and many work on large-scale survey research. However, within this last group an interesting trend has developed which appears to be linked to my own experience. Many feminist researchers working on survey research projects (often not of their own making) have added on small-scale studies of women using in-depth interviews or life histories (see for instance, the work of Catriona Llewellyn (1981), Diana Woodward and Lynne Chisholm (1981) and in particular Hilary Graham (1984)). What seems to be significant here is the way in which a desire to do valid feminist research which makes sense of women's lives and experiences has caused researchers to cut across the usual methodological boundaries between quantitative and qualitative methods. This is not to suggest that the differences are simply to do with choice of method. They do of course relate to epistemological differences. I would suggest, however, that current sociological theory rarely fully makes sense of women's lives and thus these differences become less significant as research questions are posed by feminists in quite new ways. The question still remains however: why the tendency towards qualitative research on women? Jesse Bernard (1973) for example, has argued that there is a high machismo element in the production of quantified (hard data) and that this has often led to a feminist rejection of this in line with the assumption that qualitative (soft data) is more appropriate for feminist research. (For further discussion of women and sociological research see Dorothy Smith, 1974). Moreover, many feminists feel that quantitative methods encourage an unhealthy separation between those who know and those who do not, a separation which for many feminists runs contrary to the principle and practice of feminism. I would argue, however, that this problem is not necessarily solved by a wholesale conversion to qualitative methods. Another aspect of this argument is the view that men tend to talk about their lives in unproblematic and linear ways which can be fitted into survey questions whereas women want to make connections between areas of their lives. Now, I agree that many researchers (notably male) who employ so-called hard methodology are often as interested in the technology as they are in the respondents and I suspect that research questions are even now being formulated in order to test statistical techniques. I also have a personal preference for non-statistical methods, as I really enjoy talking to people and doing in-depth interviews. However, as David Morgan (1981) points out, qualitative ethnographic methods can have their own brand of machismo, with the image of the sociologist having untrodden paths to cross in order to reach an understanding of society's folk devils.

Feminist research is often research on women (but not exclusively), see for example the work of Liz Stanley and Sue Wise (1979) and Marianne Hester (1984), and this is used as an excuse by many academic men for the ghettoization of women's work as work on women and therefore not work of world shattering sociological importance. I would argue that there is no necessary connection between research on women and feminist research.

Feminist research must take women's oppression as one of its basic assumptions and much research on women by both women and men has only served to reinforce sexist assumptions and stereotypes. I would also argue that feminist research can only be done by women out of a common knowledge and experience of oppression. Men cannot experience this form of oppression and therefore by definition cannot be feminists. Therefore, while men can do research which challenges sexist assumptions (see Pearson, 1984) this is not feminist research. Of course feminists quite rightly feel that sociology has ignored not only the 'objective' positions of women in society but also the political and cultural manifestations of male power as they apply to the lived experience of women, and for feminists doing research on women was and is necessary to redress the balance to place emphasis on women's lives and to open up debate about women's experience.

The Bias Against Qualitative Research

I now want to look in some detail at my own experience of doing qualitative research on women and men, at the problems which I encountered and at how this experience affected my views about feminist methodology. First then some of the problems connected with doing qualitative research. It may have been naive of me to think that by using qualitative methods I would be free of the pressures I associated with qualitative methodology. I still felt under a great deal of pressure to quantify, to have, for instance, 'enough' cases in each category for 'reasonable' statements to be made. At seminars and conferences my colleague Mary Porter and myself were consistently being asked for numbers, as if what we were doing was all very well, but we would still have to 'prove' it in the end. One particular occasion comes to mind when we were discussing the particular problems which women postgraduates had with their (usually male) supervisors, and rather than discuss the question of male power in academia which was the main issue we were raising, one by one the men present began to ask questions about how many women had faced these problems and were we quite sure that a similar number of male postgraduates had not had the same problems. Perhaps more importantly for the methodology itself, but not connected to the above pressures, was the reification of the interview. Doing interviews became the *raison d'etre* of the project. We developed a tendency to press on with the interviewing in the belief that this in itself was the most important part of the research even when we were already 'saturated' with data. We had fallen into the positivistic trap even though methodologically we thought we had located ourselves outside that framework. We were treating ourselves simply as receptacles for the experiences of others and often ignored as data our own experiences of the process. It is not enough to simply 'come clean' about your own real experiences of doing research in a single paper given to fellow academics at the end of the research; it needs to be incorporated into the research from the very beginning.

I am now convinced that many of the reactions which we had to the research stemmed from the twin aspects of feminism and qualitative methods. One male professor attacked us as biased because we had already written papers about aspects of the research before it was 'complete', something which no 'real' scientist would do. He was not impressed by our lack of desire to be 'scientists'. Accusations of bias have come, not only from the more entrenched positivists within sociology, but also from people who advocate naturalistic research, but who nonetheless view it as a linear process which allows little space for the researcher's interactions in the process. I would agree with Liz Stanley and Sue Wise (1983) that this is often simply positivism in disguise. The assumption being that the categories for analysis emerge from the data untouched by human hand (see Glaser and Strauss, 1967) and for discussion of this feminist researchers are criticized for preempting the data because they are already operating within a theoretical and political framework. This contradiction was a particular problem for me whilst working on the postgraduate research project as we had made a commitment at the outset to use a grounded theory approach. Much of the criticism of feminist research as biased comes from sociologists who are committed to qualitative methods and reject positivistic notions of objectivity. I would argue, however, that all researchers operate from within a theoretical framework or overview and that we affect the data at all stages. The difference is that feminist researchers tend to be much more open about this process and can therefore be seen by some as a threat to the research orthodoxy. (See for example Oakley, 1981; Stanley and Wise, 1983; and Purvis, 1985).

Interviewing Women and Men

A number of issues were raised for me while doing the fieldwork for the Postgraduate Research Project. This Project entailed conducting ethnographic interviews with postgraduate students both full and part-time, and with their supervisors, postgraduate conveners and heads of departments. I found these interviews not without their problems and perhaps the major issue was the way the interviewers worked in different ways according to the gender of the interviewee to the extent that it sometimes felt that a different methodology was being used — behind the scenes. I take it as given that my own gender had an influence on this, but this was only part of the explanation. At the outset I saw ethnographic interviews as a means of collecting data and was unprepared for the variation in the structure of the interview itself. I simply had not foreseen the issues which would be raised for us as young women interviewing men, after all, researchers did it all the time. When I interviewed women I often struck up an immediate rapport and as Anne Oakley (1981) points out, often identified with the women and their problems, especially in terms of my own similarly marginalized position within academia.

When it came to interviewing men, however, I found the same level of rapport impossible to achieve in most cases, which I now feel calls the concept of rapport into question more than my skill as an interviewer, although I did not always feel this at the time. Now, I do not want to suggest that we had any real difficulty in gaining and carrying out interviews with men; in fact we had only one direct refusal (apart from people who we just could not track down) from a male academic who claimed not to 'believe' in empirical research. What we did find (as I will go on to explain) was a difference in the form and quality of many of the interviews with men. It should also be pointed out here that in terms of the Project as a whole the balance was tilted towards men because although we attempted to interview as many women postgraduates as possible, in some departments there were very few women registered, but, of course, the majority of supervisors were men. I am not suggesting that we faced a unified set of problems with all the men we interviewed. Their styles of response varied greatly although in general the more powerful their position the more difficult the situation. What I want to do now is to illustrate some of the patterns which emerged in this process. I feel that it is important to examine the part which power has to play in the interview situation and many of the problems related to the examples of gender power. This was, of course, highlighted by the nature of the research situations. We were in fact theoretically interviewing our peers. As Jennifer Platt (1981) has pointed out, there are special problems involved with this relationship (see also Hilary Burgess in this volume) and while I certainly found similar problems to those which they outline, for me the fact of gender, particularly when combined with status was the most significant aspect.

Many of the men I interviewed attempted to control the situation from the outset by, for example, making a great issue about how busy they were and therefore placing very tight time constraints on the interview. One male professor granted me 'an audience' of fifteen minutes after I had spent days trying to see him. He was then thirty minutes late for the interview and we were interrupted three times. I felt that he had a very clear idea of what he thought I needed to know regardless of the questions I asked him, and that this was straightforward 'factual' information. Many men did, in fact, treat us rather like human questionnaires: yes, no, next question, and one in particular said at the end of the interview 'Now let me think of what you haven't asked me about', in fact he could not think of anything but made clear his assumption of being in control. Other senior men simply used the occasion of the interview to deliver a lecture on the topic of their choice, one, for instance, spent a good deal of the time attacking the SSRC while another insisted on going into endless detail about how good the graduate seminars were in his department (this was particularly interesting given the very different view of the students). One professor stated very clearly that in his view the ideal mode of postgraduate study was to be a part of a small group sitting at the feet of a 'great man' (as he had at Cambridge), thus reinforcing the view of academia as male and elitist and therefore automatically placing me in a marginal position as a mere interviewer. These are just a few examples of the issues which arose for me while interviewing powerful men. Of course we wanted their views about postgraduate research and perhaps I should not complain that this is what we got. However, what seems to be significant here is that although we thought we had set up a qualitative interview (see Measor, 1985 for a detailed discussion of the ethnographic interview) we were not in control of what actually happened and many of them seemed to be responding to a hidden structured questionnaire. The way that these experiences made me feel about myself as a woman and a researcher and the effects which this had on the research and on the rest of my life became very important. I also became increasingly aware as time passed that I had to some extent fallen for the idea of the 'objective' interviewer, and had perceived a 'need' to keep my feminism at least partially hidden (no badges, no direct confrontation of sexism, and so on) to avoid 'contaminating' the situation. After all, it was their views on postgraduate education that I wanted, not their response to feminism, or so I thought at the time. What I learnt was that senior men would react to me as a young woman in a relatively marginal position no matter what I did, and that this reaction was just as much data as anything else that happened in the interview.

Another major gender difference occurred with the postgraduates themselves. One of our main interests was in experiencing the range of non-academic pressures they were under and how these affected their work. These 'topics' included the domestic, social and political aspects of their lives. We found that in general men did not see these as legitimate topics, and simply said very little about them. Of course this lack of discussion was data in itself, but I was unable to avoid feeling that I was somehow failing to get at significant information, after all, everyone has some kind of personal life. Of course we 'knew' that in general men do not have as many outside pressures as women and suspected that those that they did have would be different, but we did not obtain the detailed data we expected because of the different responses to the interview situation and its stated focus, that is postgraduate research. Many of these men simply perceived their academic lives as separate from their 'personal' lives. Women on the other hand were very quick to make connections between different areas of their lives and to discuss problems and tensions. For example, one woman made the following comment about how she felt she had to over-compensate for the fact that she was a research student.

> Oh, yes, I think you're under tremendous pressure to be a good mother, and much more tolerant and better mother who is very careful about keeping your kids clean, well dressed, well fed... I think I'm quite an expert at giving out the image of what a good mother is.

Another woman said:

> Well, I think that women know that if the house is dirty it's the woman who is seen as the one ... it's how others perceive you, if the house is dirty it's not because your husband won't do his share.

The one man who said similar things was doing most of the child care while his wife did paid work; he said:

> In discussions they all treat me as if I'm working under the same conditions as they are ... I sometimes feel a little bitter, some colleagues just don't have worries about kids and income, it must be so easy to work.

This comment is also interesting because it shows that they (male staff) assume he is like them which means that they still have high expectations of him, whereas we found that women were expected to be different. Most men, however, had little to say about domestic matters and the following comment is a fairly typical response to a question about working at home.

> Yes, I have a study of my own ... plenty of room, yes, and facilities at home are OK. I mean you couldn't work in this hovel [his office at the Poly] I refuse to work in this.

Like many men he had a haven at home and in fact the notes attached to his transcript say 'he gave an impression of complete confidence but I (the interviewer) would like to have known more about how his wife feels about it all'.

Women on the other hand often lacked confidence and what follows is an example of the kind of comment which we heard from many women.

> In the meantime I did 'A' levels at evening classes, one a year and I suppose I kind of drifted into doing a degree because it was the next inevitable step, and as I said I always felt 'OK I

can't do 'A' levels you know that's for clever people'
... and it was sometime during the course of the
degree, again that went better than I expected, I kept doing
much better than I thought I was going to do and kept
thinking it was a fluke all the time... I mean, I still keep
pinching myself and thinking, you know, this is where I fall
down.

In a similar vein were another woman's comments when asked if she
was planning to go on to do a PhD after her MA:

Not really yet no, because to tell you the truth I've been
feeling insecure about my own position as to whether or not
I'll get through the MA, and I didn't want to broach the
subject with my supervisor because presumably they're the
ones who normally bring it up; or because he knows what my
domestic situation is like... I can't see myself in the
position of saying 'do you think I'm going to be good enough
to do a PhD?'

The following extract shows how one woman felt about her research
after she had finished.

I've learnt an awful lot, I think basically the greatest problem
I had in retrospect was not having enough confidence to do
what I wanted to do instead of being guided by my supervisor
which was never the right guidance; that's what held it up it
really was.

When it came to expectations about the future most men hoped
for an academic job or if they were more realistic about the recession
thought they would get one if there were any; at least that is what
they said, whereas the following comment sums up the position of
many women:

I would like to teach but I don't really think I'm capable of
teaching at a very exalted level.

Men and women also had different ways of dealing with conflict at
home; one woman I interviewed spoke at length about her worries
that her boyfriend felt threatened by her developing academic
interests, and her attempts to resolve this by going on holiday with
him when really she wanted to work on her thesis. At the other
extreme a male student (a vicar) whose wife had got fed up with him
never being at home whilst he was doing the fieldwork for his

previous higher degree (this was his third) had dealt with the problem by not telling her of his current registration, (she thought he was writing sermons!)

Even at the admission stage it might be made clear that men and women would be operating under different rules; as one supervisor put it:

> With a man you say 'do you realize that for six years you really have no time to do the decorating or dig the garden' and so on and you know that they will say 'I've cemented over the garden, I've just painted the house.' Whereas with a woman you ask 'Is your husband fully aware because you know it's a decision to be made jointly.'

In terms of presenting this data I have always felt that there was a danger that in outlining the ways that women talked to us about their non-academic problems, child-rearing, housework, problems with supervisors, coupled with their expressions of lack of confidence that we would give the impression (because we had no data) that men had no similar problems and as a result we would simply contribute to the sexism which states that women are not detached enough or cannot concentrate sufficiently to do 'proper' academic work. The only satisfactory way for me to handle this data was to draw both on feminist theory and my own experience as a woman and place these different sets of data in the context of women and men's lives in a patriarchal society. More specifically it was important to look at the sexism within departments and the different expectations which supervisors had of male and female students. This particular scene can be set by the following comment from a male supervisor speaking of a hypothetical student. It shows how powerful the image is of the 'normal' postgraduate as a 'bright young man':

> He will be in the department, there are postgraduate seminars going on, there are various things he can contribute to, for instance he is going to do a little bit of first year teaching and so on so he'll be about I shall see him.

Contrast this with the woman's experience.

> Informally I had a conversation with one of the lecturers about why I was being failed and not allowed to resubmit and he said something along the lines of 'you didn't come along, you weren't really interested in this were you ...'
> ... I made it very clear I suppose that actually I didn't like

to socialize with them, I didn't go to the pub with them, in fact it was held against me in the end.

Even when there is sympathy with the position which many women are in it often means that expectations are lowered.

She has a teaching load which is both heavy and erratic plus two children, you know, one of which seems to be incredibly accident prone, God, I mean, I really do admire her the way she's been at it [her PhD] for six years or something.

It's almost as if women are expected to give up under the strain.

As the material in this section reveals, collecting ethnographic data can result in very different responses from women and men. It is interesting to note that the text book description of what constitutes a good qualitative interview (Benney and Hughes, 1956) is much closer to my experience of interviewing women, whereas many men, particularly high status academics seemed to wish to disrupt this process and to assume a hidden quantitative agenda.

Analyzed in terms of feminist theory what could have been seen as a failure on the part of the interviewer or the methodology becomes a useful example of the operation of male power in a situation.

What is Feminist Research?

At the beginning of this chapter I suggested that qualitative research on women tends to be what is 'expected' from feminist researchers. I hope that in drawing on examples from my data I have shown the danger of simply displaying women's lives and problems without placing them within a feminist framework and also of the value of interviewing men for gaining an understanding of how women are oppressed in a particular context.

I would not argue that feminists should not research other women and their lives; there are obviously situations when this is valuable and necessary, but as Janet Finch (1984) points out there are ethical and methodological problems. A major problem is that we may simply use other women's experiences to further our own aims and careers. Even with qualitative research the analysis is usually unilateral and the researcher is placed in the powerful position of translator or presenter of other women's lives, searching transcripts for quotable quotes to aid in the development of an argument. The obvious attraction to doing fieldwork 'on' women is the high level of sympathy which I have described and which so often occurs between women which makes the data collection such an enjoyable process. One way of avoiding some of these problems is for feminists to engage in research with, and for, women rather than on women and to ensure that the 'findings' are fed back and publications agreed.

I have suggested throughout this chapter that doing qualitative research on men was for me, at least a tricky business. I would, however, want to argue strongly for more feminist research on men. For some time there has been debate within sociology about the importance of researching the powerful (see, for example, John Urry and John Wakeford (1975) and the debate in the journal *Race and Class*, throughout 1979) and in particular of the need to study white racism and not only black people. It is, I would argue, equally important to study male power and the exercise of that power. In relation to the research on postgraduate education; the fact that sociology and higher education in general is male defined does not mean that it has been (except in a simplistic sense) *about* male attitudes and practices. In fact masculinity is generally taken as a norm without any interrogation of the assumptions behind it and how it is achieved! Also, we cannot expect men to interrogate this male-as-norm-bias in any detail. If feminist researchers continue to focus mainly on women there is a danger that in continuing to place so much emphasis on researching the relatively powerless that we partly reinforce and rephrase what we know already. What we do not know very much about is how men 'do' sexism, exactly how they exert power and how such male behaviour can be successfully countered. Again, as David Morgan (1981) has pointed out, men can and do successfully ignore or pigeon-hole feminist research on women because they do not find it personally threatening. Feminist research should be threatening to male behaviour patterns, and one way of achieving this is to do feminist research on men. The next question of course is should this research on men use qualitative methods? There is the danger that women conducting in-depth interviews with men will be the object of subtle or even direct sexism. Although we did not suffer to any great degree from the latter during the postgraduate research project. But then, most male sociologists have at least learned to be careful about what they *say* in this context. However, one supervisor, for example, did say 'Oh, dear, are you going to tape it, that means I won't be able to chat you up' which is not a good start to an interview and made the interviewer feel undermined. Many feminists may feel that they are subject to enough sexism in their everyday lives without making themselves vulnerable in their research, and I respect this view. However, I feel that it is important to research men and that if thought is given to the most suitable methods for a given situation then this will be both possible and productive. One possibility is, of course, to engage in participant observation in a given situation which involves men, or even as Liz Stanley and Sue Wise (1983) suggest, to research yourself and your own position thus examining the processes whereby male power works in your own life (for further discussion of self-observation see Plummer (1983), especially chapter two). This leads to another aspect of doing feminist research, which I feel to be particularly important, that is the inclusion of the position of the researcher throughout the entire process. This aspect of research has been discussed within sociology for several years now (see, for example, Colin Bell and Heward Newby, 1977) but is rarely treated seriously, and is a particularly important issue for feminist researchers because of feminism's concern to explicate the politics of personal life, making it therefore insufficient to research others and to leave one's own position unexamined.

The ways in which my feminism affected the ways in which I responded to and analyzed my own marginal position as a woman researcher and the ways in which this was reinforced by male interviewees, has been particularly important for me. Although it was not until a fairly late stage in the research that I accepted the importance of this process, having previously seen myself as an analyzer of data rather than as an object of research. Latterly, however, the research became for me the process of doing the research and writing about it rather than simply the analysis of the transcripts. What I chose to write about in relation to the research and where I sought publication were similarly affected. Less than half the papers I have produced have been about research 'findings' in an orthodox sense; most of the work has been about doing research and the position of women in this process.

What then is feminist research? I stated earlier that it is not simply research on women by women, neither does it consist of qualitative methodology, for although I have a preference on an academic and a personal level (a false distinction anyway) for ethnographic methods, I have, I hope, pointed out some of the problems for feminists working in this way. I would also argue that as feminists we should use the methodology which seems to be most appropriate to the context and the questions which we are asking, but, most importantly that we should be critical of all accepted research methods as Dale Spender (1978) argues, feminists should question *all* established ways of thinking. We should not confine ourselves to the parameters of the debates between established methodologies. I see the search for *a* feminist methodology or an appropriation by feminist researchers of one particular methodology is a process which only serves to constrain feminist input into research and to contain it within existing debates. In summary, I am a feminist who does research, I hope, to avoid the constraints of one particular methodology. I will end, therefore, with a comment with which I am in complete agreement:

> Demands that feminists produce a unique methodology act to circumscribe the impact of feminism... We feel it is time to abandon what amounts to a defensive strategy. It has to be recognized that feminist research is not a specific, narrow methodology, but *research informed at every stage by an acknowledged political commitment.* (Dickens *et al.*, 1983)

References

BELL, C. and NEWBY, H. (1977) *Doing Sociological Research*, London, Allen and Unwin.

BENNEY, M. and HUGHES, E.C. (1956) 'Of sociology and the interview', *American Journal of Sociology*, 62, 2, pp. 137–42.

BERNARD, J. (1973) 'My four revolutions: An autobiographical history of the American Sociological Association', *American Journal of Sociology*, 78, pp. 773–91.

DANIELS, A. (1975) 'Feminist perspectives in sociological research', in MILLMAN, M. and KANTER, R. (Eds) *Another Voice*, New York, Anchor Books.

DICKENS, L., *et al.* (1983) 'Is feminist methodology a red herring', letter to the editor of *Network* (the newsletter of the British Sociological Association) no. 26, May.

EICHLER, M. (1980) *The Double Standard*, London, Croom Helm.

FINCH, J. (1984) '"It's great to have someone to talk to": The ethics and politics of interviewing women', in BELL, C. and ROBERTS, H. (Eds) *Social Researching: Politics, Problems and Practice*, London, Routledge and Kegan Paul.

GLASER, B. and STRAUSS, A. (1967) *The Discovery of Grounded Theory: Strategies for Qualitative Research*, London, Weidenfeld and Nicolson.

GRAHAM, H. (1984) 'Surveying through stories', in BELL, C. and ROBERTS, H. (Eds) *Social Researching: Politics, Problems and Practice*, London, Routledge and Kegan Paul.

HESTER, M. (1984) 'Anti-sexist men: A case of cloak and dagger chauvinism',

Women's Studies International Forum, 7, 1, pp. 33–7.

LLEWELLYN, C. (1981) 'Occupational mobility and the use of the comparative method', in ROBERTS, H. (Ed.) *Doing Feminist Research*, London, Routledge and Kegan Paul.

MEASOR, L. (1985) 'Interviewing: A strategy in qualitative research', in BURGESS, R.G. (Ed.) *Strategies of Educational Research: Qualitative Methods*, Lewes, Falmer Press.

MORGAN, D.H.J. (1981) 'Men, masculinity and sociological enquiry', in ROBERTS, H. (Ed.) *Doing Feminist Research*, London, Routledge and Kegan Paul.

OAKLEY, A. (1981) 'Interviewing women: A contradiction in terms', in ROBERTS, H. (Ed.) *Doing Feminist Research*, London, Routledge and Kegan Paul.

PEARSON, C. (1984) 'Male sexual politics and men's gender practice', *Women's Studies International Forum*, 7, 1, pp. 29–32.

PLATT, J. (1981) 'On interviewing one's peers', *British Journal of Sociology*, 32, 1, pp. 75–91.

PLUMMER, K. (1983) *Documents of Life*, London, Allen and Unwin.

PORTER, M. (1984) 'The modification of method in researching postgraduate education', in BURGESS, R.G. (Ed.) *The Research Process in Educational Settings: Ten Case Studies*, Lewes, Falmer Press.

PURVIS, J. (1985) 'Reflections upon doing historical documentary research from a feminist perspective', in BURGESS, R.G. (Ed.) *Strategies of Educational Research: Qualitative Methods*, Lewes, Falmer Press.

SCOTT, S. (1984) 'The personable and the powerful: gender and status in sociological research', in BELL, C. and ROBERTS, H. (Eds) *Social Researching: Politics, Problems and Practice*, London, Routledge and Kegan Paul.

SCOTT, S. (1985) 'Working through the contradictions in researching postgraduate education', in BURGESS, R.G. (Ed.) *Field Methods in the Study of Education*, Lewes, Falmer Press.

SCOTT, S. and PORTER, M. (1980) 'Postgraduates, sociology and the cuts', in ABRAMS, P. and LEUTHWAITE, P. (Eds) *Transactions of the British Sociological Association*, London, British Sociological Association.

SCOTT, S. and PORTER, M. (1983) 'On the bottom rung: women and women's work in sociology', *Women's Studies International Forum*, 6, 2.

SCOTT, S. and PORTER, M. (1984) 'Women in research: A double marginalisation', in ACKER, S. WARREN-PIPER, D, and (Eds) *Is Higher Education Fair to Women?*, London, Society for Research in Higher Education.

SMITH, D. (1974) 'Women's perspective: A radical critique of sociology', *Sociological Inquiry*, 44, pp. 7–13.

SPENDER, D. (1980) *Man Made Language*, London, Routledge and Kegan Paul.

STANLEY, L. and WISE, S. (1979) 'Feminist research, feminist consciousness and experience of sexism', *Women's Studies International Quarterly*, 2, 3, pp. 359–74.

STANLEY, L. and WISE, S. (1983) *Breaking Out: Feminist Consciousness and Feminist Research*, London, Routledge and Kegan Paul.

URRY, J. and WAKEFORD, J. (Eds) (1975) *Power in Britain*, London, Heinemann.

WAKEFORD, J. (1985) 'A Director's dilemmas', in BURGESS, R.G. (Ed.) *Field Methods in the Study of Education*, Lewes, Falmer Press.

WOODWARD, D. and CHISHOLM, L. (1981) 'The expert's view? The sociological analysis of graduates' occupational and domestic roles', in ROBERTS, H. (Ed.) *Doing Feminist Research*, London, Routledge and Kegan Paul.

5 New Songs Played Skilfully: Creativity and Technique in Writing Up Qualitative Research

Peter Woods

'Devise, wit! write, pen! for I am for whole volumes in folio'
Shakespeare

The 'Pain' Threshold

Little consideration is given to creativity in our methodological discussions. I mean by this the ability to perceive interconnections and associations among data, to provide explanations for them, and to see further ways forward. None of this is given in the material of our research. It has to be invented on the basis of various clues given to us by the research and our knowledge of other studies. This imaginative work lies at the heart of data analysis. In many ways, it is the 'make or break' activity that renders research different, useful, relevant and effective.

In this 'creative' activity there is a critical point, that falls as much within the communication of these ideas, as in their generation. Ideas can be fleeting, hazy, ill-formed, fanciful, irrelevant, inconsequential. Often, it is only when we apply the iron discipline of writing to them that we come to realize this. Like the budding author in Piers Paul Read's *Polonaise* (1977) 'The difficulty he faced with the white sheet of paper was not that he had no ideas, but that he no longer trusted his ideas to keep their shape as he gave them expression' (p. 131).

Thus we might find what we thought a particularly useful concept rather difficult to grasp; or a seemingly beautiful, but light and airy idea only wafted further away as we try to seize it; or an apparently imposing edifice encapsulating our research and all others in a totally new and discipline-shattering way, knocked over, like a castle of matchsticks, by a stroke of the pen. With others, we find, as we put on them the best constructions we can, a certain emptiness, banality, impossibility, inappropriateness, unoriginality. We may be forced back to a reconsideration of our data, perhaps to more data collection and recategorizing, certainly to reconceptualizing.

Failure, or a 'refusal', at this Becher's Brook of data analysis can be a disheartening experience. Perhaps this is why so many promising PhD studies founder, why some research studies never get reported, and why some spend so long in data collection. It is not, however, an insurmountable problem. Charles Morgan (1960) has said of the artist, '. . . no one can be effectively an artist without taking pains . . . This technical part of an artist's life may be learned, and the learning may be carried so far that it ceases to be narrowly technical and becomes a study of the grand strategy of artistic practice' (p. 119). Thus, there is a certain amount of craftwork in the creative enterprise. Also, it may be helpful to conceive of the problem not so much in terms of what you do to the data, but what you do to yourself. It is a commonplace that in qualitative work the main instrument is the researcher. Due attention has been paid to this point at the stage of data collection — less at the stage of analysis.

Pain is an indispensable accompaniment of the process. How often do we hear somebody admitting they 'sweated blood' in writing a certain piece; or the view that they know a certain stage in the research is near, and must be faced, but that they are 'dreading' and 'hating it'? This aspect of the research is best conceived as a 'rite de passage', a ritual, that is as much a test of self as anything else, that has to be gone through if the research project is to reach full maturity. If we do not feel pain at this point, there is almost certainly something wrong. Perhaps we are not progressing, and simply marking time on the spot, being satisfied with analysis at an elementary level which plays safe and avoids the risk of burning in the ring of fire, as well as the burden of hard work. But while such reports may not be entirely without value, they may not be making the best use of their material. Researchers must be masochists. We must confront the pain barrier till it hurts.

We share this experience with all kinds of creative people. I recall hearing Philip Gardiner (a Norfolk artist) describing his experience of painting as 'tense and draining — but it has to be, I wouldn't have it any other way. It's very precarious, but it adds a certain lustre to life'. The biographical annals of composers, writers, poets, artists are strewn with similar accounts of self-imposed suffering.

Once we have recognized this, we might consider our attributes as analysts. Most of us have served long apprenticeships, from junior school compositions, secondary school essays, precis, paraphrasing, comprehension tests, and language exercises, to university essays, dissertations and theses. We have spent a lifetime in trying to extract essences, order priorities correctly, express ourselves clearly and succinctly. Yet it is a curious phenomenon how on occasions such training may be completely forgotten. One such occasion I find is after an intensive piece of writing. It is as if it exhausts one's creative quota, and when it comes to the next writing enterprise, though all the ingredients are marshalled, there is no electricity, and consequently no cooking. A blank mind reflects the blank sheet of paper in front of it.

Moral Imperatives and Mental Conditioners

How, then, might we break out of this psychological state and render our chief research instrument more effective at this critical juncture? There is, firstly, a baseline of physical, mental and situational fitness without which it would be difficult to do this sort of work. I cannot write if I am tired, worried or ill, or if I am distracted. Nor does the creative urge in research and art necessarily go well with teaching. Research may benefit teaching, but the converse does not apply. As Hugh MacDiarmid (1969) has noted of art (in the general sense, and in the same sense that Nisbet, 1962, saw it as applying to sociology)

> To halt or turn back in order to try to help others is to abandon artistic progress, and exchange education for art. There is no altruism in art. It is every man for himself. In so far as he advances, the progress of others may be facilitated, but in so far as he is conscious of affording any such facilitation, his concentration on purely artistic objectives is diminished. (p. 45)

If peace is essential, so, too, is pressure. I have heard some writers (novelists) say that their best work is done in situations where time hangs heavy on their hands, but I have not found that always so. Perhaps their pressure derives from a self-generating muse, whereas I am very much a product of the Protestant Ethic. I need external motivators. In fact the danger is that, given time, I sink into even greater torpitude. Certainly one must have time for analysis and writing, and research sponsors rightly stress the need to make due allowance for it. But nothing concentrates the mind more wonderfully than schedules. We might bemoan them, but where a research report is due, a publisher's deadline to be met, a paper prepared for a certain seminar, or conference date, then there is necessity whipping the flaccid mind into activity. For this reason, it pays to contrive to have inserted in the research programme at strategic points dates for the production of papers on some aspect of the research. They must, of course, involve some investment of status, and that means addressing a public. Thus status will be lost if the schedule is not met. At the same time, it needs to be recognized that there is a fine dividing line between a nicely crowded agenda and overwork, the latter possibly having grave consequences for the quality of product and personal well-being. Writing is like making sausages. The mincing machine works more efficiently and produces better sausages when the meat is being crammed in, but we must take care we do not clog the machine or mince our fingers!

Schedules can be awesome and counter-productive if they ask for too much in too short a time. The most serviceable, possibly, are those that are staggered, that do not require a finished article at a stroke, but permit degrees of sophistication. The leap from data to presentation then need not seem too vast, and the perfectionist instincts that many researchers have can be requited and exploited in a legitimate way instead of adding to the difficulties of the task. For there is a need to take risks in the early stages of analysis, to 'play' with the data, to 'try out' certain configurations and explanations, and occasionally to back horses one is not altogether sure of — though our betting may be judicious and stop short of putting our shirts on them. This experimentation requires feedback and input from others. The ideal circumstance, of course, is the working group, when it is freely acknowledged that all are concerned in development.

Having internalized the moral imperative to write, I feel the need for some mental stimulants and conditioners. These are of two kinds, techniques and aspirations. Techniques are to do with the mechanics of communication. Here I might recall certain aspects of my training. '... where to begin, how to end, how to orchestrate, how to be simple and direct ... these things are the armoury of writers (Morgan, 1960, p. 132). And Morgan recalls his own indebtedness to his own former studies, for example, Greek and Latin

> for case, mood, tense, voice and a thousand refinements different from his own ... and while he fights his own battle for an elusive meaning, he may be fortified against

the accursed blight of 'It couldn't matter less' by the sound and memory of battles long ago.

The stimulation of mental agility no doubt varies greatly from person to person. I prefer at these times to read material other than sociology or education. To be sure, one cannot research in a vacuum, and a thorough knowledge of the relevant literature is assumed. However, academic research has a curious tendency to be all-consuming. There is so much of relevance to read, and which we feel we should know about. Thus, if there is anything at all to spare we probably invest in it that further academic article or book that we just have not as yet had time to read. But while a certain amount of such reading is essential for research context, it may not serve us very well as models of presentation. For some, of course, it may inspire. Others may find forcing themselves to embrace a wider field of literature and art productive in terms of mind-stimulation and models for writing.

For power and economy of words, for mental leaps, comparisons and metaphors, I would recommend poetry (see also Brown, 1977). For strength of description, powers of observation, ability to bring off a point, give shape to an episode, form to a story, sustained development and integration, social commentary, human insight and sheer inventiveness, I would go to a novel or to drama.

A critic made this comment about Virginia Woolf's *To the Lighthouse*:

> It is a book that has deeply influenced me. I might be walking down the street involved in a series of thoughts which probably don't seem to have any connection — the brilliance of Virginia Woolf is that she discovered there were connections and, more important, she could make sense of them and write them down.

This is essentially the same kind of creativity involved in research. Music and art are also helpful in this respect. Edward Blishen played a recording of Schubert's Octet obsessively whilst engaged in his Adaptations. Schubert 'can't have imagined that, 130 years after it was written, this enchanting music for the chamber would be used as a lenitive by a literary oddjobman' (1980, p. 38).

What all these forms of art have in common is (a) in their timeless, eternal beauty, a kind of absolute validity; (b) a perfection of form — their various parts all hang together and follow one another almost inevitably; (c) a sense of growth — as point follows point, it is not simply a matter of addition, but greater depth to the message; and

(d) human creativity — they are among the highest achievements of people. All this is neatly illustrated in the play *Amadeus* by Peter Shaffer. Salieri, in wonderment at some new Mozart compositions, is made to say 'Displace one note, and there will be diminishment; displace one phrase, and the structure will fall'. As he looked at the manuscripts he realized 'I was staring through those ink-notes at an absolute beauty'. Mozart himself realized his worth. 'Too many notes!' complained the Emperor. Replied the composer, with absolute certainty: 'There are just as many notes, your Majesty, no more, nor less than are required'. And when asked to rewrite the fourth act of Figaro, since 'that's your forte, isn't it, writing at speed?' 'Not when the whole thing's perfect!'

In all these respects, works of music, art, and so on, serve as worthy models, in their mental processes, for our ethnographic work. All forms of art have the same properties. William Trevor, for example, himself a former sculptor, likens his story-telling to moulding and chipping away at a sculpture. It is what the writer David Lodge is alluding to when he says, 'Every word must make an identifiable contribution to the whole'. And Ronald Duncan, in a poem comparing the construction of a pig-sty with poetry:

> The site: choose a dry site. Avoid building against a bank. Leaning a building to a bank may save putting up a wall, but dampness will seep through, you'll see your mortar sweat, you'll be feeding to keep your pig warm, this way she'll not fatten profitably; you may get roast out of it, but no bacon, etc. (Holloway, 1957)

Structuralists argue that there are basic common properties among these various different areas (see also Hammersley and Atkinson, 1983). Though 'transfer of training' theory was not popular a few years ago in the debate over the usefulness of Latin as a school subject, Levi-Strauss, for example, believes that the receipt by the brain of musical messages can serve as a model for the receipt of all other kinds of cultural message. For example, he argues that melody and harmony illustrate the structural linguist's distinction between sequence and content. Interestingly, Levi-Strauss himself is often described as an artist as well as a scholar, and 'his style remains a baroque combination of order and fantasy' (Sperber, 1979, p. 24).

There is a further point — that whatever we select to consider in the area of art will reflect our own personal concerns and make-up, and encourage reflexivity. Thus it not only helps put our research on a broader plane of people's affairs, but helps give it depth. Ethnographic work is extremely personal. To a greater extent than other forms of research, it allows a working out of one's own destiny within the context of 'public issues'. In other words, it offers insight into problems and anomalies one may have experienced in the past in a structured way aligned to general human experience, and thus avoids the excesses of self-indulgence.

Cranking-Up

These models are the Rolls Royces of the artistic world. When I come to address myself to writing-up research, I am reminded of my first car, an ancient Morris 1000, which had to be cranked up before it would start. It was rather erratic in its running (largely, I eventually discovered, because of the tendency for its tappetts to seize up), and boiled over on occasions, but it usually got there in the end, though not very quickly.

The 'cranking up' is a necessary preliminary. Analysis is multi-layered — it does not all take place on the same mental plane. Writing is such a different activity from other responsibilities of academic life (such as teaching and administration) that we are not usually in the right frame of mind, nor do we fall into it naturally. It has to be artificially induced. We might regard it as a challenge and as poten-tially very rewarding intellectually. We might persuade ourselves that we actually enjoy writing, though any intellectual reward or enjoy-ment usually comes afterwards, certainly not at the beginning. 'Writing-up' research is nothing like the delightful essays we used to do at junior school, or the cathartic bits of biography or magazine articles we may compose from time to time, which have a stronger measure of self-indulgence and journalese about them. Academic writing is a strongly disciplined activity, and we have to gear ourselves up for it.

I might have to set anything from a day to a week aside for 'cranking up'. I might find that I have two or three clear days that I can give over to making a start on writing, to generate a bit of impetus that may then be carried on over the next two-three weeks. This is an average time for getting to grips with a writing project, and in general, I find I have to devote all my attention to it during that period if I am to master it. I am very unsociable and rather ill-tempered during this time. Some of us may actually have to appear to undergo profound personality changes in order to do the work. Unlike Dr Jekyll, however, we have no magic potion.

I find it is done almost by default. That is, I always delude myself into thinking that I am actually going to commence writing on those first days. I rarely do. For what happens is confrontation and engagement with the pain barrier. Part of this is to do with forcing oneself into psychological overdrive. What these initial two-three days consist of, then, might be a reconsideration of all the research material, a continuous sifting and re-sifting, clearing out the debris, identifying the strengths, aligning the material towards them, checking on key associated work, reclassifying, having one or two attempts at an introduction, and, if that fails, putting together one of the more complete, coherent and interesting sections. If the latter works, it can snowball, and provide a comparatively easy passage. More typically, it is only the beginning of the struggle.

What one is doing, then, in these early stages, is firstly undergoing a process of 'psyching up' to writing pitch, (a process attended by some disorder and discomfort), and secondly, going through the initial stages of preparing one's material for presentation. The cranking-up process is partly systematic and consolidating, partly disorderly and adventurous as one searches for new configurations. This latter indicates a third activity, therefore, one of creativity. It comes from reading and rereading fieldnotes, transcripts, summaries, categories; examining comments made along the way, perhaps in a research diary, made at the time 'for future reference'. One tests out a few more ideas, seeing what they look like on paper. Diagrams are useful in trying to show interrelationships. The waste-paper basket fills up rapidly. Robert Graves was told by an early mentor that his 'best friend was the wastepaper basket' and this, he later discovered, was 'good advice'.

At the end of the first day, therefore, all that may have been produced is a side of A4, which will probably be at once discarded the following day. But a great deal of mental preparation and ground clearing of data will have been done. I have a standard 'production rate' of five written pages, or a thousand words a day. I think this is a kind of writer's norm I have somehow internalized, and it seems to be about right when I am working properly. The quality may be variable, especially to begin with, but I do not worry about that at this stage as long as the brain is being oiled into gear and some ideas are beginning to come. The 'quota' stands as some tangible and identifiable product of the work of the day. While this is a stage for throwing ideas around in the mind and testing out alternative constructions, the acid test for them is whether they retain their potential value in communication. The quota is a reasonable amount to provide for such a test — long enough to require sustained and coherent thought and to reflect fairly large-scale organization, and short enough to tackle in a day without exhausting front-line concentration.

Protestant Ethic person also internalizes time regulation. When I was schoolteaching, this was beautifully controlled externally by the 'nine to four' and 'termly' requirements. You knew when you were working and when not. As an academic, management of time is more personal, but I find I am still governed by Protestant Ethic standards. The ritual of sitting down to work at 9.00 a.m. and working through to 12.00 or 12.30 p.m., and then a further two hours in the afternoon, is a good mental discipline. Without this moral impulsion behind the ritual I doubt whether I would ever get round to writing at all. However, it is a curious thing that while I keep to the ritual, 'off-duty' hours can be vastly more productive. Thus, winter evenings, weekends, late at night and occasionally early morning are all comparatively high productivity times. Protestant Ethic standards dictate that these are 'free time', and the psychology of it is that I cannot make a mess of them, or it does not matter if I do. I am consequently more relaxed, and usually therefore more productive. Periods before holidays are also useful. Holidays must be earned, and if a project is unfinished, will not be enjoyed. There is, too, a strong practical impulsion, for a partially finished project means that 'cranking up' has to commence again on the same piece after the 'limbering down' of the holiday — hardly the best use of scarce resources.

Having got cranked up, successfully engaged a gear and begun moving, I will at various points meet a roadblock. I take comfort, however, from the fact that this happens to the best of authors. In one of his novels, Tchekov agonized for days over how he was going to get one of his heroines across the threshold of a house. Conrad had terrible torments. He sometimes wished to be a stone breaker, because 'There's no doubt about breaking a stone. But there's doubt, fear — a black horror, in every page one writes' (Karl and Davies, 1983). Edward Blishen (1980) speaks of a highly capable novelist of his acquaintance who, after writing 'a hundred splendid pages would be overtaken by literary dread at its worst' — fear of reviewers, and fear that 'the narrative had come to a halt' (pp. 118–9). He would beg Blishen 'to tell him frankly if I thought his skills were in decline ... And at the end, always, as I made the noises necessary to keep him writing, he'd ask, "Does it move? It does move, doesn't it?"' The moral here is that we need good friends, mentors, trusted colleagues whom we can rely on for good advice and moral support.

This kind of therapy does not rule out the equally valuable constructive criticism one looks for from colleagues, which at times might be quite trenchant — though that is addressed to a different problem.

Writers develop their own psychological boosters. John Mortimer (1983, p. 9) has his study plastered with his own playbills. 'I've never been strong on confidence. When the page is blank and you fear, as I regularly do, that it may never be filled again — it does help to look up and think at least I wrote *that*!' For those of us who have not got that far, we must have recourse to basic elements of character — confidence in one's ability to pass the threshold; patience, in not expecting too rapid a return and in tolerating difficulties and hold-ups; stamina and determination, to keep at the task exploring all avenues and employing all one's resources in countless configurations to find a way ahead. At such junctures, we might recall Masefield's optimistic lines:

Therefore, go forth, companion: when you find
No highway more, no track, all being blind,
The way to go shall glimmer in the mind.

— though it is as well to bear in mind the old adage that the 'light at the end of the tunnel may be an oncoming train!'

There are strategies one can bring to bear on blockages. The first thing is to analyze the problem. Is it because you are tired (even though perhaps you have not reached your quota)? The answer, clearly, is rest, or a change of activity. Is it because of a lack of preparation or inadequate groundwork, so that you really do not know what you want to say? One is thrown back into a reconsideration of data, more reading perhaps, and certainly more preliminary thought. Or perhaps one gets an uneasy feeling that the account is going up a blind alley, that what seemed like the right direction in planning, now in writing turns out to be a mirage. There is no alternative but to return to the beginning of the faulty line. The important thing is not to get consumed by the blockage, but to master it.

Otherwise, there are numerous little ploys that I am sure we all use to avoid such blockages. Gazing out of the window at the panoramic vista ('I will lift up mine eyes unto the hills from whence cometh my help'), drinking numerous cups of coffee (as much for the breaks as for the caffeine), pacing the room, listening to a cheerful thrush, examining distant activity on the allotments through binoculars (Damn! The coalman is getting ahead of me again!), conversing with the dog, explaining a point or making a speech to an imaginary audience (Mills, 1970, recommended this), holding a conversation in one's head, taking a walk around the garden, playing the violin ... and so on. Thomas Keneally has a snooker table in his study for such moments. Some recommend a bout of strenuous exercise, almost as if thrashing the ennui out of one's system — squash, swimming, running. One headmaster I knew used to keep a punch-bag in his office for 'insoluble problem' times.

However, one needs to distinguish genuine blockages from self-induced ones. Work-avoidance strategies are particularly subtle in writing activities. In a study of student methods Bernstein (1978, p. 30) describes the 'creativity fritter':

> It is best to wait until you are bursting with ideas or are sufficiently motivated, even if the motivation is guilt due to unsuccessful previous application of fritter techniques. This is therefore the let-it-brew-for-a-while fritter (closely related to this is the I'll-lie-down-and-think-about-it fritter; the possible danger in this tactic is, of course, very clear; listing all things people are designed to do horizontally, studying is one of the lowest on the list.)

We might take heart again from the fact that even the best writers 'fritter', indeed they excel at it. Coleridge wrote to a friend,

> Tomorrow morning, I doubt not, I shall be of clear and collected spirits; but tonight I feel that I should do nothing to any purpose, but and excepting Thinking, Planning and Resolving to resolve — and praying to be able to execute (Letter to John H. Morgan, 1814).

William Cowper similarly

> ... difficult (I say) for me to find opportunities for writing. My morning is engrossed by the garden; and in the afternoon, till I have drunk tea, I am fit for nothing. At five o'clock we walk; and when the walk is over, lassitude recommends rest, and again I become fit for nothing. The current hour therefore which (I need not tell you) is comprised in the interval between four and five, is devoted to your service, as the only one in the twenty-four which is not otherwise engaged (Letter to the Rev. William Unwin, 1781).

Work-avoidance strategies may indicate a genuine need for relief, or an only too human reaction to steer clear of pain. We might at least recognize them for what they are. As for blockages, one might try to head them off by ensuring a stream of options. Pen and paper should be carried at all times. Ideas may be sparked off by auto-suggestion when watching television, listening to the radio, cooking a meal, digging the garden, and should be noted down before forgotten. I find driving in the car a particularly productive situation, and here, a recording machine is helpful. When writing, I often find the mind playing with future possibilities at the same time as concentrating on the point in hand. Even as I write, I scribble down a key word at the bottom of the paper to remind me of them, lest they be lost.

If a blockage is unavoidable and immovable, I go elsewhere, to some other part of the analysis where the going is easier. This helps recovery of fluency and confidence and helps salve the Protestant Ethic conscience as it fills out more of the quota, or I may go back over what I have done filling out a point here and there, and further rationalizing my plan. I shall then return to the blockage later, with new-found impetus. The whole report, paper, article or book is then put together later like a film at cutting and editing stage. I rarely write an article sequentially. The introduction is usually written last, for only then will I be sure of what the article is about. My final handwritten manuscript will be a mass of deletions and inserts, some written overleaf, some on extra pages, which themselves will have inserts, deletions and perhaps, extra pages. A secretary once described my manuscripts as like a game of Monopoly — 'Go to …' 'Do not …' 'Go back to …' 'See over …', with lines, arrows, bubbles etc.

If all else fails, the blockage may lead to discarding that particular element, or at least pigeon-holing it for future reference. However, it is as well to bear in mind that these are likely to be the most gratifying, worthwhile and celebrated aspects of the work if the problems are overcome. They should not be set aside lightly.

Planning

I recall in my school days the requirement to 'plan' an essay in rough. It was a one-off activity. You did your plan — you 'thought' — and then you followed it, and 'wrote'. Planning in writing up research is immensely more complicated. The former is secondary work, and not particularly creative. The latter is a search for new formulations, and almost by definition cannot be planned in advance. For the creative process continues into writing up. In fact, it may be *the* most creative part of qualitative work, and at times it is difficult to distinguish between planning and writing.

However, like patios and paint, as I have found over the years, you cannot apply the finish successfully without a good foundation. One's whole research, of course, involves planning. But in qualitative work, data collection ranges in a free and relatively uncommitted way. Plans for the final product usually begin to take shape during initial analysis. That is not my concern here, but it will be understood that fairly firm plans may be laid at this stage.

Beyond the preliminary analysis, I find four main planning stages; (a) a preliminary, partly systematic, partly randomized, speculative scheme; (b) a provisional working plan; (c) a reworked plan at first draft stage, which may be repeated in subsequent drafts; and (d) a final tidying up plan. Their nature is as follows:

(a) The initial scheme attempts to combine the solidity of the work already done with more speculative attempts to theorize and conceptualize. One must be heavily selective, reducing the data to a manageable size for the presentation vehicle in mind. Ideally, the plan should present an all-inclusive, see-at-glance picture of all the most important features of the research. This facilitates seeing what relates to what, and in what way various elements might hang together. Weak, unsupported elements are discarded. Data are marshalled to support others, and examples chosen. At the same time, this fairly mechanical work is accompanied by 'brainwaves' — attempts to see the data in a new light. I will make plenty of notes at this stage, scribbling down these brainwaves as and when they come to me. I shall end up with a file of these, which I duly go through on an appointed 'planning' day. They will be annotated and classified, added to as further thoughts occur, and reduced as I find similar points repeated. The preliminary plan may be fairly detailed, and certainly the more thoroughly it is done, the easier the passage into writing, even though that particular plan may soon be radically altered. For it is performing another function — preparing the mind. It is not only giving it a grasp of the whole enterprise, but forcing it to concentrate on the mechanics of construction. In the next stage, 'writing' will combine with this to produce the more lasting plan.

(b) The provisional working plan is abstracted from this. It consists, in essence, of a number of major headings, with sub-headings where appropriate, and an indication of the content (and where it is to be found) to be included under them. I may have a special chart for points I wish to emphasize in the conclusion. These are not easily written, yet are one of the most important sections. One solution therefore is to carry forward an ongoing plan of the conclusion to which notes are added as writing proceeds.

All the notes and data headings are systematically reconsidered to check for omissions or misrepresentations. Then the working plan is reexamined for order and for connecting links. These are not too strong at this stage, for the working plan will inevitably be changed once writing commences. In qualitative work especially, it is important to carry this divergent cast of mind through almost to the end product.

(c) A reworked, 'realized' plan emerges in writing the first draft. The preliminary plan will not be slavishly followed, for improved ideas will emerge as you begin to write. Some sections may prove very productive, others less so. In fact, one may suspend or bracket temporarily any overall plan while one follows promising lines of thought, which themselves have several branches. One may wish, in consequence, to afford these greater prominence within the scheme, and relegate others. The first draft may thus have a kaleidoscopic quality about it which is stitched together to provide an element of coherence and continuity, and which may bear little resemblance to the preliminary plan. This coherence, however implicit, should be real, and available for strengthening in subsequent drafts. But what you may find yourself doing at this stage is indulging the development of the component parts. You have a notion of the finished product, but its eventual quality depends on the quality and strength of its component parts as well as the way they are put together. You cannot make a Rolls Royce out of Morris 1000 parts.

(d) It follows that there must be a further plan, where the linkages, development and explanation are strengthened, and the material, possibly, again reordered. It sometimes pays to set the first draft aside for a while, to 'mature'. Returning to it with a fresh mind, it is easier to spot strengths and weaknesses. One also brings new resources to bear in the form of new thoughts, more 'focused' research and reading, and, most importantly, the reactions of others. Also, by this stage, one is well past the pain barrier and the tidying up can be done with greater confidence and equanimity. You have successfully externalized the product, and can now relax, and chip away at its improvement, deleting here, adding a further word of explanation there, finding more mellifluous and accurate phrase perhaps, reordering, tightening up, fitting it in to the general framework of research to which it relates, adding references, drawing conclusions. At this stage one applies the severest tests. What is missing here? What is wrong with this argument? What does it need to strengthen it? How else could this material be interpreted? How could this be criticized? What prejudices am I indulging? What do I really mean by this? Here there is a nice quote — but is it really needed? Here are some impressive sounding sentences — but what are they saying? There are some good points in this paragraph — but do they really relate to what goes before and after? Though in some ways easier to do than initial composing, in some ways it is still quite hard to summon up the resolve to rewrite sections once they have been typed. Nonetheless, it has to be done.

The twin principles here, I think, are that one must plan at each stage, but also maintain flexibility. It is important to have some sense of the overall scheme — we cannot just sit down and start writing — but equally important to realize that as the intensity of mental involvement with the data increases at each stage, so the previous plan may be amended or discarded. William Walton said he had not wanted to do *Facade* at the time. His comment later was, 'One sometimes happens to do something very good by mistake'. This is equally true of writing. One must aim for a productive tension between constructive planning and anarchic, but potentially highly productive, freedom.

With all these stages of writing and levels of thought, it is helpful to the psychological management of one's output to have several projects under way at the same time, all at different stages (see Glaser, 1978). Malcolm Bradbury, for example, has various projects in different typewriters around his house. It is comforting to have the satisfaction of publication just around the corner for one, and the option of 'chipping away' at a second draft for another, when one is working up inspiration for assaulting the pain barrier with a third. If they are related, they might 'feed off' each other, and they allow for ease of switching between psychological states, and thus maximizing the use of one's time and energies. This, however, calls for careful scheduling. Overproduction can lead to underachievement.

Common Failings in First (and Sometimes Later) Drafts

In countering pain and meeting the difficulties of writing up, there is a natural tendency to have recourse to some false solutions. This is another reason why it is so difficult to produce a finished paper in one or even two drafts. Among these are:

(i)   The 'Straw Person'

There is a strong temptation to work on a principle of contrasts. Thus in an attempt to highlight one's own argument, and increase its purity and force, one may construct an apology of an opposing one which does not really exist. It is a kind of bastardized ideal type, drawing on the evils of certain positions and glueing them together into a Frankenstein's monster of a case. The straw person typically draws on the work of a number of people and in itself is recognizable as nobody. Another similar form of misrepresentation, common amongst book reviewers, is to seize on only those points within one person's position that serve the present purpose, ignoring their context which may well modify those points. This is error enough in itself, but the major sin is inadequately contextualizing one's own work within the field. Of course, people who disagree with the representation of their position and one's analysis also, on occasions, shout 'Foul! Straw person!' when it is real flesh and blood.

(ii)   Overclaiming

This often accompanies a straw person. One gets carried away by excitement and enthusiasm as ideas emerge, and in attempting to make the most of one's argument in the strongest terms, overstates the case. It is often only when one sees the product in type that this is recognized. The initial exuberance has faded, and a more rational evaluation can take place. It is worth noting that there are pressures on us to overclaim. It has often been remarked that only positive research gets reported. We need to make our research tell and count. We are therefore looking for opportunities to 'excel'.

(iii)   Underclaiming

This derives from an unwarranted modesty or failure to perceive possibilities. The report may be written 'down' in an inconsequential way, set in a rather lugubrious context with the disadvantages of the method stressed over the advantages, and the weaknesses rather than strengths, stressed in conclusion. By oversight, there may be missed opportunities, unspotted connections and relevances. Here especially one stands to gain from the comments of others.

(iv) Utopianism

This is an imaginary state of ideal perfection. It is not necessarily a fault if recognized for what it is. At times, however, Utopian suggestions are put forward as practical possibilities. The research then becomes predicated on an other-worldly base and loses credibility. As in (a) however, there might be arguments as to what is Utopian and what not.

A form of Utopianism leads, on occasion, into mysticism. Unwilling to commit thoughts to the impurity of the printed page, we may cloak them in obscurity and advance them as an 'ongoing exploration of minds'. Unfortunately it is a journey without end, on which we are likely to be lone travellers. As Mills (1970, p. 243) notes, 'the line between profundity and verbiage is often delicate, even perilous'. At times, too, we may indulge in excessive jargon. One may fall into this in straining to show some theoretical richness in one's work — but it is the strain that shows not the theory. I am reminded of Shakespeare's character who 'draweth out the thread of his verbosity finer than the staple of his argument'.

(v) Sloppiness

This is too casual writing, showing inadequate thought during analysis and planning. There might be wild claims without proper evidence, ambiguities, inconsistencies, non sequiturs, contradictions. Many of the latter can be ironed out in later drafts, but if the general structure has not been adequately conceptualized, there is no alternative but to start again.

(vi) Overzealousness

I have argued for a productive tension between planning and freedom. Too much of the latter leads to sloppiness, too much of the former to overzealousness. The ideal situation is where the free-ranging mind can produce ideas that are then subjected to methodological rigour. It is difficult to work the process the other way round. Too much concern with the proprieties of method and 'le mot juste' at this early stage can lead to a barren product. It is like batting immediately for a whole session, yet scoring no runs. Or rigorously scrubbing some clothes — your product ends up scrupulously clean, but threadbare. Ideas must be allowed space and time to germinate. They will quickly rot if they are no good. But they will certainly never take root if not sown and cultivated.

(vii)   Overexactness

This is too neat an account. There is pressure on us — from research sponsors, from publishers, from the academic world at large — to be meticulously tidy, to present our work in ordered packages, duly itemized, sectionalized and sequenced. However, qualitative data above all is not like that. The problem is how to convey the sense of flux, process, messiness, inconsistency, ambiguity and so on, which is the very essence of everyday life. This is difficult to do whilst also trying to derive some theoretical order from the material. It is easy to slip into a previous, inappropriate, presentational framework, and make categories and types too sharp and distinct, and one's account rather too foursquare. The greatest danger of this comes when seeking to use earlier models or theoretical constructions. An extreme example of this I saw recently involved a 4×4 matrix where the author had felt pressured to produce a type for every square. The result was to make a nonsense of the matrix, for most of the types could have gone anywhere.

(viii)   Theoretical Inadequacy

Common forms of this among ethnographic research include:

(a)   Exampling
All that is done is to provide further illustrations of somebody else's concepts or theoretical constructs. Unless deliberately set up as a replication study, or seeking to develop formal from substantive theory, there is little worth in this. What should be done is to reexamine the data carefully to tell us what *else* it tells about these. More appropriate, if one knew the research was going to involve these theoretical areas, would be a prior consideration of them on the

Popperian lines already suggested — how might they be tested, falsified? What considerations do they omit? How adequate are they as representations of the data?

(b)   Theoretical lag or mismatch

Some of us have had to be dragged kicking and screaming, or yawning and rubbing our eyes, into the proper season of ethnography. A good illustration of this 'lag' is the 'characteristics' model noted by Hargreaves (1977) attending much of the early 'interactionist' work in schools, as opposed to a more purist 'process' model. The characteristics model was a hang-over from psychological approaches, especially interaction analysis, which had certain affinities with ethnography. Theoretical 'lag' may come about through one's own biography. Steeped in certain methods and approaches by training, experienced and 'internalized' through successful research, which may have brought some acclaim and established a personal niche, it is difficult to make a complete break and view the world otherwise.

(c)   Undertheorized description

Ethnography is description by definition. But it is description that is theoretically informed (see Hammersley, 1980). The description I have in mind here is little more than a presentation of the data as it stands, with little attempt to analyze, explain, draw out common features across situations, identifying patterns of behaviour, syndromes of factors, and so forth. It is journalistic, and quite appropriate in that kind of market, but it is inadequate as academic research. Of course, marshalling the data is an appropriate step in research analysis, but it comes at an earlier stage.

Conclusion

The point where rich data, careful analysis and lofty ideas meet the iron discipline of writing is one of the great problem areas in qualitative research. While true to some extent of all kinds of research, it is more of a difficulty in qualitative approaches because of (a) the emphasis in them on the investigator as the chief research instrument, which tends to make such problems appear more personal than they really are; (b) the nature of the research as process — an open-ended ongoing dialogue between data collection and theory, where the search for ideas militates against early foreclosure; and (c) the necessity, in view of this, to regard the 'writing-up' process as an important inducement to the production of ideas, as well as to their communication.

The disjuncture produces pain, which I have argued is the inevitable corollary of the rites of passage we must go through in our quest for a fully matured product. Regarding it like this externalizes and demystifies the problem, making it less personal. Further analysis then reveals the patterned nature of the complexities involved, which renders them susceptible to treatment. I have made suggestions, from my own experience, of the form that this 'craftwork' might take — the cultivation of amenable situations; pandering to the Protestant Ethic (if a 'Protestant Ethic person') one minute with schedules and quotas, and outflanking it the next with productive use of 'free' time; calculated risk-taking; giving special attention to models of excellence in areas, perhaps, outside that of the research, such as literary or other artistic work; 'cranking up' to the appropriate mental state, and undergoing apparent personality changes; meeting 'blockages' in similar analytical style and applying to them a range of techniques; maintaining flexibility in the complicated planning procedures without loss of rigour or impetus; and recognizing some common errors that attend our first efforts at writing.

Such are the strategies that go toward the attempts to produce 'a new song, played skilfully with a loud noise' (Psalm XXXIII). An essential part of the apparatus, however, is a healthy scepticism and a recognition of our ultimate imperfection, that we never quite make the song 'new' enough, or play with sufficient skill, or make a 'loud' enough noise. For if we thought otherwise, we might never produce anything. As the poet said,

And what is writ, is writ, —
Would it were worthier!

References

BERNSTEIN, S. (1978) 'Getting it done: Notes on student fritters', in LOFLAND, J. (Ed.) *Interaction in Everyday Life*, Beverley Hills, California, Sage.

BLISHEN, E. (1980) *Shaky Relationships*, London, Hamish Hamilton.

BLISHEN, E. (1983) *Donkey Work*, London, Hamish Hamilton.

BROWN, R.H. (1977) *A Poetic for Sociology*, Cambridge, Cambridge University Press.

GLASER, B. (1978) *Theoretical Sensitivity: Advances in the Methodology of Grounded Theory*, Mill Valley, California, The Sociology Press.

HAMMERSLEY, M. (1980) 'On interactionist empiricism', in WOODS, P. (Ed.) *Pupil Strategies*, London, Croom Helm.

HAMMERSLEY, M. and ATKINSON, P. (1983) *Ethnography: Principles in Practice*, London, Tavistock.

HARGREAVES, D.H. (1977) 'The process of typification in the classroom: Models and methods', *British Journal of Educational Psychology*, 47, pp. 274–84.

HOLLOWAY, J. (Ed.) (1957) *Poems of the Mid-Century*, London, Harrap.

KARL, E.R. and DAVIES, L. (Eds) (1983) *The Collected Letters of Joseph Conrad, Volume One: 1861–1897*, Cambridge, Cambridge University Press.

MACDIARMID, H. (1969) in GLEN, D. (Ed.) *Selected Essays of Hugh MacDiarmid*, London, Cape.

MASEFIELD, J. (1932) *The Collected Poems of John Masefield*, London, Heinemann.

MILLS, C.W. (1970) *The Sociological Imagination*, Harmondsworth, Penguin (originally published in 1959 by Oxford University Press).

MORGAN, C. (1960) *The Writer and His World*, London, Macmillan.

MORTIMER, J. (1983) 'Wig, pen and wisdom', *Radio Times* 27 August–2 September, London, BBC Publications.

NISBET, R. (1962) 'Sociology as an art form', *Pacific Sociological Review*, Autumn.

READ, P.P. (1977) *Polonaise*, London, Pan Books.

SPERBER, D. (1979) 'Claude Levi-Strauss', in STURROCK, J. (Ed.) *Structuralism and Since*, Oxford, Oxford University Press.

Part Two
Issues in Policy
and Practice

6 Social Policy and Education: Problems and Possibilities of Using Qualitative Research

Janet Finch

This chapter argues that there is significant potential for qualitative research to have an impact upon social policy in the field of education — a potential less than fully realized in recent years — and considers some of the difficulties which are likely to be encountered by qualitative researchers who engage in social policy, drawing upon my own study of pre-school playgroups.

My use of the phrase 'social policy in the field of education' is deliberate. I am concerned in this paper, not with 'educational policy' as narrowly defined, but with education as part of the broader social policy enterprise through which governments and other policy-makers seek to produce change in social as well as educational outcomes or to preserve the social and economic status quo (Finch, 1984a). Pre-schooling is a particularly apposite example of the importance of considering education as part of the wider social policy enterprise, since the links have been drawn very visibly in the past two decades, especially in the Plowden Report and the EPA experiments which followed it. There is no need to go over this ground again, which has been extensively discussed elsewhere (see most recently Mortimore and Blackstone, 1982). The centrality of pre-schooling to both educational and social policy has not, however, guaranteed it a substantial allocation of public resources Despite the commitment to expansion of nursery education confirmed in the 1972 White Paper (DES, 1972), voluntary playgroups have come to occupy an increasingly central place in the spectrum of pre-school provision, as part of the search for 'low cost solutions' in this sector (DHSS/DES, 1976). Since they are provided on a voluntary not a statutory basis, and since they fall in a rather ambiguous area between 'day care' of the under fives and pre-school 'education', playgroups are often excluded from discussions of educational provision. However, their relevance to education, especially to strategies of compensatory education, should not be under-estimated. It was, after all, at an annual meeting of the Preschool Playgroups Association that Sir Keith Joseph made his 'cycle of deprivation' speech.

My own study of playgroups was not concerned with their pedagogic aspects but arose from an interest in exploring the notion of self-help provision in the pre-school sector, and what it meant in practice for localities in which there is a high concentration of the urban poor — in inner city areas and on run-down council estates. My method was a longitudinal, small-scale study of four self-help, voluntary playgroups in such areas, plus one 'middle class' comparison group. The study lasted for three years: for the first two years I made regular observational visits to the groups, and then I conducted semi-structured interviews with all the women who ran groups, plus a sample of mothers who used them.[1] The relevance of these playgroups to pre-school education became evident, amongst other things, from the consumers' view of them: mothers who used the groups almost all told me that they did so because they hoped that their child would gain some sort of preparation for school.

Qualitative Research and Social Policy in the Field of Education

Within social policy generally (with the possible exception of studies of crime and deviancy) studies using qualitative methods have made relatively little impact, as can be seen from Martin Bulmer's (1978a) survey of the field. The reasons for this lie partly with the dominant position which statistical work has long held in British government policy-making (Abrams, 1968) and partly with the intellectual splits which occured in academic social science in the 1950s and 1960s, when social problems were sharply distinguished from sociological problems, and the latter were identified as the proper topic of academic study (Finch, 1982). This intellectual split occured in education along with other sub-disciplines of sociology (Floud, 1957). The predictable consequence of this split was that policy-oriented research was regarded with some indifference if not distaste and in the academic division of labour it was assigned to the discipline of social administration, with its strong empiricist orientation.[2]

As far as the study of education is concerned, despite its well-established ethnographic tradition and the fact that it has a rich tradition of policy-oriented research (Glennerster and Hoyle, 1972), the two have not often come together: in social policy studies in the field of education, a relatively small part has been played by studies employing qualitative, especially ethnographic, techniques. Conversely, the expanding tradition of ethnographic research in education during the 1970s, appeared to concern itself rather little with specific questions of educational (still less of social) policy. Although the early studies of David Hargreaves (1967) and Colin Lacey (1970) perhaps had some influence upon the development of comprehensive education, subsequent work has had little apparent impact, nor has it necessarily been intended for such use.

At this point it seems useful to distinguish between two meanings of 'social policy research'. The first is the academic study *of* some area where social policies are operating, or perhaps are not operating very effectively. The purpose of such studies is to document and analyze the impact of social policies upon their target populations. The second meaning is, studies conducted with a view to influencing the future direction of the policy; that is, studies which aspire to feed directly into the policy-making process, usually with a view to producing some kind of policy *change*. Such studies may sometimes be commissioned by government, the DES, and LEA or some other interested party such as a pressure group. This chapter is concerned with social policy research of both types but especially the second, since this highlights particular issues about the presentation and use of findings, especially with policy-makers.

I am, therefore, identifying 'policy-makers' as a key audience which researchers have to address. By this phrase I mean essentially, politicians, officials and administrators who operate at all levels of decision-making and service delivery including (for certain purposes) senior teachers in schools. I fully accept that policy is implemented and therefore to an extent 'made' and remade in the daily practice of teachers and other professionals (see Andy Hargreaves, in this volume). But the question of how professional practice can be changed as a result of research raises a whole separate set of issues, such as those discussed by Kelly in her contribution to this volume. My principal focus is the more formal and explicit processes of policy-making which take place in central and local government, and in headteachers' offices.

Of course, the actual composition of the relevant policy-making audience will vary somewhat according to topic. In the case of playgroups, it involves not only the DES at central government level, but also the DHSS; and at local government level, the social services

as well as the education department. This is because of the administrative split in the pre-school sector, which designates certain activities as 'day care' and others as 'education'. One task for any
researcher who aspires to feed into policy-making, therefore, is to
identify relevant audiences. Another is to find ways of both formula-
ting and presenting data which will commend as is relevant and
important to that audience — it is this issue which is discussed in the
later part of this chapter. It seems reasonable to assume that whatever
the potential audience for the outcomes of qualitative research, they
will need to *be* convinced of the value of the work. A parallel
illustration is given by Threadgold (in this volume) where she
indicated that, as a headteacher, she finds ethnographic work very
useful in informing her thinking about policy and practice in her own
school; but that teachers in the classroom often need to be convinced
of the relevance of such studies and the research methods which they
employ.

So although the potential 'policy-making' audiences may still
need to be convinced, as far as the academic community is concerned.
It seems to me that the prospects for developing policy-oriented
qualitative work are more auspicious in the 1980s than they were in
the 1970s. In the academic study of social policy, space has been
opened up in recent years for a wider conception of what constitutes
appropriate research, as the dominant empiricist tradition in social
administration has increasingly been challenged, principally by Marxists and feminists, both of whom have been concerned to place the
study of social policy in a clear theoretical context (see, for example,
Mishra, 1977; McIntosh, 1981; Taylor-Gooby, 1981). *Inter alia*, this
has served to create an environment more conducive to questioning
what constitutes appropriate research for social policy, and in particular, for more sophisticated notions of what constitutes 'facts' and
how they are created. At the same time — and indeed partly as a
result of such changes in the discipline of social administration —
other social scientists, especially sociologists, have apparently begun
to review the study of social policy with rather less suspicion and
hostility (Finch, 1982). In other words, I am suggesting that the
climate is now right for a degree of intellectual reintegration of social
problems with sociological problems, and that qualitative research
can make an important contribution to this.

In the rest of this chapter, I shall explore the nature of the
contribution which qualitative research can make to social policy in
the field of education looking first at studies *of* social policy, and
second at research contributions *to* the policy-making process and at

some of the problems which this raises for researchers doing qualitative work.

Providing Accounts of the Consequences of Social Policies

The potential of research based on qualitative, rather than quantitative, methods can be seen clearly in relation to the study *of* social policy, and especially the consequences for human beings of particular social policies. It can do this because it can provide theoretically grounded, analytical accounts of 'what happens' in reality, in ways which statistical methods cannot accomplish.

First, methods of qualitative research can be seen as complementary to other kinds of research, with their special contribution to make more comprehensible accounts based upon statistical measures or formal interviewing: as James (1977) puts it, ethnography 'provides perspective, insight and understandable description' (p. 193). The complementary nature of quantitative and qualitative methods was recognized by the early researchers into social policy, including Charles Booth:

> I think I should say that the statistical method was needed to give bearings on the results of personal observation, and personal observation to give life to statistics. It is not so much verification — the figures or facts may be correct enough in themselves — but they mislead from want of due proportion or from lack of colour. (quoted in Simey and Simey, 1960, p. 78)

Second, in providing the 'colour', qualitative studies reflect the subjective reality of the people being studied. They can therefore make a special contribution to an understanding of what it is actually like to be a recipient of supplementary benefit, community care, compensatory education, or whatever. This rather implies that qualitative studies in the field of social policy most appropriately will take the underdog perspective, with the aim of making visible the consequences of decisions made by the socially powerful about the socially powerless. This may be impeccable for the analysis of social policy, but it is less promising for the social scientist who wishes to contribute to policy formulation, as I shall suggest in the next section.

Third, good qualitative research must essentially be theoretically grounded, and should be less open than quantitative work to the charge of abstracted empiricism. Of course, work informed by interactionist perspectives *has* been accused of empiricism, especially by Marxists. But as Hammersley has argued, although some inter-actionist work in the sociology of education has been empiricist, this is not an inherent feature of the approach. In fact, in his view, interactionist study has a substantial contribution to make to theory, both at macro and micro levels (Hammersley, 1980). Meanwhile, an interest in ethnography has developed among Marxists, especially among academics associated with the Centre for Contemporary Cultural Studies, but several of them are now arguing strongly that not only are Marxist theoretical orientations and ethnographic methods quite compatible, but that such methods can lead to distinctive theoretical developments in their own right (Grimshaw *et al.*, 1980, p. 74). Paul Willis has further argued that only ethnography which *is* theoretically grounded, and utilized by a researcher who is able to theorize on his or her feet, is capable of producing incisive accounts of social life (Willis, 1980, p. 92–4). From a different theoretical stance, the contribution of Hammersley, Scarth, and Webb to this volume, argues that the development and testing of theory can and should take place as part of ethnographic study, and that this can best be accomplished by the comparative method.

To extend this argument to research which concerns social policy, I would argue that ethnographic and other qualitative work is capable of producing accounts of 'what happens' which enable us to understand as well as describe it, because they are theory-led. At the very least, such accounts complement quantitative work; and often they may be able to uncover underlying social processes which are concealed from the kind of qualitative work which can only docu-ment correlations, but of itself cannot account for them.

My study of playgroups provides, I believe, an illustration of the potential of qualitative research for providing theoretically-grounded critical accounts of 'what happens' as a consequence of social policy. The particular focus of my interest was the significant shift from statutory to voluntary self-help provision in the pre-school sector. Statistically, it looks as if the playgroup movement has been highly successful in providing a viable alternative to statutory provision: by 1982, they were catering for almost half a million children, far more than any other form of pre-school provision, unless one counts those children admitted to primary schools before their fifth birthday — also about half a million (Central Statistical Office, 1982, table 3.37). Statistical studies can tell us how many children are being catered for in playgroups and something about their social profile; questionnaire studies can tell us what parents say when asked formal questions about their experiences of playgroups. But only studies which include an element of observation — and probably over a fairly long period of time — can tell us what playgroups are *actually like*.

My particular interest was in what 'self-help' provision would mean for working class women living in economically deprived areas. This is a particularly interesting group, given that in the post-Plowden initiatives they were the target population for compensatory education programmes which concentrated on pre-schooling. Through observation and semi-structured interviewing, I was able to document the character of self-help playgroups in such areas, and I found that they diverged wildly from the image of what a playgroup 'ought' to be like as promoted, for example, in PPA literature (for full discussion of this see Finch, 1984d).[3] One consequence was that — although it was not part of my study to measure actual educational outcomes — it seemed most unlikely that they would ever be able to provide the preparation for schooling which was the overwhelming aspiration of mothers who used them. Briefly, they developed on one of two models — the 'unsupervised' and the 'oversupervised'. The former were groups in which the children and adults had very little direct contact except for very instrumental purposes like the mid-morning drink. Mothers used words like 'rowdy' and 'disorganized' to describe these groups, and at times regarded them as physically dangerous, so that they stayed during sessions to make sure that their own children did not get injured. These playgroups it seemed to me, essentially the extension of the unsupervised groups of children who play in the street, noted as a phenomenon characteristic of working-class child-rearing practices from the Newsons onwards (Newson and Newson, 1968). The alternative, 'oversupervised' model contrasted with the former, in that the children were actually quite rigidly supervised (therefore making these playgroups a less dangerous place), but the contact between adults and children was essentially limited to the giving and receiving of orders, and there was little 'educational' practice which would characterize a 'good' nursery school, in which adults listen *to* children, act as resources *for* them, and sensitively capitalize upon their enthusiasm in order to extend the children's learning. The 'oversupervised' playgroup was characterized above all by an emphasis upon production, with the whole session geared principally to ensuring that each child made 'today's special product' to take home at the end of the session.

This brief description does little justice to the complexity and richness of the data generated in such a study. I have perhaps said enough, however, to demonstrate that research of this sort provides accounts of 'what happens' as a consequence of social policy (in this case, a shift from statutory provision to self-help in the pre-school sector) in ways which cannot be provided by more quantitative methods: they reflect the subjective reality of the recipients of policy, they show the meaning of that reality, and they necessarily integrate data with theoretical questions.

However, when we consider not merely *providing* such accounts but also *using* them to inform the policy-making process, quite different issues arise. Can qualitative studies in social policy move easily from critical analysis to the provision of data and reports in a form which will feed directly and effectively into this process? And what are the problems of so doing?

Qualitative Research and Policy-Making: Some Problems for the Researcher

Although getting policy-makers to take note of one's findings may be partly a matter of issues extraneous to the content of the research (such as the status of the research director or the institution from which it was mounted), the nature of the research itself does seem to have some bearing upon the ways in which it can be used. One of the features of qualitative work from the perspective of the policy-maker is that it is likely to look unrepresentative — ethnography, for example, may look indistinguishable from anyone's personal, subjective account. As Shipman has noted, ethnographic work in schools may look to the policy-makers very much like the kind of thing which inspectors or journalists or even teachers themselves produce; and its claim to offer something distinctive must rest not so much on the methods employed, as upon its use of insights from theory and knowledge about related fields of study (Shipman, 1985). Quantitative work, by contrast, appears to provide 'the facts'. The capacity to provide objective facts has long been the basis upon which social scientists have been regarded as useful to governments and, as Bulmer has noted, it relegates the social scientist to the role of technician, with decisions about what facts are relevant to a particular issue lying firmly with the policy-makers (Bulmer, 1978, p. 43; Cherns, 1972, pp. 16–17). This is a situation with which qualitative researchers are unlikely to feel comfortable, since the integration of data and theory is the foundation of good qualitative work, as I have already argued.

Another problem for researchers using qualitative methods is that there can be acute ethical and political dilemmas about how the material produced is *used*, both by the researcher her/himself, and by other people. Such questions are not absent in quantitative research, but greater distancing of the researcher from the research subjects may make them less personally agonizing. Further, in ethnographic work of depth interviewing, the researcher is very much in a position of trust in being accorded privileged access to information which is usually private or invisible. Working out how to ensure that such trust is not betrayed is no simple matter, as I have argued elsewhere (Finch, 1984c). Where qualitative research is targeted upon social policy issues, here is the special dilemma that findings could be used to *worsen* the situation of the target population in some way.

This was very much the situation with which I was faced in my playgroup study, and I found it so difficult to handle that for a while I thought that I did not want to publish anything at all about this study, for fear that (if it was noticed at all) it might be used in ways with which I would be very uncomfortable. I think that my experience is instructive in relation to questions about how qualitative research can feed into the policy-making process.

My particular dilemma was that, in studying 'working-class' playgroups I uncovered situations where practice diverged wildly from bourgeois standards of child care and education which most policy-makers and academics would take as the norm, and at times were downright dangerous. Further, in observing the groups and talking to the women who ran and used them over a period of time, I became convinced that I was not simply studying a handful of particularly 'poor' playgroups which by some stroke of bad luck had turned up in my sample; rather I began to view them as characteristic examples of how a playgroup *will* develop, when the principle of self help is applied to pre-school provision in poor urban areas. In particular, I could see very clearly that these playgroups and the way they were run replicated very clearly characteristic modes of working class child-rearing, followed cultural rules about how women handle each other's children and relied necessarily upon women whose own educational experiences left them in a weak position to be able to provide facilities which would prepare their own and other women's children for school (Finch, 1984d). At this point I began to get worried. I could well see that the publication of such conclusions could well mean that I was further reinforcing those assumptions deeply embedded in our culture and political life that working class women (especially the urban poor) are inadequate mothers and too incompetent to be able to organize facilities that most normal women could manage (Lewis, 1980). The implied insult to these women who had welcomed me for three years seemed very much like a betrayal of the trust which they had placed in me, and would mean that I was effectively condemning women whose economic, environmental and personal circumstances were grim in comparison with my own, and with which I personally would have coped very badly. Small-scale, qualitative longitudinal research does actually expose the researcher to that kind of knowledge, and — without coming anywhere near the total suspension of critical judgment which 'going native' implies — creates a rounded understanding of what it is actually like to *be* a mother in such circumstances, which places the researcher very much 'on their side' (Finch, 1984c).

The policy implications of this interpretation of my work, I suppose, would be that — as far as the education of the children of the urban poor is concerned — it is indeed mothers who constitute 'the problem'. The appropriate response, therefore, would be to find some way of compensating for their inadequacies. I feared that, in the circumstances of the early 1980s, this would probably mean the infusion of middle-class volunteers into 'self-help' schemes in poorer urban areas, to ensure that pre-school facilities were still provided at low cost, while at the same time educating working-class mothers in proper modes of child care.

In the end, I did work through these questions sufficiently to feel able to write about these playgroups. Essentially, I recognized that my data not only posed moral and political dilemmas for me personally, but also some important intellectual questions which I should not duck. In a sense, the issues here concern the classic problem of how one can deliver good education and social services to the children of the poor, without involving a 'deficit' model which implies that the recipients of the service are inadequate, rather than the services themselves (Finch, 1984a, chapter 4). How was I to make sense of the social processes which I had uncovered without 'blaming the victim' in inappropriate ways (Ryan, 1971)?

One possible interpretation is that I had imposed an inappropriate model of 'the playgroup' upon these groups — I had taken the middle-class model as the norm, measured the working-class groups by this model and then found them wanting, rather than assessing the working-class playgroups in their own terms. I should perhaps have substituted a 'cultural difference' model for a 'deficit' one. Quite apart from objections which can be made to 'cultural difference' in general terms (see, for example, Robinson, 1976, pp. 14–16), in the case of the playgroups in my study, the 'middle-class' model *was* the one to which the women who ran the groups appeared to aspire, and it certainly was the model by which they would be judged by the statutory agencies responsible for registering and inspecting them. The model, in other words, was the participants' model, not merely mine. Moreover, the participants' strong aspirations that their playgroups should prepare children for school pointed in a direction very different from the playgroups which they were actually running. I was pushed back, therefore, onto the 'deficit' dilemma.

I am not certain that I have fully resolved these issues, but the article which I finally wrote on the educational aspects of these playgroups (Finch, 1984d) argues that to view working-class mothers as incompetent is improper and naive, first, because the women whom I studied were being asked to produce self-help nursery education without the appropriate material resources, a point which Joyce Watt makes about *all* playgroups, but which applies with particular force in localities where material and environmental resources are seriously lacking (Watt, 1977; Finch, 1984b). Second, they were being asked to prepare children for an educational system which had rejected *them* as 'failures'. Precisely because of that, they wanted their own children to have a good start, but the self-help solution throws the onus straight back on them. Where women are in this situation, their lack of confidence in their own abilities to contribute to their children's education is well documented and cannot be easily overcome: on the evidence of one study at least, professional interventions to help mothers are likely to make them less (not more) confident (Raven, 1980). Third, I argued that the constraints which these women were under made the reality of their lives a grim struggle in many cases, and it is well-known that working-class mothers with pre-school children are a high-risk category for clinical depression and less measurable problems. To see working-class women's conduct of playgroups as evidence of their individual or collective incompetence is to repeat the process whereby women have had various expectations laid upon them which they could not possibly fulfil, and then have been labelled as inadequate if they do not do so. The 'policy' conclusion of this position, it seems to me, is to argue that there is no substitute for state-provided nursery education, not by invoking a 'deficit' model of compensation, but because working class parents have the right to demand good pre-schooling for their children, resourced collectively since there is no prospect that they can resource it themselves — and that working-class mothers have the right to be given a choice of whether they wish to be full-time mothers (Finch, 1984b).

To argue like this is to take a frankly moral stance, far removed from the model of the objective scientist, or the technician-researcher. It seems to me that qualitative research on social policy issues will lead inevitably to explicit moral stances of that sort, and that it can never simply provide 'the facts' because the 'facts' which it creates are by definition complex and subtle, and suffused with conceptual and theoretical understandings. Simply to offer raw ethnographic data or other qualitative material as 'facts' without interpretation could well lead to conclusions far removed from any the researcher herself would support, as was very clear to me in relation to my playgroup data.

This line of argument is reminiscent of Becker's 'Whose side are we on?' question, and the whole debate about whether it is appropriate for the sociologist to side with the 'Underdog' (Becker, 1967; Gouldner, 1973). I think that this is a debate which cannot be ducked by qualitative researchers who engage with social policy. In this chapter, I have discussed the particular form which my difficulties took in this instance and clearly this was related to the fact that I was studying a group of women living in particularly powerless circumstances: the particular form which my dilemma took was a product of the relationship between feminist commitments and research, some aspects of which are discussed by Scott in this volume (see also Finch, 1984c). But whilst the *form* might be different in another instance, it seems to me very likely that any research project which focuses upon issues of social policy will encounter something similar, since in studying the recipients of social policy, one is almost by definition studying relatively powerless groups. So, on the one hand one has a strong pull of sympathy for those whose situation one has studied; on the other hand, there is the question of one's credibility with policy-makers. Bulmer (1978) highlights the dilemma here when he writes,

> If the legitimacy of political scientists is not recognized by administrators, and if many sociologists champion the under-dog and are suspicious of the State, then something of a vicious circle develops, where social scientists fail to contribute to policy deliberations (though they may have an important effect upon the climate of opinion) and this is then cited by policy-makers as a good reason for not involving them. (pp. 19–20)

The researcher who wishes to engage directly with the policy-making process therefore may find it impossible to do so without being prepared to observe not only the minimal rules of the game, but also to work with the basic definitions within which policy-makers and administrators work. But this may well mean adopting a frame of reference which objectifies 'working class mothers', 'unqualified school leavers', or whoever as 'the problem' — that is, precisely the perspective which one's own work challenges. One has done violence to one's own work by presenting it in a form acceptable to policy-makers.

Developing Acceptable Compromises

Does the choice then become either to abandon the underdog perspective in order to engage to some effect with social policy-makers; or to stay entirely clear of social policy questions, retaining one's moral purity and intellectual integrity, but making no attempt to change the situation of the people whom one has studied? The most attractive option for many researchers, I think, is to try to steer a course between those two, since many researchers who study questions of social policy also have some moral investment in social change. As Colin Lacey (1976) puts it in discussing his interest in studying Hightown Grammar:

> My concern was to promote those sorts of intervention that would lead towards egalitarian society ... This concern has remained a central underlying purpose. It predates my interest in sociology as such and it provides support for my continuing interest ... If I felt that sociology was not useful in this way, I would probably turn to politics or journalism or something. (p. 54)

I suspect that this will strike a chord with many other researchers in education whose work is related to current issues of policy, and the issue then becomes one of acceptable compromises: can we find ways of engaging directly in social policy which involve neither abandoning our own analyses nor demolishing our credibility with the first word we utter?

It seems to me that there are three possible ways of working out 'acceptable compromises' of this sort. The first is to define oneself publicly as an advocate, at least as far as the use of one's research is concerned. This is the position which Jennifer James (1977) adopts in her discussion of ethnography and social problems. She argues that such ethnography can, and should, lead to advocacy on behalf of the 'problem' group because 'it is the only reasonable justification for probing the life-styles of these human-beings' (p. 198). The qualitative researcher, it seems to me, is particularly well placed to act as an advocate on behalf of the group whom he or she has studied because he or she can both reflect the subjective reality of these groups and also can operate on their behalf from a less vulnerable position. The advocacy stance implies a direct engagement with issues of policy and perhaps with policy-makers.

The problems with the advocate compromise seem to be, first, that it may not be sufficient of a compromise — that is, one's identification with the oppressed or 'problem' group may remove one's credibility with policy-makers from the very beginning. Second, to act as an advocate on behalf of a group of which one is not a member may serve to perpetuate the very processes which one wishes to challenge since it reinforces the view of the working-class mothers or unemployed school leavers as people who have to have things done *for* them — by implication, because they are incapable of acting for themselves. Third, one's claim to be an advocate may not be (and perhaps cannot be) endorsed by the group themselves. One is, in other words, a self-appointed advocate, basing one's actions on one's own interpretation of the needs of the group as they have emerged through a research project, not necessarily the needs which the group itself defines. As a researcher, one can argue for statutory pre-school provision whether or not that demand has been specifically articulated by the majority of people who would benefit from it. But as a political advocate, to articulate views which one's research group have not expressed is essentially paternalistic and therefore again falls into the trap of reinforcing the very definitions which one is seeking to challenge.

The second possible compromise is to define oneself rather more as a provider of knowledge upon which policy-makers and others can act, but not as a direct or active participant in the policy-making process. Lacey (1976) appears to take this line when, in discussing the use of the Hightown Grammar study he writes:

> It was not the intention of the researcher to be directly interventionalist ... but to provide teachers and students in general with an insight into their own world that would lead to further debate, the redefinition of problems and the development of new solutions. (p. 83)

The implication here is that the researcher is the provider of knowledge, not just in the sense of 'facts' but, more importantly, of *insights* which invite participants to reconceptualize their own world, and therefore possibly to devise ways of changing it. Similarly,

Cherns (1972) has argued that the appropriate point of entry into the policy-making process for the social scientist is to increase and clarify policy-makers' understanding of the situation in which they are operating, and thus to increase the range of available options for change (p. 19).

The strategy being developed by these writers can perhaps best be expressed in Janowitz's (1970) formulation, when he speaks of the 'enlightenment' model (as opposed to the 'engineering' model) of the relationship of sociology to policy. He suggests that in the enlightenment model, the relationship between the two is diffuse and complex, with sociologists essentially providing a sophisticated form of social intelligence, by charting complex trends and conceptualizing social processes so as to 'help society to clarify or even alter its social and political goals and objectives' (p. 251; see also Bulmer, 1982). As Bulmer (1978) has pointed out, this model rather blurs the distinction between theory and research, and emphasizes creating the right intellectual conditions for problem-solving, not just the provision of technical solutions (p. 26).

I suspect that this particular compromise holds attractions for many of us, and it certainly avoids the paternalistic trap associated with the advocacy strategy. On the other hand, one's input into the policy-making process is by definition indirect, and therefore one is rather dependent upon the participants and/or the policy-makers actually to accept one's insights and act upon them. The danger here is the one which I experienced in my playgroup study: that there is real potential for the researcher's insights to be reinterpreted and translated into the policy-making process in ways quite contrary to those which she or he would have wished. Even if the 'correct' message is understood, there is, of course, no guarantee that it will be acted upon; although such guarantees are unlikely to be available to us whichever strategy we adopt. But the researcher who acts as the provider of knowledge only (albeit quite radical knowledge) essentially abdicates responsibility for the use of that knowledge — which at best is a weak strategy for engaging policy-making, and at worst, counter productive.

The third possible 'acceptable compromise' is to get one's own hands dirty, to take up a frankly reformist stance, and to engage directly in the development of social engineering strategies which attempt to alleviate some of the worst features which one has identified. This may prove an unattractive model to social scientists for a variety of reasons, both practical and ideological. The idea that 'experts' can come in and manipulate social structures in ways which they believe to be appropriate is an approach which many would oppose on political and moral grounds, although in fact it was a major motivating force behind the development of social science. The Webbs (1932) provide a prime illustration of this: in their book on methods, they argue that an 'applied science of society' is possible, and they document a number of areas in which, in their view, the systematic study of social facts has led to social change (pp. 242–7). They do, however, seem somewhat to regret that one cannot change the habits of a population as easily as one can change legislation (p. 251). In other words, a concern to engage with strategies of social engineering can very easily slide into an attempt to change the *people* with whose 'problems' one is concerned, not the *situation* of which they are part. It is very easy to see how this slippage can occur, and it must be an ever-present danger for any researcher who does try to use her work to press for some kind of policy change: one can begin, for example, with a clear view that arguing for statutorily provided nursery education does not imply a victim-blaming approach to working class mothers, but in the process of negotiation and compromise which such a strategy necessarily implies, it is all too easy to agree to settle for something rather less than one had hoped for — for example, the provision of full-time, paid and qualified supervisors for voluntary pre-school provision — which does imply precisely that.

So engaging directly with strategies for policy change can turn out to be profoundly conservative by comparison with one's aspirations. Even if it is more successful than that, it is unlikely to result in more than small reforms which only scratch the surface of the changes which one might ideally like to see. The charge of being gradualist and piecemeal has long been levelled at this essentially Fabian approach to social policy, by those who see it as an unpromising route to more fundamental change. The classic dilemma for those who are attracted to this kind of reformism is to decide whether it is better to do something rather than do nothing — which is effectively the outcome of many proposals which are apparently more radical but require fundamental social change before they could happen. In arguing here that we may produce only small changes, I do not mean to imply that I am against more fundamental change in principle but simply that, in relation to a single research project, a relatively small change may be all that one can realistically accomplish. Also, I wish to avoid an overcrude dichotomy between 'small-scale' and 'large-scale' change. Individual instances may well fall between the two extremes; and especially since educational provision in Britain is relatively decentralized, similar 'small' changes taking place in several local authorities may eventually amount to something quite substantial.

Of course, the dilemmas which I have been discussing are not peculiar to qualitative research. However, there is a sense in which researchers who undertake such studies are likely to be attracted to reformist rather than revolutionary solutions. Payne *et al.* (1981) argue that the ethnographic tradition 'is a liberal and gradualist one in which the complexity of social questions is seen to demand piecemeal and partial answers' (p. 108). In this they follow Albion Small, who believed that a sociological education, based upon observations of the social world inductively generalized to larger issues, was likely to make reformist citizens out of students, because it 'instructs students in the complexities of the social process, complexities which utopians and amateurs and agitators leave out of view'. (Dibble, 1975, p. 34)

Ethnography — and allied types of qualitative research — may be an intellectual style which aligns most closely with reform rather than revolution, but the kind of data it produces, as I suggested earlier, may not commend itself to politicians and policy-makers committed to social engineering strategies. Therefore, the qualitative researcher who tries to engage with them undoubtedly will have a difficult task, but one that is *possible* — at least in terms of her or his own intellectual position. Some of the likely difficulties can easily be anticipated from the foregoing discussion: one will have to find ways of fighting off being relegation to a technician role, whilst being required to produce different sorts of data (probably quantitative). This means finding ways of presenting one's qualitative work which show that it is pertinent and important even if no claims are made that it is be representative. This is a task which undoubtedly will be necessary, and we must expect to go on the offensive and find ways of accomplishing it which are both imaginative and convincing. We also need to anticipate that if we attempt to engage with policy-makers in reformist strategies for social change we *will* have to use our work to be prescriptive as well as analytical — unless, that is, we are content with relegation to the technician role. This perhaps is the most difficult part of the process for a qualitative researcher to contemplate, committed as we are to exploring the complexity of human existence and social processes. However, to adopt the reformist stance does require that we find ways of reconceptualizing and presenting our work so that it can be potentially translated into practical policies, and (in contrast with the 'provider of knowledge' strategy) requires that we do this ourselves.

Conclusion: Why Bother?

In this chapter, I have tried to develop a discussion which explores both the problems and the possibilities of making links between qualitative research and social policy. One reading is that I have demonstrated that it is impossible. I would not share that view: difficult, complex, demanding, perhaps, but not impossible. My argument has been essentially that as qualitative social scientists we can develop ways of analyzing and presenting our work which commends it to policy-makers, and that this probably involves accepting that — at least as far as our academic work is concerned — our orientation essentially is reformist.

Others of course may still wonder why we should bother at all. To this, I would reply, that to study education is necessarily in many cases to uncover issues of social policy and the fact that it has been unfashionable in recent years for 'pure' social scientists to recognize this (the division, that is, between social problems and sociological problems) has been damaging both to our credibility and to our understanding of educational processes and the political contexts in which they are set. As Payne *et al.* (1981) put it, making a strong case for the development of a new 'policy sociology', we should stop being content with a critical-spectator sociology and recognize that sociology *is* involved in the policy field of necessity, because the knowledge it produces can always be used there (p. 156). Moreover, if as qualitative researchers, we are not prepared to engage with the social policy implications of our own work, we leave the field completely open to other social scientists who will be quite happy to sustain the long-standing dominance of quantitative work in the eyes of policy-makers. In many cases this may well mean that only atheoretical theoretical, statistical or demographic work continues to be used; but even good quantitative work, theoretically informed and well executed, necessarily suffers from the 'lack of colour' which Charles Booth so readily recognized. We do not have to be engaged in a vendetta against quantitative researchers to see that we should be denying them the right to have the last word in every instance.

Notes

1 I am grateful for the support of the SSRC who funded the interview stage of the research. Only two of the five playgroups (one of them the middle-class comparison group) were still open after the two-year observational

period, and interviews were conducted in those two plus another group which had only just closed: a total of forty-eight interviews.

2 I discuss the historical background to the relative lack of impact of qualitative research upon social policy more fully in Finch (1986, forthcoming).

3 In comparing the playgroups in my study with this 'ideal' model, I do not intend to imply that all such groups in wealthier areas necessarily match that ideal. However, it must be noted that the one 'middle-class' comparison group in my study, although not in an especially wealthy area, did differ substantially from all the other groups in many ways, and came very much closer to the PPA ideal (see Finch, 1984d).

References

ABRAMS, P. (1968) *The Origins of British Sociology 1834–1914*, Chicago, University of Chicago Press.

BECKER, H. (1967) 'Whose side are we on?', *Social Problems*, 14, pp. 239–47.

BULMER, M. (Ed.) (1978a) *Social Policy Research*, London, Macmillan.

BULMER, M. (1978b) 'Social science research and policy-making', in BULMER, M. (Ed.) *Social Policy Research*, London, Macmillan.

BULMER, M. (1982) *The Uses of Social Research: Social Investigations in Public Policy Making*, London, Allen and Unwin.

CENTRAL STATISTICAL OFFICE (1982) *Social Trends No. 12*, London, HMSO.

CHERNS, A. (1972) 'Social sciences and policy', in CHERNS, A., SINCLAIR, R. and JENKINS, W.I., *Social Science and Government*, London, Tavistock.

DEPARTMENT OF EDUCATION AND SCIENCE (1972) *Education: A Framework for Expansion*, Cmnd. 5174, London, HMSO.

DEPARTMENT OF HEALTH AND SOCIAL SECURITY/DEPARTMENT OF EDUCATION AND SCIENCE (1976) *Low Cost Day Provision for the Under Fives*, papers from a conference at Sunningdale, January.

DIBBLE, V.K. (1975) *The Legacy of Albion Small*, Chicago, University of Chicago Press.

FINCH, J. (1982) 'The sociology of welfare', in BURGESS, R.G. (Ed.) *Exploring Society*, London, British Sociological Association (Second edition published by Longman, 1986)

FINCH, J. (1984a) *Education as Social Policy*, London, Longman.

FINCH, J. (1984b) 'The deceit of self help: Preschool playgroups and working class mothers', *Journal of Social Policy*, 13, 1, pp. 1–20.

FINCH, J. (1984c) '"It's great to have someone to talk to": The ethics and politics of interviewing women', in BELL, C. and ROBERTS, H. (Eds) *Social Researching*, London, Routledge and Kegan Paul.

FINCH, J. (1984d) 'A first class environment? Working class playgroups as preschool experience', *British Educational Research Journal*, 10, 1, pp. 3–17.

FINCH, J. (1986) *Qualitative Research and Social Policy: Issues in Education and Welfare*, Lewes, Falmer Press, (forthcoming).

FLOUD, J. (1957) Report of discussion at the British Sociological Association Annual Conference, *British Journal of Sociology*, 8, p. 172.

GLENNERSTER, H. and HOYLE, E. (1972) 'Educational research and educational policy', *Journal of Social Policy*, 1, 3, pp. 193–212.

GOULDNER, A. (1973) 'The sociologist as partisan: Sociology and the welfare state', in GOULDNER, A., *For Sociology*, London, Allen Lane.

HALL, S., HOBSON, D., LOWE, A. and WILLIS, P. (Eds) (1980) *Culture, Media, Language*, London, Hutchinson.

HAMMERSLEY, M. (1980) 'On interactionist empiricism', in WOODS, P. (Ed.) *Pupil Strategies*, London, Croom Helm.

HARGREAVES, D.H. (1967) *Social Relations in a Secondary School*, London, Routledge and Kegan Paul.

JAMES, J. (1977) 'Ethnography and social problems', in WEPPNER, R.S. (Ed.) *Street Ethnography*, Beverley Hills, California, Sage.

JANOWITZ, M. (1970) *Political Conflict*, Chicago, Quadrangle.

LACEY, C. (1970) *Hightown Grammar*, Manchester, Manchester University Press.

LACEY, C. (1976) 'Problems of sociological fieldwork: A review of the methodology of "Hightown Grammar"', in SHIPMAN, M. (Ed.) *The Organisation and Impact of Social Research*, London, Routledge and Kegan Paul.

LEWIS, J. (1980) *The Politics of Motherhood 1919–1939*, London, Croom Helm.

McINTOSH, M. (1981) 'Feminism and social policy', *Critical Social Policy*, 1, 1, pp. 32–42.

MISHRA, R. (1977) *Society and Social Policy*, London, Macmillan.

MORTIMORE, J. and BLACKSTONE, T. (1982) *Disadvantage and Education*, London, Heinemann.

NEWSON, E. and NEWSON, J. (1968) *Four Years Old in an Urban Community*, London, Allen and Unwin.

PAYNE, G., DINGWALL, R., PAYNE, J. and CARTER, M. (1981) *Sociology and Social Research*, London, Routledge and Kegan Paul.

RAVEN, J. (1980) *Parents, Teachers and Children: A Study of an Educational Home Visiting Scheme*, Sevenoaks, Hodder and Stoughton.

ROBINSON, P. (1976) *Education and Poverty*, London, Methuen.

RYAN, W. (1971) *Blaming the Victim*, London, Orbach and Chambers.

SHIPMAN, M. (1985) 'Ethnography and educational policy', in BURGESS, R.G. (Ed.) *Field Methods in the Study of Education*, Lewes, Falmer Press.

SIMEY, T.S. and SIMEY, M.B. (1960) *Charles Booth, Social Scientist*, London, Oxford University Press.

TAYLOR-GOOBY, P. (1981) 'The empiricist tradition in social administration', *Critical Social Policy*, 1, 1, pp. 6–21.

WATT, J. (1977) *Co-operation in Pre-School Education*, London, Social Science Research Council.

WEBB, S. and WEBB, B. (1932) *Methods of Social Study*, Cambridge, Cambridge University Press.

WILLIS, P. (1980) 'Notes on method', in HALL, S., HOBSON, D., LOWE, A. and WILLIS, P. (Eds) *Culture, Media, Language*, London, Hutchinson.

7   Action Research: What Is It and What Can It Do?

Alison Kelly

Action research is back in fashion. The last few years have seen an explosion of action research projects, books, papers and conferences. But action research means many things to many people. In this chapter I want to examine some of these different definitions and practices. My aim is not to decide what is 'true' or 'real' action research, but rather the opposite — to argue that action research is a 'broad church' and no one type should be allowed to pre-empt the term. I will then discuss some of the advantages and disadvantages of the particular model of action research employed in the Girls into Science and Technology (GIST) Project.

Models of Action Research

Educational action research in Britain has two main strands. Both of these trace their origins to Kurt Lewin's pioneering work on social disadvantage, but there the similarity ends. One strand is that of 'experimental social administration' exemplified by the Educational Priority Areas, and having close links to compensatory education programmes in the United States. The other strand is the teacher-researcher model, stemming from the curriculum development work of Lawrence Stenhouse and his colleagues in East Anglia. The GIST project has elements of both of these, but it resembles more closely a type of action research employed in business studies, which I shall call the 'simultaneous-integrated' approach.

Experimental Social Administration

Halsey (1972), writing about Educational Priority Areas (EPAs) describes action research as 'an experimental or quasi-experimental version of futurology as design. Ends are stated together with means to their achievement... Ends and means are modified and explicated in a programme of action and the relation between them is analyzed by research monitoring of the action programme' (p. 4). In the EPAs the problem (educational under-attainment) was identified by an official body (the Plowden Committee) outside the school system. Suggestions for tackling it were derived from the research literature, and were implemented by project teams consisting of action workers and research workers. The aim was to 'bring together two professions, social research and administration ... in what we can call experimental social administration ... to change the world by understanding it' (Halsey, 1972, p. 165). The practitioners, the teachers, are nowhere in this description. Indeed, Halsey argues that 'to work through existing educational institutions and teachers is ... to put a major feature of the project at risk' since teachers would probably not implement the action in the way that the researchers intended. Although the organization of the EPA projects varied, the general aim was to take a research-based hypothesis, test it in an experimental action project, and evaluate its effects. Ideally, both theoretical and practical conclusions should emerge.

The EPA projects have not generated a tradition of educational research, but similar accounts of action-research can be found in other fields. Powley and Evans (1979), discussing the National Children's Bureau's Intermediate Treatment Centres, argue that the project must start with a clear plan based on hypotheses derived from research and that 'action and research have distinct roles'. George Smith (1982) comments in his review of four action research projects between 1968 and 1981 that 'action research is not itself a method of research ... the term refers to a setting for research where it operates in close proximity to a setting for action'. And Ray Lees (1975) suggests that 'the research group is intended to assist the action team in the assessment of the locality's needs ... it is concerned with the continuous monitoring and final evaluation of the project's work and recommendations'. The common features of these projects are that research and action have separate functions, which are clearly planned from the start of the project, and that the research workers maintain their role of outsiders to the situation under study.

Teacher-Researcher

Teacher-researcher action research stands in complete contrast to experimental social administration. As developed at the Centre for

Applied Research in Education and elsewhere, educational action research is essentially teacher-based. Elliott (1983) argues that it should be 'practitioner-based and characterized by an absence of a division of labour between practitioners and researchers' and Dave Ebbutt (in this volume) suggests that educational action research is 'the systematic study of attempts to improve educational practice by groups of participants by means of their own practical actions and by means of their own reflections upon the effects of those actions'. The teacher's perspective is central and s/he defines the problem as s/he sees it — Elliott (1982) says 'problem definition in action research should not be controlled by an external agency'. The crucial step is for teachers to become reflective about their own practice. Indeed, in an earlier paper Elliott (1978) defines action research simply as 'reflection related to diagnosis'.

These ideas have now been implemented in a range of projects, both large and small. In this volume Dave Ebbutt, Carol Cummings and Margaret Threadgold all describe teacher-research action research projects. Other examples include the Ford Teaching Project (Elliott, 1975), the School Accountability project (Elliott *et al.*, 1981) and the collection of papers edited by Jon Nixon (1981).

Teacher-researcher action research differs from experimental social administration in several ways other than those of who defines the problem and whether action and research roles are separate or combined. Teacher-research action research does not typically start with hypotheses derived from the research literature, and is not usually concerned to contribute to the corpus of social science knowledge and theory. Thus, Carol Cummings (in this volume) describes how the 'problem' emerged in the course of her research, rather than being planned from the outset. She argues that questions of academic respectability and generalizability are irrelevant to the teacher-researcher. Similarly, Sharples (1983) suggests that action research should concentrate on the 'evidencing of practice' and that it is an integral part of good teaching. He argues that an enhanced understanding of the particularity of a teacher's situation is more important than generalizability, and that replicability and transferability are less important than authenticity and accountability. For Sharples, action research is a crucial feature of professional development, and he implies that school-based action research is the only sort of educational research which has validity for practitioners. These views are not necessarily shared by all advocates of teacher-researcher action research Dave Ebbutt maintains that there *is* a distinction between good teaching and action research. He suggests that teachers' reflections on their own practice must be made public in the form of a report if they are to be labelled 'research'. His criteria for an 'action' project remain implicit, but it is arguable that critical reflection and classroom monitoring does not necessarily lead to marked alterations in behaviour. Carol Cummings only admits to 'frequent small shifts of emphasis and changes in practice' as the result of her involvement in action research. In general, the 'action' is much less planned and formal in the teacher-researcher mode of action research than in the experimental social administration mode.

Simultaneous-integrated

Simultaneous-integrated action research (SIAR) has been used quite extensively in organizational research, and has developed along distinct lines. Rapoport (1970) suggests that 'action research aims to contribute *both* to the practical concerns of people in an immediate problematic situation and to the goals of social science by joint collaboration within a mutually acceptable ethical framework'. Hult and Lennung (1980) have added further refinements. In their view

Action Research
1 simultaneously assists in practical problem solving and expands scientific knowledge;
2 as well as enhances the competencies of the respective actors;
3 being performed collaboratively;
4 in an immediate situation;
5 using data feedback in a cyclical process;
6 aiming at increased understanding of a given social situation;
7 primarily applicable for the understanding of change processes in social systems;
8 and undertaken within a mutually acceptable ethical framework.

Despite (or perhaps because of) its complexity I find this an extremely useful definition. It combines a strong research component with a respect for participants' knowledge and understanding. Action and research are integrated and proceed simultaneously. This approach has not been widely employed in educational research, but it does characterize the Girls into Science and Technology Project quite well. By describing this Project I hope to clarify the definition of simultaneous-integrated action research and suggest that it can be a useful method for work in education.

GIST as Simultaneous-Integrated Action Research

Girls into Science and Technology was an action research project aimed at encouraging more girls to continue with physical science and technological subjects when these become optional at the end of third year of secondary school. We worked with teachers in eight coeducational comprehensive schools in Greater Manchester to devize and implement a range of intervention strategies in the first three years of secondary school. Interventions included visits from women working in scientific and technical jobs who could provide positive role models for the girls, development of curriculum materials utilizing girls' interests, attitude changing sessions with teachers, the provision of material on famous women scientists, observation of classroom interaction with feedback to the teachers and careers advice to the children on the consequences of dropping scientific and technical subjects. Our research interests in the project covered topics such as the reasons for girls' avoidance of these subjects at school, the way children's attitudes develop over the first three years of secondary schooling, classroom interaction between the sexes, teachers' behaviour towards, and opinions about, girls in science and technology, and the way teachers' attitudes develop and change. Both qualitative and quantitative methods were used, including questionnaires, classroom observation, discussions with teachers and curriculum innovation. The project and its outcomes are described more fully elsewhere (Kelly *et al.*, 1984; Smail *et al.*, 1982; Whyte, 1985q). In this chapter I want to concentrate on the methodological issues.

The GIST Project was not designed in the light of Hult and Lennung's definition of action research — indeed we were not aware of their definition until about half-way through the project. GIST developed as an action research project in response to our own desire to tackle a practical problem in education and our scepticism about the relevance of conventional research for teachers. Nevertheless GIST fits neatly into the simultaneous-integrated action research framework, and can be used to illustrate Hult and Lennung's definition. Like them I will consider the definition phrase by phrase.

(I) Simultaneously Assists in Practical Problem Solving and Expands Scientific Knowledge

In the GIST Project we were concerned with the practical problem of encouraging girls to study science and technology; we were also investigating why girls tend to avoid these subjects. A thorough understanding of the determinants of girls' choices may help us to devize appropriate intervention strategies; alternatively it may help us to explain why some interventions are less successful than hoped and avoid the kind of backlash which followed the apparent failure of Headstart in the United States. The intervention strategies were developed on the basis of previous theoretical research into the origins of girls' underachievement in science and technology (see Kelly, 1981); by putting these interventions into practice some of the theories could be tested. In this way action and research were interwoven. Research was used to evaluate action, and action provided an experimental situation for research. But the design was not rigid. Actions changed on the basis of research findings and research plans changed to fit the actions which had been taken. The GIST team was not divided into 'action' and 'research' workers — we all tried to work on all aspects of the Project (although it is only fair to say that some of us were more heavily involved in one side or the other depending on our interests and previous experience).

(II) As Well as Enhances the Competencies of the Respective Actors

Successful action research, which develops strategies to achieve some desired social goal, obviously enhances the competencies of those seeking to achieve that goal. Thus we hope that through their involvement in the GIST Project teachers have improved their classroom management skills and developed ways of capturing girls' interest in science and technology. But this is to stress the action side of the Project. We also hope that teachers have learned something of research techniques such as questionnaire design and classroom observation. Perhaps more importantly we hope that teachers have come to question their taken for granted assumptions about the world (that is, to take a research stance on their experience), and will continue to examine and evaluate their own actions now that the formal Project is finished. But the Project team are also actors within this particular drama and action research should be a learning experience for all those involved. As academics we are forced to come out of our ivory towers and learn some hard lessons about the possibilities and limitations of action in school. Again this should have lasting effects after the Project has finished in providing a practical grounding for our theorizing.

(III)   Being Performed Collaboratively

In traditional educational research the teachers' role is defined by the researcher. Either the researcher asks the teachers to behave in a particular way, teach a particular syllabus or adopt a particular style. Or the researcher observes the teachers going about their daily business and gives them only a vague idea of the object of the research so as to minimize interference in the process being studied. A hierarchy of power and knowledge is set up between researchers and researched. In the GIST Project the model was different. The purpose of the research was discussed with the teachers and their ideas about how it should be implemented were just as — if not more — useful than those of the Project team. The initial idea for the GIST Project came from outside the schools and our first task was to convince teachers, many of whom had never consciously thought about the situation, that this was indeed an educational problem which could be tackled in schools. Later on we hoped, and constantly stressed our hope, that teachers would initiate interventions appropriate to their own schools. In practice, this took a long time and most of the ideas came from the Project team. Teachers did select which of the possible strategies to adopt. But because the impetus for the Project came from us, and our commitment was, at least at the beginning, greater than theirs, the choice was certainly guided. Collaboration does not mean that our roles were identical. The Project team did not in general (although we did upon occasion) take classes; the teachers did not in general analyze data and write research reports (although the data is available to them and a few have written short articles). Both teachers and the Project team are involved in evaluating the Project and the success of the various interventions, but not necessarily by the same criteria.

The notion of collaboration could, in theory, be extended to pupils and parents as well as teachers, although this was not attempted on the GIST Project. Parents are clearly an important group which it would have been advantageous to involve if we had had the resources to do so. Pupils are more problematic. Teachers and parents are adults who can form their own opinions and withdraw from the Project (either formally or informally) if they disagree with the aims. But pupils in schools have less freedom of action; moreover, they are more influenced by passing fads and fashions. Although we wanted the girls to make informed decisions about their option choices and future life styles, we did not want them to choose to study science simply to help the project succeed. This would be the Hawthorne effect with a vengeance and ethically extremely dubious. So we encouraged teachers to discuss sexism and the reasons that girls tend to avoid science with their classes; but we did not involve the pupils directly in discussing the aims or implementation of the project.

(IV)   In an Immediate Situation

Many researchers, including myself (Kelly, 1981) have studied the causes of girls' under-achievement in science and made recommendations for change arising from that research. But traditional research stops with the causes, or, at the latest, with the recommendations. Whether or not they are implemented is not seen as any part of the researcher's responsibility. In general they are not. Teachers often rightly see such recommendations as impractical because they have not been tried out in schools. In simultaneous-integrated action research this divorce between research and practice does not occur. Researchers are responsible for implementing their own recommendations and have to work within the schools rather than studying them from the outside.

(V)   Using Data Feedback in a Cyclical Process

Most researchers do their best not to influence the system they are studying. In experimental designs there is a pre-test, some action, and a post-test. In observational studies the observer tries to merge into the background, become a fly on the wall, and let events take their normal course. In both cases precautions are taken to avoid the subjects finding out what the researchers are looking for, because if they knew they might helpfully provide it. As Ackroyd and Hughes (1981) say, 'These days the methodological injunction to the researcher not to influence the subjects he or she studies is emphasized whatever the methodological device or technique employed'. Once the data are collected it becomes the property of the researchers who take it back to their university or college. Several years later the results emerge. Perhaps a book is written and a complementary copy sent to the school which was studied. But the school has little, if any, say over what is done with the results.

In the GIST Project we wanted the subjects to know what we were looking for and to provide it. We employed 'reactive' measures. For example, we used a simple classroom observation schedule to monitor teachers' interactions with girls and boys in the classroom. The teachers knew that previous research (for example, Spender, 1978 and 1982) had shown that teachers usually spend more time with boys than with girls; they knew that we were assessing them in this respect. And so they made an effort to apportion their time evenly between the sexes. At the end of each period of observation the quantitative results and our more interpretive observations were discussed with the teacher concerned so that s/he got feedback on her or his behaviour. This was both a research and training exercise. Our presence and comments gave the teachers a chance to practice behaving equally to both sexes and suggestions on how to deal with sex stereotyped behaviour on the part of the pupils. For example, we noticed that boys were more likely than girls to 'call out' the answer to questions so we suggested that girls could get a fair share of the teacher's attention if questions were directed to specific individuals rather than to the class as a whole. Our research results challenged conventional wisdom on the impossibility of distributing teacher attention equally to girls and boys, and threw light on the ways in which science comes to be seen as a masculine subject in school (Kelly, 1985; Whyte, 1984).

Survey data can also be fed back to teachers. The children in the GIST Project schools completed a number of attitude and achievement tests in their first term at secondary school. These tests were analyzed on the computer as rapidly as possible. By the end of the third term we had visited each school to describe what we had found, and how their children compared with others in the study. By September we had produced and distributed to the schools a booklet describing the test results (Kelly *et al.*, 1981). On the basis of these results we suggested possible courses of action in each school. For example, we found that at age 11 girls were already far less interested than boys in learning about physical science. However, both sexes turned out to be interested in human biology. So we suggested that teachers might approach physical science topics through their links with human biology. Boys were found to be more sex stereotyped than girls in their attitudes towards careers and boys were much more likely than girls to consider science unsuitable for women. So we decided that more of our work should be geared towards changing boys' attitudes in this area. Analysis of the results of spatial and mechanical tests enabled us to pick out girls with special skills in these areas who were subsequently told of their talent and specifically encouraged to study technical subjects higher up the school. In all these ways the data was used cyclically: our actions were influenced by our research, and the research then had to be adapted in turn to reflect the new actions.

(VI) Aiming at an Increased Understanding of the Totality of a Given Social Situation

Most educational research which is concerned with improving practice has adopted an experimental model. However, by controlling for all variables except those under consideration, by pouring in money for curriculum materials, or demanding a certain allocation of time and facilities, the normal school situation is distorted and becomes artificial. Schools are constantly changing in unpredictable ways which destroy any neat experimental design; they have limited resources and constraints of staffing and building which vary from school to school. Simultaneous-integrated action research does not attempt to control for these factors or minimize their effects. In the GIST Project we were trying to find out what ordinary schools with ordinary teachers and ordinary resources could do to improve girls' take-up of scientific and technical subjects. There was no massive input of resources and no standardized research design. Each school adopted a different package of interventions to suit their individual needs, because we believe that interventions work best if the staff feel committed to them. All the GIST schools experienced staff changes and four suffered major reorganization during the course of the project. But this is the nitty-gritty of life in schools. If innovations cannot survive in these conditions they are useless; and if they do succeed it suggests that they might also work in other schools with similarly unpredictable conditions.

(VII) Primarily Applicable for the Understanding of Change Processes in Social Systems

Clearly, action research is only applicable to systems which can change. But this applies to the great majority of the educational field.

Action research is a way of trying out changes and seeing what happens. As such it has a particular appeal to researchers motivated by a philosophy of social change such as feminism, multi-culturalism or socialism. GIST was a feminist research project and we wanted to use a research method which would allow us to express our commitment to improving women's position. Simultaneous-integrated action research met this criterion because we were taking practical steps to help girls as well as studying them. We were working to change pupils' and teachers' attitudes and choices, and simultaneously researching into how change comes about, so that our experience could be generalized and applied more widely. The modern feminist movement also stresses the importance of non-hierarchical organization and sharing knowledge and skills; again simultaneous-integrated action research is appropriate because it involves collaboration and sharing of data between researchers and researched. I do not want to argue that simultaneous-integrated action research is *the* feminist methodology — like Sue Scott (in this volume) I believe that a political commitment is more important than the specific methods employed — only that it has certain features which may give it a particular appeal for feminists.

(VIII)   Undertaken Within a Mutually Acceptable Framework

If researchers and teachers are to collaborate together it might seem axiomatic that they share a common ethical framework. In practice, this is not always so. One can be concerned to encourage girls in science and technology for a variety of different reasons; as part of a wider change in women's position in society; as part of a move towards sex equality in school; to get more good pupils into your department at school; because you think girls will civilize the boys in class or you like having pretty faces around; because your inspector/ headteacher/head of department is pushing the idea. Most of these positions were found among the 200 or so teachers involved in the GIST Project. While the project team was unambiguously committed to changing women's position in society, this was not true of all our collaborators. A mutually acceptable ethical framework had to be negotiated around our common ground. A major part of the Project was concerned with working with teachers to increase their awareness of sex stereotyping as an educational issue. Part of the action research was thus to change their ethical framework. Simultaneously they have charged our understanding of the extent to which sex stereotyping is a response to pupil behaviour and a useful administrative device. A mutually acceptable ethical framework sometimes means compromises and is continually under discussion.

As this description has shown, simultaneous-integrated action research incorporates aspects of both experimental social administration and teacher-research approaches, but also differs from them. Like experimental social administration it is concerned with the growth of scientific knowledge, theory building and cumulation — the traditional concerns of educational research. But it does not demand that the researcher remains uninvolved or impose a strict experimental design on the project. Feedback between research and action is a vital part of the simultaneous-integrated approach, and in this it resembles the teacher-researcher model. However, simultaneous-integrated action research does not require the teachers' perspective to be central. Teachers must be active collaborators in the research, not passive recipients of it, but they need not be the initiators. The Project team should not be an external agency, but may provide an external impetus for action. Indeed it could be argued that the GIST Project started at an earlier stage than most teacher-researcher projects, with the need to make teachers aware that a problem exists. Whereas teacher-researcher action research 'takes' teachers' problems as its subject matter, simultaneous-integrated action research starts by 'making' a social issue in this case girls' underachievement in science — problematic for teachers. Once this is done the initiative passes to the teachers as they begin to examine and change their own practice.

Advantages and Disadvantages of Simultaneous-Integrated Action Research

Writers from all three action research traditions have commented on the tensions between action and research, whether these roles are separate or combined. For example, Lees (1975) from the experimental social administration school suggests that 'the researcher's commitment to rigorous procedures may run counter to the practitioner's need for flexibility and intuition in dealing with practical situations' and 'research neutrality poses a problem with practitioners, who typically consider a strong value commitment to their projects important'. In his view, 'the danger of [an] integrated approach is that research could give way to advocacy'. Similar comments are made by Halsey (1972), Powley and Evans (1979) and Smith and Barnes

(1970). The conflict of interests and of loyalties felt by teacher-researchers, whether they are researching their own or their colleagues behaviour, raises issues such as 'should the teacher/researcher insist on tape recording the lesson if it clearly embarrasses and inhibits the pupils?' (Nixon, 1978) and a 'relative lack of commitment to the here and now participant identity' (Smetherham, 1978). From a simultaneous-integrated perspective, Rapoport (1970) discusses 'Three Dilemmas in Action Research', concerned with ethics, goals and initiatives. Most of these authors are committed to the further development of action research, but their accounts seem to stress the disadvantages rather than the advantages of this type of research.

In my opinion, one of the main advantages of action research over more conventional methodologies, is that it goes a long way towards breaking down the traditional hostility of teachers to researchers. As Cope and Gray (1979) comment 'it is difficult to overestimate the legacy of suspicion that surrounds much educational research as far as teachers are concerned'. They are discussing quantitative research, but the same can be said of qualitative methods. For example, McNamara (1980) claims, that 'whatever the intellectual or theoretical value of [ethnographic] work to the community of social scientists, it is of no intellectual, theoretical or practical value to the teaching profession'. Carol Cummings and Margaret Threadgold (in this volume) make similar points. This cannot be said of action research where the relevance of the research to teachers' practical concerns is obvious. Teachers are far more likely to co-operate in a research project when they can see that its purpose is to improve a situation which is worrying them. In simultaneous-integrated action research the proposed interventions can often be justified by research-based arguments, and in the GIST Project we found that this lent credibility to our suggestions. This deference to research may be a peculiarity of science teachers, whose own discipline is research-based, but I suspect that it also applies more generally.

Thus, one of the advantages of action research is that it is more acceptable to teachers and this can make it easier for researchers to gain access to schools. On the other hand action research makes more demands than traditional research on the teachers' time and energy. This can lead to a reluctance to become over-involved. In the GIST Project we noticed that the control schools, where by definition no action was taking place, responded much more promptly to requests for information than did the action schools. In the action schools there was sometimes a certain sense of 'not you again'.

In a simultaneous-integrated action research project, research and action can be mutually supportive. Research can point the direction for action and increase its credibility as well as evaluating its effects. Action can make school-based research more acceptable to teachers and test its theories. But this is not to imply that conflicts between the needs of research and the needs of action do not occur: they do. One source of conflict in the GIST Project was over how much time and energy should be spent on research (narrowly conceived as theoretical concerns) compared to action in schools. Both action and research are greedy activities which will expand endlessly if not checked. Compared to the urgency of solving a practical problem, the expansion of scientific knowledge can seem an unwarranted luxury. It is sometimes necessary to protect the research component of the project by withdrawing from action for a period. In this respect school holidays are a great boon!

Writers in the experimental social administration tradition often see the tensions between action and research in terms of the researchers' need for a well-designed experiment, with random allocation of subjects to groups and clearly-defined treatments in each group. From a simultaneous-integrated perspective the fact that these conditions are seldom met is one of the bonuses of action research. Experimental situations are, by definition, artificial; action research takes place in far more naturalistic settings. Thus the results show what can be achieved in a normal school setting. Obviously if the research design is messy, and liable to change in midstream, it is difficult to get clear-cut results. In the GIST Project we are not able to compare the effectiveness of the different interventions in any formal way, because we have not insisted that each school use one and only one. But we would argue that this is a futile exercise anyway, since what matters is the cumulative effect of interventions on the whole atmosphere of a school. Situations such as girls underachievement in science and technology are 'over-determined', with many interlocking causes, and any single intervention will only have a marginal effect. Moreover, a strategy which worked well in one school, where the teachers were enthusiastic about it and where it fitted in with other aspects of school life, might be disastrous if imposed on another school.

Many people find this approach hard to appreciate. We have frequently been asked, both by teachers and researchers, how we are going to 'prove' which is the 'best' intervention. They have wondered why we did not have a control group in each school or at least a single strategy in each school. The answer is that the only thing we hope to prove by the GIST Project is that girls' under-achievement in science and technology is an educational problem that can be ameliorated (not eliminated) by ordinary teachers working in ordinary schools. As Smith (1975) has argued, we need to reduce our expectations. Research will not tell us the best way to achieve some desired end; but it may be able to point us a few steps up the path and describe how we got there.

This does not mean that action research should abandon all attempts at evaluation. In the GIST Project we have two control schools where children have completed attitude and achievement tests but where no interventions have taken place. By comparing the results in these schools with those in the action schools we can demonstrate the effect of intervention as compared to non-intervention. We also have qualitative information from our collaborators — the teachers — on how effective they feel each intervention has been with their children. But we will not be surprised if the results vary widely from school to school or from teacher to teacher, reflecting the uniqueness of each situation.

Problems of random allocation and control groups are clearly only relevant to researchers in the quantitative tradition. But simultaneous-integrated action research also presents problems for the qualitative researcher. Principal among these is the practical difficulty of taking field notes. A neutral observer can sit quietly in a classroom noting what goes on around her/him. Even a participant observer can, in classical fashion, make frequent trips to the toilet to record observations. In practice it is seldom as simple as this, but the problems are multiplied for the action researcher who is often, almost by definition, at the centre of the action. It is difficult, if not impossible, to simultaneously run a workshop on, for example, sex-stereotyping in schools, and observe teachers' reactions to it. The workshop leader inevitably gets a different picture to the participants. Given unlimited resources, two of the project team could attend each session, one to initiate action and one to observe. But in practice this is a luxury which can seldom be afforded. On the GIST Project our notes were written in retrospect, with all the imperfections that entails.

Action research has substantial attractions for a socially committed researcher because it enables her/him to work towards social change as well as the expansion of knowledge. In the teacher-researcher model the teacher's perspective is central and so the social commitment must come from her/him. This limits the range of issues which the teacher-researcher can investigate. It is all very well to speak of stepping outside your own taken-for-granted reality to 'see ourselves as others see us', but without an outside input this can be impossible, simply because the reality *is* taken for granted. Where I might see sexism in a classroom, a group of teachers who have never questioned the patriarchal basis of our society will probably not notice it. This is evident in much of the writing by teacher-researchers who continue to use 'he' to describe all their pupils! The issues which teacher researchers study tend to be questions of classroom management rather than socially or sociologically important problems. I do not accept that action research should be restricted to the questions which are important to practitioners, or that the practitioners' viewpoint is necessarily 'right'.

In both experimental social administration and simultaneous-integrated action research a social commitment can be built into the plans of the project team. The idea that the researcher's value system enters into all research work is now well accepted amongst academics — although much less so among teachers — but traditional research designs still seek to minimize the influence of the researcher's individual views. This can be personally frustrating as Sue Scott (in this volume) points out. In the GIST Project, our personal commitment was well known to the teachers we were working with. Advocacy was part of the job. It can be argued that this is less ethical than a neutral position which implies respect for the participant's views. I disagree. It seems to me both unethical and condescending to pretend to be neutral about issues which one personally feels to be important. To confront the differences of opinion implies greater respect for the extent to which teachers have thought out and can defend their viewpoints, than does the assumption that these views will change the moment a researcher disagrees with them. In general researchers do not have the power to impose their way of thinking on teachers. The other argument for neutrality is that one loses data by making one's own position clear. Again, I do not think this is necessarily true. On the GIST Project, because our position was known, we were told a lot of stories supposedly illustrating either the immutable or the changeable nature of sex roles. The data certainly changed because we were arguing a case, but except in the very rare instance where the discussion degenerated into personal hostility, it was not lost.

However, to balance this value loaded approach we found it essential to employ 'hard' data to support our case. Science teachers in particular are not persuaded by general arguments, or by ethnographic data. They need statistics and percentages to convince them that we are not part of the lunatic fringe, that we know what we are talking about. Classroom incidents are often dismissed as atypical, or at least, not true of *their* classrooms. Harding and Randall (1983) argue that ethnographic observations and theories based on these observations are only convincing to teachers who already accept their basic premise. Our experience on the GIST Project is similar. Case-studies and consciousness-raising exercises are frequently dismissed as 'waffle'. Statistically-based psychological studies (such as Dweck *et al*'s (1978) work on classroom interaction) are less easily accused of bias and seem to be taken more seriously by sceptical teachers. As Janet Finch (in this volume) argues, qualitative data can have relevance to policy makers, but quantitative data has more immediate appeal. In the GIST study we made instrumental use of whatever methods and data appeared to be most effective in convincing any individual teacher.

Teacher-researcher and simultaneous-integrated forms of action research also have attractions for feminist researchers because of the way that equality between researchers and practitioners is built into the project. Elliott (1983 and personal communication) suggests that in teacher-researcher action research there should be no fixed boundaries between the two groups in terms of roles or tasks. Simultaneous-integrated action research does not necessarily seek to eradicate these distinctions. Nor does it take it as axiomatic that teachers should generate their own research problems, or that the research should be approached wholly from the practitioners' viewpoint. But it does emphasize that teachers should be collaborators in the research, who are fully informed about its purpose and results, and whose ideas are crucial for planning actions. The overall idea for the research may come from the project team, but the working out of that idea in practice is a joint effort.

Although the philosophy is different, in practice this approach has much in common with teacher-researcher action research projects, particularly those with outside funding. Writers in this tradition have discussed the problems of encouraging teachers to define issues with remarkable frankness. Elliott (1982) admits that 'members of the central team [of the Teacher-Pupil Interaction and the Quality of Learning (TIQL) project] experienced some pressure from teachers to give them direction' and includes the following comment from one of his collaborators: 'I am not sure that the approach you advocate in theory is really translatable into practice very generally'. Similarly Adams (1980) found that 'after one term of working schools [it became] clear that little progress in the [Ford Teaching] Project seemed possible without intensive and heavy intervention by the team'. Rudduck and Stenhouse (1979) report considerable difficulty in disseminating the teacher-researcher *approach* — audiences generally preferred to talk about substantive results.

However, the notion of collaboration can raise particular problems within simultaneous-integrated action research because of its commitment to social science as well as action. This is especially true where a major part of the project is concerned with increasing teachers' awareness of a particular problem. In the GIST Project we were working with all the science and technical craft teachers in a school, not just with volunteers (as happens in teacher-researcher projects). Although in theory all the staff were involved in the decision to cooperate with GIST, in practice some were more enthusiastic than others. We consider that teachers' attitudes towards boys and girls are a vital ingredient in encouraging or discouraging girls from choosing science and technology. A major part of our intervention, particularly in the early stages, was to sensitize teachers to the problem of sex stereotyping in the classroom through workshops and informal chats. As Hearn (1979), a practising science teacher, has pointed out 'the most difficult stage in the whole exercise is accepting the problem and resolving to do something about it'. Ferguson (1981) has called this process of making a problem visible by discussing it and associated pieces of research 'deliberative enquiry', and it has some similarities to feminist consciousness-raising. As part of our research interest in ways of bringing about change in teachers' attitudes, the Project team kept notes on most of our discussions with teachers, and these notes form part of the overall Project evaluation. But this is one-sided. The teachers did not (as far as we know) go away and write notes on our reactions to suggestions.

This can produce severe ethical problems. If we treat the teachers as collaborators in our day-to-day interactions, it may seem like a betrayal of trust if these interactions are recorded and used as evidence. Particularly if the evidence is negative. With a project like GIST with a clear overall aim, there is frequently a definite 'right' and 'wrong' teacher reaction, and teachers may well feel that they are being judged. One way out of this could be to submit all our reports and evaluations of teachers' reactions to the teacher involved for comment; to get them to assess their own changing attitudes. This might work well with teachers who have become 'converts', but is more problematic if teachers remain indifferent or even hostile to the aims of the project. How does one write an honest but critical report of teachers' attitudes if one hopes to continue to work with the people involved? We face many of the same problems as Helen Simons (1983) and Gordon Griffiths (in this volume) of a conflict between the pursuit of truth and the maintenance of trust with the teachers in schools. I do not think we have yet found a satisfactory way of resolving this dilemma. Our position lies uncomfortably between that of the internal evaluator whose main loyalty is to colleagues and the school, and the external researcher for whom informal comments and small incidents may provide the most revealing data.

The teacher-researcher solution to the problem of assessing change in teachers' attitudes is to rely on teacher self-monitoring. This can also be built into simultaneous-integrated action research. On the GIST Project a number of teachers have written accounts of their own reactions to the projects. We also cooperated with a team of independent evaluators who interviewed teachers about their perceptions of GIST (Payne *et al*, 1984). While these methods have produced some fascinating insights, we are reluctant to accept them as the whole story. Teachers' perspectives are as partial as ours, and as liable to distortion through modesty, politeness, guilt or self-justification.

A more concrete measure of change in teachers' attitudes is changes in behaviour. These can take the form of altered classroom management (as seen in classroom observation sessions), organizational changes (such as the institution of single sex physics classes which were initially rejected as sexist) or curriculum revision. But many attitude changes are more subtle than this, and the problem of assessing them remains.

A final question about action research, of all varieties, is whether it diverts attention and resources from more fundamental questions. By concentrating on reforms within schools it may seem to ignore the societal causes. A position which appears to blame the individual teacher or the school for the problem of girls' underachievement in science can be seen a deeply conservative in discounting the influence of patriarchy and capitalism. But action research does not necessarily fall into this trap. Janet Finch (in this volume) argues cogently that researchers ought to 'get their hands dirty' with social policy, and I agree. Small improvements are better than no change at all. Moreover action research in schools can reveal rather than disguise the societal cause of educational problems. Many teachers espouse an 'out-there' philosophy which suggests that the causes of girls' underachievement in science lie in the homes, in the primary schools or in the labour market — anywhere but in the secondary school. But patriarchy is not something that operates 'out-there' — it is all pervasive. Action research can raise teachers' conciousness about the processes they are involved in, and the ways in which secondary schools are a link in the chain by which patriarchal relations are reproduced. Exposing the connection between micro and macro structures can be anything but conservative. If successful, it enables teachers to break out from the determinism which says 'its too big for me, there's nothing I can do', and yet avoid disillusion if their efforts produce only small effects. Action research may be one way of creating a 'transformative' school which aims to transform social relations rather than simply reproduce them.

Conclusion

In this chapter I have tried to sketch out some of the advantages and disadvantages of simultaneous-integrated action research. As is probably obvious, to my mind the advantages outweigh the disadvantages. Simultaneous-integrated action research has advantages for educational researchers in reducing the communication gap between teachers and researchers. Currently, many teachers consider educational research an expensive irrelevance. They mistrust its conclusions because they are obtained in artificial conditions; they consider most of its concerns marginal to the actual business of teaching in schools; and they resent the resources it seems to command. In this climate of suspicion it is hard to justify the usefulness of much conventional educational research. Simultaneous-integrated action research, by working in ordinary school conditions and attempting to find answers to teachers' practical problems, may provide one way out of the impasse. Any losses in research rigour are more than compensated for by gains in the acceptability of the research. The method also has advantages for feminist researchers in that it enables us to take concrete steps to improve women's position, and to put our theories about the egalitarian organization of research into practice. As a method for the generation of sociological knowledge I think the main advantage of simultaneous-integrated action research is that it deals with total situations and recognizes the complexity of interlocking relationships, while still allowing theories to be tested and evaluated. The specific methodology employed is less important than the overall approach to action and research.

This is beginning to sound like a eulogy. I do not want to argue that simultaneous-integrated action research is the 'only' or even the 'best' way of doing research. For different situations and different problems other forms of action research and conventional research are more appropriate. However, I do want to suggest that simultaneous-integrated action research should be seriously considered by educational researchers, and used more widely than it has been in the past. The term 'action-research' is currently in danger of being captured by teacher-researchers to the exclusion of other models, and this would be unfortunate.

Acknowledgements

Many of the ideas in this chapter have been developed in discussion with my colleagues on the GIST Project, Barbara Smail and Judith Whyte. I am grateful for their contributions. However our discussions are seldom conclusive, and this article represents my synthesis, not theirs. I am also grateful to Peter Halfpenny for commenting on an earlier Draft of this paper and to the participants at the Whitelands College seminar for a lively discussion which helped to clarify my ideas.

References

ACKROYD, S. and HUGHES, J.A. (1981) *Data Collection in Context*, London, Longman.

ADAMS, E. (1980) 'The Ford Teaching Project', in STENHOUSE, L. (Ed.) *Curriculum Research and Development in Action*, London, Heinemann.

COPE, E. and GRAY, J. (1979) 'Teachers as researchers: some experience of an alternative paradigm', *British Educational Research Journal*, 5, pp. 237–51.

DWECK, C. *et al.* (1978) 'Sex differences in learned helplessness' *Developmental Psychology*, 14, pp. 268–76.

ELLIOTT, J. (1975) *Ford Teaching Project*, Cambridge, Cambridge Institute of Education.

ELLIOTT, J. (1978) 'What is action research in schools?' *Journal of Curriculum Studies*, 10, 4, pp. 355–7.

ELLIOTT, J. *et al.* (1981) *School Accountability*, London, Grant McIntyre.

ELLIOTT, J. (1982) 'Facilitating action-research in schools: some dilemmas', working paper no. 12, Teacher Pupil Interaction and the Quality of Learning Project, October.

ELLIOTT, J. (1983) 'Paradigms of educational research and theories of schooling', paper presented at Westhill Sociology of Education Conference, January.

FERGUSON, J. (1981) 'The science education of girls in Canada: A strategy for change', paper presented at First GASAT Conference, Holland, November.

HALSEY, A.H. (Ed.) (1972) *Educational Priority: Vol. 1 EPA Problems and Policies*, London, HMSO.

HARDING, J. and RANDALL, G. (1983) 'Why classroom interaction studies?' paper presented at Second GASAT Conference, Norway, September.

HEARN, M. (1979) 'Girls for physical science: A school based strategy for encouraging girls to opt for the physical sciences', *Education in Science*, April, pp. 14–16.

HULT, M. and LENNUNG, S. (1980) 'Towards a definition of action-research: A note and bibliography', *Journal of Management Studies*, 17, 2, pp. 241–50.

KELLY, A. (Ed.) (1981) *The Missing Half: Girls and Science Education*, Manchester, Manchester University Press.

KELLY, A. (1985) 'The construction of masculine science', submitted to *British Journal of Sociology of Education*, 6, 2, 133–54.

KELLY, A., SMAIL, B. and WHYTE, J. (1981) *Initial GIST Survey: Results and Implications*, mimeo, Manchester, Manchester Polytechnic.

KELLY, A., WHYTE, J. and SMAIL, B. (1984) *Girls Into Science and Technology Final Report* Dept. of Sociology, University of Manchester.

LEES, R. (1975) 'The action-research relationship', in LEES, R. and SMITH, C. (Eds) *Action Research in Community Development*, London, Routledge and Kegan Paul.

McNAMARA, D.R. (1980) 'The outsider's arrogance: The failure of participant observers to understand classroom events', *British Educational Research Journal*, 6, pp. 113–26.

NIXON, J. (1978) 'The teacher as researcher: Methods and procedures', paper presented to British Educational Research Association Conference, September.

NIXON, J. (Ed.) (1981) *A Teachers' Guide to Action Research*, London, Grant McIntyre.

PAYNE, G., HUSTER, D. and CUFF, T. (1984) *GIST or PIST: Teachers' Perceptions of the Project Girls Into Science and Technology* Manchester Manchester Polytechnic.

POWLEY, T. and EVANS, D. (1979) 'Towards a methodology of action research', *Journal of Social Policy*, 8, pp. 27–46.

RAPOPORT, R.N. (1970) 'Three dilemmas in action research', *Human Relations*, 23, pp. 499–513.

RUDDUCK, J. and STENHOUSE, L. (1979) 'A study in the dissemination of action research', SSRC Final Report HR3483/1, November.

SHARPLES, D. (1983) 'An overview of school based action research', paper presented at Action Research in Classrooms and Schools Conference, Manchester Polytechnic, March.

SIMONS, H. (1983) 'Club rules: The limits of positive evaluation', paper presented to Qualitative Methodology and the Study of Education Workshop, Whitelands College, London, July.

SMAIL, B., WHYTE, J. and KELLY, A. (1982) 'Girls Into Science and Technology: the first two years', *School Science Review*, 63, pp. 620–30.

Smetherham, D. (1978) 'Insider research', *British Educational Research Journal*, 4, pp. 97–107.

Smith, G. (1975) 'Action research: Experimental social administration', in Lees, R. and Smith, G. (Eds) *Action Research in Community Development*, London, Routledge and Kegan Paul.

Smith, G. (1982) 'Action research 1968–81: Method of research or method of innovation', *Journal of Community Education*, 1, 1, pp. 31–46.

Smith, G. and Barnes, J. (1970) 'Some implications of action research projects for research', paper presented to World Congress of Sociology, Varna, Bulgaria.

Spender, D. (1978) 'Don't talk, listen', *Times Educational Supplement*, 3 November.

Spender, D. (1982) 'The role of teachers: What choices do they have?' in (Ed.) *Sex Stereotyping in Schools*, Council of Europe Swets & Zeigler.

Whyte, J. (1984a) 'Observing sex stereotypes and interactions in the school lab and workshop', *Educational Review*, 36, 75–86.

Whyte, J. (1985) *Getting the GIST*, London, Routledge and Kegan Paul (forthcoming).

8 Educational Action Research: Some General Concerns and Specific Quibbles

Dave Ebbutt

We shall not cease from exploration
And the end of all our exploring
will be to arrive where we started
And know the place for the first time

Little Gidding
by T.S. Eliot

Introduction

The context which gave rise to the issues discussed in this chapter was a collaborative educational action research project which ran from January 1981 to March 1983.

Teacher-pupil Interaction and the Quality of Learning (TIQL) was funded by Programme 2 of the Schools Council. Teacher researchers were organized in the main as teams or groups within an inner network of ten schools. These schools — one sixth-form college, five upper/secondary schools, one middle school and two junior/infant schools — were selected by invitation in consultation with local education authorities. The project was coordinated by a central team of consultants based at the Cambridge Institute of Education. The Project focused on problems of teaching for under-standing, with particular reference to a dilemma we believed teachers faced at all levels of the school system; namely, between teaching for understanding and teaching for assessment (DES 1979; Doyle 1979 and 1981). The Project aimed by a process of action research to support teacher researchers in:

(i)   collecting and analyzing evidence about the problems of implementing understanding tasks in the classroom;
(ii) generating hypotheses and testing teaching strategies in order to attempt to resolve the problems in the above process;
(iii) identifying significant contextual or organizational constraints;
(iv) developing organizational and curricular strategies for resolving these constraints.

Publication of comprehensive documentation of the Project's work is currently under negotiation. This includes accounts of the vicissitudes of the research process in schools (Ebbutt and Elliott) and a selection of the case studies written by teacher researchers (Elliott). Many of the chapters in the first of these accounts originally appeared in draft form as a series of in-house working papers which were written by Project consultants and widely circulated from time to time throughout the life of the Project.

In this chapter I want in Part 1 to organize and clarify my own thinking about some general aspects of educational action research. Subsequently in Part 2 I want to think about specific aspects of educational action research which became of interest as the TIQL Project progressed. In order to focus my thinking in Part 2 I want to take a reflective look, informed by the benefit of hindsight, at the first and to date most widely circulated TIQL Project Document *Action-Research: A Framework for Self-Evaluation in Schools* (Working Paper No. 1) written by John Elliott the TIQL Project Director. It would be inappropriate to do this without paying some attention to a similar document *The Action-Research Planner* (Kemmis *et al*, 1981). My reason for taking this approach resides in the history of the TIQL Project. Sometime between December 1980 and the end of January 1981, Elliott received from Deakin University, Australia, a draft of what was shortly to be published by them as the *Action-Research Planner*. Receipt of this draft provided a stimulus to Elliott's planning of the TIQL Project, and by the end of February 1981 he had written his *Framework*, which fully acknowledged the parentage of the Kemmis Planner.

It is important to point out that both Kemmis and Elliott acknowledge their debt to the pioneering work in the field of action research of the American social psychologist, Kurt Lewin. It is through a brief consideration of his work that I want, in Part 1, to organize and clarify my own thinking about aspects of action research in educational settings.

Part 1 — Early Work on Action Research

Corey (1953) maintains that there was at least one other pioneering influence on the field of action research in the United States.

The expression *action research* and the operations it implies come from at least two somewhat independent sources. One is the activities and writings of Collier during the period (1933–45) when he was Commissioner of Indian Affairs. Collier represented a group that was emphasizing the importance of social planning, and he insisted that 'research and then more research is essential to the program ...' He used the expression *action research* and was convinced that 'since the findings of research must be carried into effect by the administrator and the layman and must be criticized by them through their experience, the administrator and the layman must themselves participate creatively in the research impelled as it is from their own area of need'.

The second source is Lewin (1948) and his students, many of whom have attempted to study human relations scientifically and to improve the quality of human relations as a consequence of their enquiries (p. 7).

An important facet of Lewin's work was its concern with practical situations of social conflict. In particular he was interested 'in the psychological problems confronting any minority group whose space of free movement is restricted by barriers of caste and prejudice' (Lewin, 1948, Foreword). Much of his work was carried out with Jewish or black minorities. The action component of his work derived from his insistence on democratically guided social change and his belief that 'remedial efforts should be introduced into a community prepared to study the results of its own social action'. In order to facilitate such a process he developed change experiments designed to allow groups from the communities in question, with the guidance of external consultants to 'learn to become detached and objective in examining the foundations of their own biases'.

After his death in 1948, Lewin's ideas were developed and refined by co-workers and one strand found its expression in the work on conflict in industrial relations settings developed in the United Kingdom at the Tavistock Institute.

Performance Gaps

The parallels between these developments during the 1930s and 1940s and the concurrent growth of mainstream psychiatry and clinical psychology are striking. The notion of a performance gap is as central to action research in social settings as it is to psychiatry and clinical psychology. In the latter specialisms, trained consultants 'deal with the problem of helping *individuals* into more adequate communication with their inter-personal worlds, helping them gradually to discover the distortions or discrepancies of perception and relationships that have been maintained by themselves and by inadequate communications from others' (Lippit, 1949). By the same token, change experiments implemented by Lewin and successors helped *groups* to diagnose facts about their relations with other *groups*. Then consultants subsequently helped the groups to turn these diagnostic discoveries, perhaps for example distorted minority group perceptions of the ideologies or stereotypes of the majority group, into new practical patterns of group action and collaboratively to study the effects.

It is my contention that it is via the notion of a performance gap — a gap between espoused theory and theory-in-action — by which advocates of action research locate its niche as an appropriate mode of research in schools and classrooms. For instance Kemmis (1981) in his Planner uses this illustrative example:

> There is a *gap* between the idea and the reality of inquiry teaching in my own classroom. Recognizing this *gap*, I must develop a strategy of action if improvements in this kind of questioning are to be achieved ... (p. 2) (my emphasis)

Similarly the Ford Teaching Project (1972–75, also directed by Elliott) emphasized practical strategies for monitoring the performance gap between a teacher's aspirations and practice. For example the technique of triangulation for comparing and contrasting three points of view of a classroom episode — the pupil's view, the teacher's view, and an external observer's view — is premised on the idea of a performance gap. Indeed this project team of Elliott and Adelman explicity developed an empirically grounded schema or typology of formal and informal teaching. They were able to show that some of the project teachers' 'theories' logically entailed a gap between aspiration and practice (Elliott, 1976, p. 15). For instance, they claimed that some teachers who professed an aim to foster independent reasoning in their pupils, nevertheless operated a theory-in-action which could be described as informal, structured and guided; that is, a theory-in-action which logically encourages pupil dependence.

Taking a similar approach the current Open University Course *Curriculum in Action* (Open University, 1980) articulates its stance in terms of a performance gap in this case between the curriculum in action and the curriculum as intention. It does so by framing six simple questions. These are:

(I)   What did the pupils actually do?
(II)   What were they learning?
(III)   How worthwhile was it?
(IV)   What did I do?
(V)   What did I learn?
(VI)   What do I intend to do now?

By the same token the performance gap which the TIQL Project team articulated in some of their early documents and which was also seen to exist across the school system by others, including HMI, was that between teaching for understanding and teaching for assessment. More specifically, the focus for our teacher researchers in their own classrooms was again articulated as a performance gap at the classroom task level, between the tasks teachers set for pupils and the task the pupils eventually come to work upon.

Definition of Educational Action Research

So far, my argument is intended to indicate the bridge between what I will call classic (or Lewinian) action research and educational action research. Now I need to consider what educational action research is seen to be. Both Elliott and Kemmis more or less agree about working definitions for what constitutes the essence of educational action research. That is I think they would concur with my synthesis that it is about *the systematic study of attempts to change and improve educational practice by groups of participants by means of their own practical actions and by means of their own reflection upon the effects of those actions.*

> The study of a social situation with a view to improving quality of action within it. (Elliott, 1981, p. 1)

> Put simply action research is the way groups of people can

organize the conditions under which they can learn from their own experience. (Kemmis *et al.*, 1981, p. 2)

Action research is trying out an idea in practice with a view to improving or changing something, trying to have a real effect on the situation. (Ibid, p. 8)

Much earlier, Corey (1953) observed that 'The process by which practitioners attempt to study their problems scientifically in order to guide, correct and evaluate their decisions and actions is what a number of people have called action research'. (p. 6)

There is no mystery underlying the idea of improvement in practice. It involves, as Schön (1983) so simply puts it

transforming the situation from what is to something he (the practitioner) likes better. (p. 147)

It seems to me that a vital element is missing from some of these working definitions. That missing element is; what is it about the activities they seek to define which allows the legitimate use of the term *research*? This is obviously an aspect of a much bigger question about the distinguishing features of research from other forms of discourse, which will only be dealt with superficially here. Stenhouse (1984) defines research 'as systematic enquiry made public' (p. 77). Meanwhile, Shulman's (1980) conception of what counts as research is that it is 'a family of methods which share the characteristics of disciplined enquiry'. For the distinguishing characteristics of disciplined enquiry he summarizes Cronbach and Suppes (1969):

1 Arguments and evidence can be examined.
2 Not dependent solely on eloquence or surface plausibility.
3 Avoids sources of error when possible and discusses margin for possible errors in conclusion.
4 Can be speculative, free wheeling and inventive.

Given that these are at least some of the characteristics of disciplined enquiry, then there is one clear and simple implication for educational action research which flows from them. If action research is to be considered legitimately as research, then participants in it must, it seems to me, be prepared to produce written reports of their activities. Moreover these reports ought to be available for some form of public critique. I would go as far as to say that if this condition is not satisfied by participants then no matter how personally and professionally valuable the exercise is in which they are engaged, it is not action *research*. I am emphasizing this condition because re-

Dave Ebbutt

searcher lore holds that it is notoriously difficult to encourage teachers to write accounts. Such reluctance on the part of teachers to write up an account of research has been the exception rather than the rule in the TIQL Project. However, current or forthcoming developments in information technology may sooner rather than later render the condition of the production of a written report redundant (see Bell, 1982). But such developments will equally affect all forms of disciplined enquiry, they will not solely apply to educational action research. So for the moment the production by participants of written reports remains important.

Classification of Types of Insider-Research in Schools

At this point it is important that the reader be clear about what I am trying to do here. I am trying to clarify *my own* thinking about educational action research. I am not seeking to arbitrate or prescribe what title various groups of teachers or research projects ought to give themselves. Consideration of definitions and necessary conditions does facilitate *my own* thinking about a classification of where I see educational action research fitting within the whole spectrum of what might be termed insider-research-related activity, currently taking place in schools. I have attempted to represent this classification diagrammatically (see table 1).

The broad classification is intended to be more or less self-explanatory. Nevertheless, there are a few points which perhaps need to be emphasized. It is only a broad classification of insider-teacher research not of all educational research. The necessary but not sufficient condition which separates an activity legitimately labelled research from one which is not (for example C from A) is, it has been argued, the production of a report which fulfils Cronbach and Suppes' criteria and which is available to some form of public critique. The demarcation between 'traditional' research [E] from action research [C and D] lies in the purpose of the activity — to contribute to the canons of social science knowledge in the former — to contribute to practical knowledge, to change and improvement in the latter. This distinction is explained more fully by Kemmis and Grundy (1981), more polemically by Delamont (1981), and with greater balance by McCormick and James (1983). The sort of teacher research which falls into this pure research mode is typified, I suggest, by some advanced diploma or master's theses carried out largely on a part-time basis where the researcher has access only to his/her own

Table 1: Broad Classification of a Range of Insider Activity Currently Occurring in Schools

TEACHER

Category 1	Category 2	Category 3	Category 4	Category 5
Works in isolation of own classroom	Works in isolation of own classroom	Works in isolation of own classroom	Works in isolation of own classroom as part of a coherent group who meet regularly	Works in isolation of own classroom
and	*and*	*and*	*and*	*and*
Reflects on own practice from time to time, may implement action steps	Regularly reflects on own practice. May implement action steps	Regularly reflects on own practice. Systematically implements action steps	Systematically reflect about own practice and systematically implement action steps	Reflects about aspects of practice. Selects hypotheses from formal theory
but	*and*	*and*	*and*	*and*
No use of external consultant	May use external consultant or a critical friend	May request help from consultant or critical friend	Almost certainly uses consultant or critical friend	May request help from consultant or supervisor
and	*and*	*and*	*and*	*and*
No systematic data collection	Informally collects some data	Systematically collects data	Systematically collects data	Systematically collects data
→	*and* →	*and* →	*and* →	*and* →

159

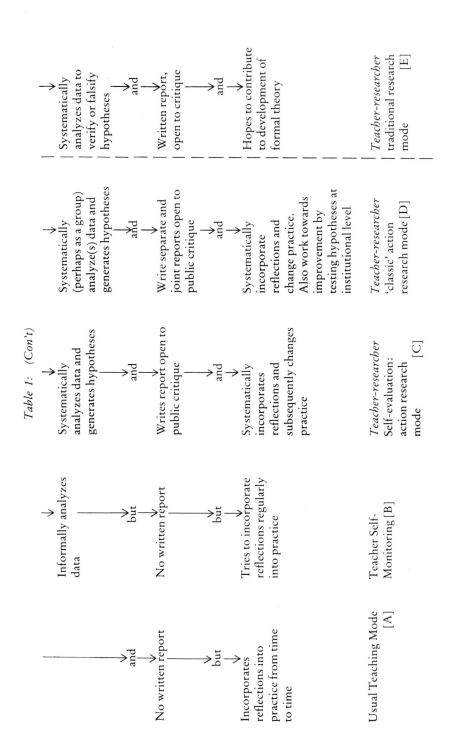

Table 1: (Con't)

Usual Teaching Mode [A]	Teacher Self-Monitoring [B]	Teacher-researcher Self-evaluation: action research mode [C]	Teacher-researcher 'classic' action research mode [D]	Teacher-researcher traditional research mode [E]
→	→ Informally analyzes data	→ Systematically analyzes data and generates hypotheses	→ Systematically (perhaps as a group) analyze(s) data and generates hypotheses	→ Systematically analyzes data to verify or falsify hypotheses
and → No written report	but → No written report	and → Writes report open to public critique	and → Write separate and joint reports open to public critique	and → Written report, open to critique
but → Incorporates reflections into practice from time to time	but → Tries to incorporate reflections regularly into practice	and → Systematically incorporates reflections and subsequently changes practice	and → Systematically incorporate reflections and change practice. Also work towards improvement by testing hypotheses at institutional level	and → Hopes to contribute to development of formal theory

institution. What separates 'classic' action research [D] is the collaborative group nature of the enterprise and, to an important extent, the scale and political location of the changes envisaged. I think that it must be admitted that much of the action research activity in most of the TIQL Project schools fell squarely into the self-evaluation/action research mode [C]. Finally, what the classification does for me is that it clarifies a difficulty which arises repeatedly at conferences where teachers present their research (the public critique condition) but to which I never know how to respond. Practitioner sceptics in the audience invariably ask:

Isn't this what the good intuitive teacher does all the time?

The question is often prefixed by 'surely'. The classification makes clear the increased degree of systematization and collaboration involved as one moves from the usual teaching mode through teacher self monitoring to 'classic' action research.

Part 2 — How Educational Action Research is Seen to Proceed

Kemmis (1981) in his *Planner* and Elliott (1981) in his *Framework*, adopt and adapt, with minor variations, the Lewin (1948) description of how action research proceeds by a sequence of spiral steps. This is how Lewin describes the process:

Planning starts usually with something like a general idea. For one reason or another it seems desirable to reach a certain objective. Exactly how to circumscribe this objective; and how to reach it is frequently not too clear. The first step then is to examine the idea carefully in the light of the means available. Frequently more fact-finding about the situation is required. If this first period of planning is successful two items emerge: namely an 'overall plan' of how to reach the objective and secondly, a decision in regard to the first step of action. Usually this planning has somewhat modified the original idea.

The next period is devoted to executing the first step of the overall plan.

... this second step is followed by certain fact-findings ...

... This reconnaissance or fact-finding has four functions. First it should evaluate the action. It shows whether what has been achieved is above or below expectation. Secondly it gives the planners a chance to learn, that is, to gather new general insight, ...

Thirdly, this fact-finding should serve as a basis for correctly planning the next step. Finally it serves as a basis for modifying the 'overall-plan'.

The next step again is composed of a circle of planning, executing, and reconnaissance or fact finding for the purpose of evaluating the results of the second step, for preparing the rational basis for planning the third step, and for perhaps modifying again the 'overall-plan'.

Rational social management, therefore, proceeds in a spiral of steps each of which is composed of a circle of planning, action and fact-finding about the result of the action. (p. 205)

These remarks are interesting in several respects. It is clear from his description how Lewin envisaged that the process of action research proceeds, and where feedback of information occurs. He maintains that information gained as a result of reconnaissance following an action step feeds back to influence and amend decisions previously made about the general idea or the overall plan or both. What is also interesting, however, is Lewin's mix of metaphors. He mentions *steps* of action and a *circle* of planning, executing and reconnaissance which together proceed in a *spiral*. It seems to me that the metaphor which Lewin had in mind was that of a spiral staircase. Both Kemmis in his *Planner* and subsequently Elliott in *Framework* take up and emphasize the spiral form of the research process. Kemmis in his *Planner* represents the process diagrammatically as shown in Figure 1.

Elliott revises this diagram in his *Framework* because he feels that 'it can as set out above allow those who use it to assume that "the General Idea" can be fixed in advance, that "Reconnaissance" is merely fact-finding and that "Implementation" is a fairly straight-forward process'. He goes on to argue for a modification of the diagram to take into account his feeling that:

The general idea should be allowed to shift. Reconnaissance should involve analysis as well as fact-finding and should con-stantly recur in the spiral of activities, rather than occur only at the beginning.

Figure 1

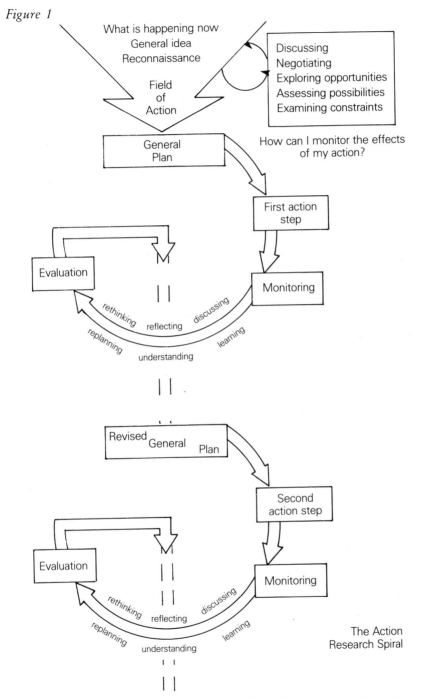

What is happening now
General idea
Reconnaissance

Field
of
Action

Discussing
Negotiating
Exploring opportunities
Assessing possibilities
Examining constraints

General
Plan

How can I monitor the effects
of my action?

First action
step

Evaluation

Monitoring

rethinking reflecting discussing
replanning learning
understanding

Revised General Plan

Second
action step

Evaluation

Monitoring

rethinking reflecting discussing
replanning learning
understanding

The Action
Research Spiral

Source: Kemmis, S et al (1981) *The Action Research Planner*, Deakin, Deakin University Press, p. 4, figure 1.

> *Implementation of an action step is not always easy, and one*
> *should not proceed to evaluate the effects of an action until one*
> *has monitored the extent to which it has been implemented.*
> (Elliott's emphasis)

I would argue that it is not the case that Kemmis equates reconnaissance with fact finding only. The Kemmis diagram clearly shows (and the text pp. 17–21 also) reconnaissance to comprise discussing, negotiating, exploring opportunities, assessing possibilities and examining constraints. In short there are elements of analysis in the Kemmis notion of reconnaissance. Nevertheless, I suggest that the thrust of Elliott's three underlined statements is an attempt on the part of a person experienced in directing action research projects to recapture some of the 'messyness' of the action–research cycle which the Kemmis version tends to gloss. In this respect — the shifting general idea and the recurrent nature of reconnaissance — Elliott brings educational action research back closer to the 'classic' Lewinian model. In so doing however he remains faithful to the Lewinian metaphor of the spiral staircase. Diagrammatically Elliott represents the process as shown in Figure 2.

But is a spiral really the most appropriate, rather than merely an adequate metaphor? If interpreted literally I suggest that it is not for the following reason. If in moving along a spiral (or a spiral staircase) one wishes to return to an original starting point, then one must retrace or repeat one's steps back up or down the spiral. This is not what Lewin, Elliott or Kemmis have in mind. Their spiral metaphor has some of the characteristics of an Escher illusion, where visually 'the trick' is that one imagines one is proceeding up a stairway without ever getting any higher. It seems to me that a more appropriate way to conceive of the process of action research is to think of it as comprising of a series of successive cycles, each incorporating the possibility for the feedback of information within and between cycles. Personally I am inclined to think that the manner in which action research proceeds is more analogous to the way in which certain biological processes progress, and are regulated within living organisms. I have in mind, for example, the way in which hormonal feedback loops regulate and control the menstrual cycle and or pregnancy. In my view the idealized process of educational action research can be more appropriately represented as shown in Figure 3.

Figure 2

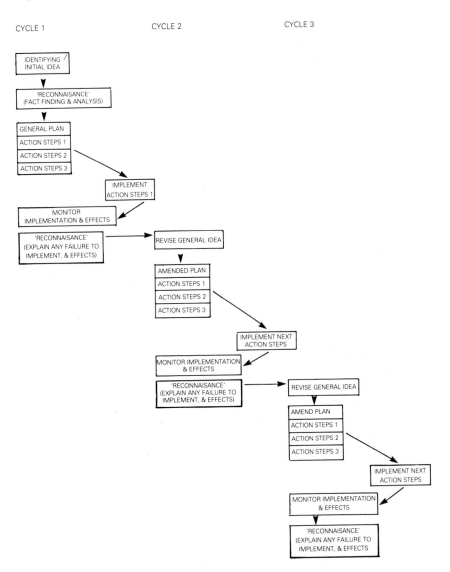

Source: Elliott, J. (1981) *Action Research: A Framework for Self-Evaluation in Schools*, TIQL Working paper no. 1, mimeo, Cambridge, Cambridge Institute of Education, p. 3, figure 2

Figure 3: Idealized Representation of the Process of Action Research

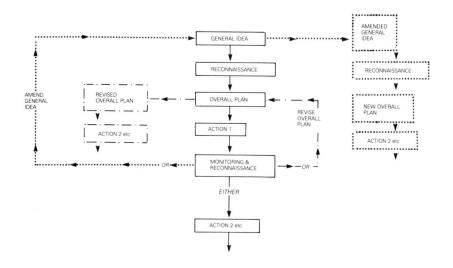

The Dynamics of Educational Action Research

At this point I want to consider another issue, or more accurately an omission with regard to action-research as revealed in these two documents, which I personally find problematic. An interesting aspect of both the Kemmis version and the Elliott representation of how educational action research proceeds is that there is no consideration given as to what provides the dynamic to drive the process through its successive cycles. The Lewin model is qualitatively different in this respect. His model evolved as a response to social conflict particularly as experienced by minority groups. It does not require too much thought to imagine the range and depth of feeling experienced by members of a black minority continuously living with the effects of overt discrimination year in, year out. The imperative for change in such situations was, and is, a community-wide wish individually and collectively to improve one's lot. One can hear and feel the imperative for change in the songs of such minorities right up to the present, for example blues and reggae. The Lewinian model of action research was developed in order to harness the energy of that imperative in a particular democratic way in accordance with social psychological principles. A similar argument applies with respect to action research and the resolution of conflict in industrial relations settings.

It seems to me that no qualitatively comparable dynamic for educational change exists within the teaching profession in schools in the United Kingdom. Moreover, it is the norm for teaching to take place in isolation behind closed doors, to a large extent the autonomy such isolation confers on the teacher is valued within the profession. As Hargreaves (1982) only half jokingly argues ... 'teaching is like sexual activity: it is a highly intimate act, best conducted in private, and to be watched by intruders is to inhibit one's performance ... Autonomy then, is the polite word used to mask teachers' evaluation apprehension and to serve as a rationale for excluding observers'. There is simply no qualitative connection with respect to an imperative for change when moving from a consideration of minority groups to a consideration of institutionally isolated and insulated teachers. For example, the feminist dynamic which Kelly brings to the work which she describes in this volume as simultaneous-integrated action research is hardly comparable. Certainly her interventionist strategies are designed to provide a dynamic for change. It seems to me, however, that the energy and commitment required for change to occur all stems from herself and her co-workers and is invested in order to *activate* the system, rather than as in the examples quoted above to *harness* an already present imperative for change. I suggest that Elliott, again drawing upon his experiences in earlier educational action research projects, tacitly realised the absence of a collective dynamic. He developed a strategy whereby teacher researchers in the TIQL Project schools could move through the action research process. His strategy centred on the previously acquired research knowledge and research management skills in combination with the authority position of the school coordinators. Their expertise, energy and skill was amongst other roles to function in order to provide the dynamic to drive the action-research cycle.

In his *Framework* Elliott (1981) foresaw the tasks of the co-ordinator as:

(a) convenes approximately three team meetings per cycle, for example, at the beginning, middle and end of a term;
(b) keeps a record of any agreed 'General Plan' which emerges;
(c) coordinates negotiations between individual team-members and the headteacher, other staff, external consultants etc;
(d) helps individuals to share insights and research strategies;
(e) coordinates the writing up of research reports and papers. (p. 26)

I have written extensively on how the coordinators interpreted their role in the TIQL schools. Suffice to say that where these co-ordinators were not tempted away by promotion and where they remained on site in school, they did provide the dynamic to initiate and sustain the action research cycle. An interesting side effect of this strategy, as I see it, was that to some extent the centrality of the co-ordinator's research management role rendered the role of the central consultant problematic. It was problematic only in the sense that the central consultants chose to explore the implications of a more collaborative relationship than usually obtains between researchers and practitioners. This was not so much the case in the Ford Teaching Project where the two members of the central team were altogether more directive and themselves provided the dynamic to urge the process along. The foregoing argument only serves to underline my view that the significant organizational innovation of the TIQL Project in terms of the management of educational action research was Elliott's conception of the coordinator's role.

Another apprehension I have about both documents, the Elliott *Framework* and the Kemmis *Planner* , derives from my observations of how teachers reacted to the former. I am thinking in particular about the appropriateness of using such documents during the early negotiation phase of an educational action research project. My apprehension is fuelled specifically because I feel that the documents, and especially the diagrams, engendered and contributed to an atmosphere of mystification about the process of educational action research. If this is a fair observation it is ironic, in that action research in all its applications is centrally concerned with the demystification of participants in the process. I have no evidence that the observations of some teachers' reactions to the document and its diagrams point to mystification, rather than to anger or tiredness or overwork. I am inferring it to be the case. This inference is partly based on my own initial reactions to the diagram in *Framework* ,and partly based on memories of the earliest phases of the Ford Teaching Project when I was a potential participant. What seems to me to have been over-looked in the way *Framework* is drawn up and certainly was overlooked when we (the team of consultants) talked through the document with teacher groups before the TIQL project commenced, was that potential participants have to ask themselves at least two fundamental questions simultaneously, whilst they are reading or being talked through it. I suggest that these are:

Am I capable of understanding correctly how they say this Project is meant to work?

Am I capable of making it work correctly in my own classroom?

These questions are prior to and of a different order than the sort of cost-benefit questions which Doyle and Ponder (1977) say all pragmatically sceptical teachers ask themselves when faced with the decisions about adopting an innovation.

My view is that parts of the Elliott *Framework* tend to mystification because the argument is pitched as a detailed elaboration of how educational action research ought to proceed, and because it adopts a diagrammatic representation of the action research 'spiral' which when first encountered appears novel and strange. I suggest the novelty and strangeness stem from its unfamiliarity when compared with everyday diagrams — curriculum flow charts, fault finding charts for a video recorder or a central heating boiler. The spiral diagram, in my view further contributes to mystification because it gives the impression (denied in the text) that each of its stages is discreet; that it is a refined and authoritative representation of a complex systematic and sophisticated process. Three types of teacher reaction (all complicated and coloured by other factors) to the document which occurred when it was being used as a basis for discussion during the negotiation phase of the project were:

    (i)   bemused or daunted acquiescence;
   (ii)   literal critique;
  (iii)   dissociation.

These need little elaboration. Typical of the first was a general reaction of eighteen teachers who attended one meeting, less than half of whom eventually became part of the Project. It was also, I suggest, a reaction of teachers in another school who subsequently became active and productive within the Project but who recurrently over time articulated worries about where precisely their activities could be fitted onto the action research spiral. They were unclear if at any one time they were engaged in reconnaissance or monitoring. The literal critique reaction was essentially that the diagram purported to be a spiral but was a bad representation of a spiral — if the project could not even draw spirals their thinking must be deficient. Dissociation from the project occurred in one instance during the second term and resulted from a feeling that the methodology failed to satisfy the needs of objective analysis and that the unclear aims encouraged involvement from people who showed only a superficial initial understanding.

Dave Ebbutt

The Logic of Educational Action Research

Until recently I harboured a further difficulty about educational action research, which the writing of this chapter has helped me resolve. This problem did not stem specifically from anything written in either the Kemmis *Planner* or the Elliott *Framework* and yet is implicit in both. It was about 'the logic' of educational action research. Elliott tended to use this phrase from time to time as a justification for a particular strategy or policy on how some aspect of the TIQL project should proceed. Conversely, he has used the phrase 'against the logic of action-research' to reject other strategies. The difficulty stemmed from my own inability to pin down what this 'logic' was seen to be, and where it stemmed from. Was the 'logic' of educational action research no more than a set of unstated conventions or edicts? The use of the term 'logic' was, I felt, contributive towards even greater mystification. The 'logic' of educational action research in the sense that I now understand Elliott to be using it, inheres in, and is presupposed by the definition: *the systematic study of attempts to change and improve educational practice by groups of participants by means of their own practical actions and by means of their own reflection upon the effects of those actions.* Once one begins to think of action research in these terms and to separate it out from normal practice, teacher self-monitoring and from teacher research in the traditional mode as I have attempted to do in my classification then the nature of the 'logic' becomes clearer.

The source of my earlier confusion stemmed from my interpretation of logic in the restricted sense of *formal* or *propositional* logic. Lacking a background in philosophy I was mistakenly interpreting Elliott's use of logic to be the same as the Aristotelian ideal of logic as a formal science comparable with geometry. Toulmin (1958) describes this ideal in its fully realised form:

> According to this view, it is not enough that the propositions of formal logic should themselves be timelessly true. The subject will not have reached its ideal, mathematical condition until the units between which these logical relations hold have also been transformed into change free, time independent objects. (p.179)

Clearly the utterances teachers make about their own practice, the very stuff of educational action research, are not timeless propositions. They are as Toulmin says, 'dependent in all sorts of ways on the context or occasion on which they are uttered'. My dilemma, shared I suspect by many practitioners reading about the logic of action research, was that I could not square my Aristotelian conception of logic with my understanding of what action research is about. Having got over this particular hurdle it is possible to see that such enterprises as action research or enquiry teaching have their own special informal logic. Toulmin again gives the nice example of such an enterprise — jurisprudence which 'elucidates for us the special logic of legal statements, yet it eludes mathematical treatment . . .'.

It seems to me that Schön (1983) in the context of what he terms reflection-in-action, goes to the heart of the matter when he asks:

> What is it then that is distinctive about the experimenting that goes on in practice?
>
> The practice context is different from the research context in several important ways all of which have to do with the relationship between changing things and understanding them. The practitioner has an interest in transforming the situation from what it is to something he likes better. He also has an interest in understanding the situation, but it is in the service of his interest in change. (p. 14)

As I understand it, Elliott uses the term 'the logic of action research' to mean much the same as other people might use the term 'the spirit of the game' presupposed by the laws of cricket. Thus, for Elliott a particular decision on the part of external consultants might be said to be against 'the logic of action research' if it was shown to be contrary to the spirit or requirements of action research as enshrined in, or presupposed by, the definition. This can be illustrated with two examples from Elliott's (1978) article in which he sets out the bones of the logic of action research under the heading 'Characteristics of Action Research in Schools'.

> (6) *Since action research looks at a situation from the participants' point of view it will describe and explain 'what is going on' in the same language as they used; namely, the commonsense language people use to describe and explain human actions and social situations in everyday life.*
>
> It is by virtue of this fact that the accounts of action research can be validated in dialogue with participants. A research report couched in the language of abstract disciplines is never a product of genuine action research.
>
> (7) *Since action research looks at a problem from the point of*

> *view of those involved it can only be validated in unconstrained dialogue with them.*
>
> Action research necessarily involves participants in self-reflection about their situation, as active partners in the research. Accounts of dialogue with participants about the interpretations and explanations emerging from the research should be an integral part of any action research report. (p. 356)

Kemmis, on the other hand, talks not about the logic of action research but about 'maxims' which he recommends as useful to keep in mind when carrying out action research. (Maxim — A proposition expressing some general truth of science or experience — *Shorter Oxford Dictionary*). He (in press) presents a list of thirteen such maxims, which he has adapted from Fitzpatrick and McTaggart (1980) of which the following are but three:

(b) Responsibility for the action rests with participants. They must create conditions in which this responsibility is recognized and maintained.

(g) The group should understand and feel in control of any monitoring techniques used — only then will insights they develop be authentic (that is, accepted on the basis of their meaning for participants, not their legitimacy as technical measures).

(m) The group should summarize the review progress systematically to determine what new directions are appropriate.

I had made the assumption that Elliott's logic and Kemmis' maxims were being used synonymously to describe the same thing. But as I now understand it, maxims are little more than rules of thumb, or rules of the art. Maxim (m) (above) tells us something about successfully operationalizing action research but it does not determine the practice of action research. Maxim (m) has been derived empirically by successful practitioners of action research, whereas the logic of action research determines the practice upon which they came to engage.

In this chapter I have attempted to tackle the questions and apprehensions about educational action research which were uppermost in my mind. I appreciate that I have only skimmed the surface of the agenda of possible questions. Other people will put other questions at the top of their agenda, for example the relationship of action research to critical social theory, or what is the relationship between the micro world of the classroom and change in society at large? For the moment, however, I feel I have aired, and even resolved, some of the issues which were concerning me.

References

BELL, G.H. (1982) *Information Technology and Teacher Research*, TIQL working paper no. 9, mimeo, Cambridge, Cambridge Institute of Education.

COREY, S.M. (1953) *Action Research to Improve School Practice*, New York, Teachers' College, Columbia University.

CRONBACH, L.J. and SUPPES, P. (Eds) (1969) *Research for Tomorrow's School: Disciplined Enquiry for Education*, London, Macmillan.

DELAMONT, S. (1981) 'All too familiar? A decade of classroom research', *Educational Analysis*, 3, 1.

DEPARTMENT OF EDUCATION AND SCIENCE (1979) *Aspects of Secondary Education in England and Wales*, London, HMSO.

DOYLE, W. (1979) *The Tasks of Teaching and Learning in Classrooms*, mimeo, North Texas State University.

DOYLE, W. (1981) *Accomplishing Writing Tasks in the Classroom*, mimeo, North Texas State University.

DOYLE, W. and PONDER, G.A. (1977) 'The practicality ethic in teacher decision-making', *Interchange*, 8.

EBBUTT, D. and ELLIOTT, J. (Eds) (forthcoming) *Issues in Teaching for Understanding*.

ELLIOTT, J. (1976) *Developing Hypotheses from Teachers' Practical Constructs*, mimeo, University of North Dakota.

ELLIOTT, J. (1978) 'What is action-research in school?', *Journal of Curriculum Studies*, 10, 4.

ELLIOTT, J. (1981) *Action-Research: A Framework for Self-Evaluation in Schools*, TIQL working paper no. 1, mimeo, Cambridge, Cambridge Institute of Education.

ELLIOTT, J. (Ed.) (forthcoming) *Case Studies in Teaching for Understanding*, Cambridge, Cambridge Institute of Education.

ELLIOTT, J. and EBBUTT, D. (Eds) (forthcoming) *Supporting Action Research in Schools*.

FITZPATRICK, M. and McTAGGART, R. (1980) 'The requirements of a successful action program', paper given at Australian Association for Research in Education, November.

HARGREAVES, D.H. (1982) *The Challenge for the Comprehensive School*, London, Routledge and Kegan Paul.

KEMMIS, S. *et al.* (1981) *The Action Research Planner*, Deakin, Deakin University Press.

KEMMIS, S. (in press) 'Research approaches and methods: Action-research', in ANDERSON, D. and BLAKERS, C. (Eds) *Transition From School: An Exploration of Research and Policy*.

KEMMIS, S. and GRUNDY, S. (1981) 'Educational action research in Australia: The state of the art', paper given at Australian Association for Research in Education, November.

LEWIN, K. (1948) *Resolving Social Conflicts*, New York, Harper.

LIPPIT, R. (1949) *Training in Community Relations*, New York, Harper.

McCORMICK, R. and JAMES, M.E. (1983) *Curriculum Evaluation in Schools*, London, Croom Helm.

OPEN UNIVERSITY, (1980) *Curriculum in Action*, Milton Keynes, Open University Press.

SCHÖN, D. (1983) *The Reflective Practitioner: How Professionals Think in Action*, London, Temple Smith.

SCHULMAN, L.S. (1980) 'Study guide and audiotape for disciplines of inquiry in education', in American Educational Research Association, *Alternative Methodologies in Educational Research*, New York, AERA.

STENHOUSE, L. (1984) 'Evaluating curriculum evaluation', in ADELMAN, C. (Ed.) *The Politics and Ethics of Evaluation*, London, Croom Helm.

TOULMIN, S.E. (1958) *The Uses of Argument*, Cambridge, Cambridge University Press.

Part Three
Issues in Teacher Research

9   Case Study and Curriculum Research: Some Issues for Teacher Researchers

Hilary Burgess

The last decade has witnessed the emergence of a style of educational research and reporting which has come to be known as the 'case study'. In considering the usefulness of this style of investigation we need to examine as MacDonald and Walker (1975) suggest, the 'case' for the case study. Indeed, Skilbeck (1983) claims that as a style of research it is doubly effective as:

> Taken in one direction, it leads us to the perfection of observation and documentation; in another, it is a key factor in the revitalisation and democratization of educational practice and educational knowledge. (p. 18)

Here Skilbeck suggests that the case study, while perfecting the use of observational methods and documentation also illuminates the process of schooling and opens it up to evaluation by all those concerned with education. However, the methods employed by the case study researcher may raise a number of particular issues and problems. For example, the use of observation and unstructured interviewing can lead to a close liaison between those being studied and an involvement in the events or issues being researched. Furthermore, as Adelman, Jenkins and Kemmis (1980) argue, anonymity can often be a 'non-solution' because if it is impenetrable the research does not provide feedback to those who are the subject of investigation. These issues, and others concerned with gaining access, negotiating entry to classrooms, interviewing peers and questions concerning the ethics of research may pose numerous problems for the researcher. In turn, these issues are also faced by teachers who engage in research activities (see also the chapters by Cummings and Griffiths in this volume) but it is necessary to understand how these problems arise and how they can be handled during an investigation. It is the purpose of this chapter, therefore, to examine some of the problems that I faced as a teacher researching the work of other teachers in a primary school.

The Research Setting

While a number of studies have focused upon secondary schools (Hargreaves, 1967; Lacey, 1970; Ball, 1981; Burgess, RG, 1983) few in depth case studies have been conducted in primary schools: the exceptions being those by Sharp and Green (1975), King (1978) and Pollard (1979). However, these case studies highlight particular aspects of primary education, for example, Sharp and Green were concerned with the way in which education is used as a form of social control and King wished to interpret the meanings which infant teachers assigned to their actions, while Pollard has studied the procedures of everyday life in the primary classroom and the way in which pupils and teachers learn to accommodate to each other. In these terms, the focus of these studies is not specifically upon the curriculum. My study, therefore, attempted to begin to fill this gap by examining the mathematics curriculum through a detailed case study of a primary school.

My research focused upon the primary school mathematics curriculum with special reference to the published scheme *Mathematics for Schools*, (Howell, Walker and Fletcher, 1979) popularly known as Fletcher, and widely used in Britain and in the local authority in which the school was located (*cf.* Burgess, H.M.M, 1983). The way in which this scheme was used by teachers was examined through a case study of one primary school. Classroom observation, unstructured interviews and documentary evidence were the main methods of social investigation which I used, while the focus of the study was upon the way teachers defined and redefined the mathematics curriculum.

Several linking themes were selected in order to examine the mathematics curriculum: aims and objectives in teaching mathematics, school and classroom organization, and the use of practical work and language in mathematics. The social processes and social organization of the case study school were also researched in order to provide a context in which to view the definitions of the mathematics curriculum that were provided by the Headteacher and teachers of Elm Park Primary[1] (*cf.* Burgess, HMM 1983).

To provide a starting point for the research the question was posed: How do teachers define and interpret the mathematics curriculum within their primary school? The selection of this question follows on from King's work (1978) in infant schools. For as Hargreaves (1980) has suggested, ethnographic research can only become cumulative if researchers use previous themes and questions in a new area of study.

A research approach needed to be adopted, where the methods used were appropriate for the questions that were posed. Indeed, as Bechhofer (1974) remarked, the fundamental principle involved in the use of research methods is that any method of social investigation has to be selected for use in relation to the sociological problem that confronts the researcher. In this sense, the evaluation of the strengths and weaknesses of different research methods can only be done effectively in relation to real problems and real research. For Gouldner (1971) argues:

> When viewed from one standpoint, 'methodology' seems a purely technical concern devoid of ideology; presumably it deals only with methods of extracting reliable information from the world, collecting data, constructing questionnaires, sampling, and analyzing returns. Yet it is always a good deal more than that, for it is commonly infused with ideologically resonant assumptions about what the social world is, who the sociologist is, and what the nature of the relation between them is. (pp. 50–1)

Gouldner emphasizes that the processes involved in doing research are not only inseparable but also intrinsically connected with those carrying out the research, and therefore, highlights the relationship between the processes of research and the researcher. In this sense, the methods employed to study the mathematics curriculum at Elm Park Primary School were selected in relation to the problem posed and took into account the character of the researcher and the researched who were all primary school teachers. However, the initial problem to be resolved was how to gain access to a primary school in the local education authority in order to begin the research.

I used the criteria advocated by Schatzman and Strauss (1973) for 'casing the joint' to ensure that the school I selected included all the attributes that I wished to study. In these terms, Elm Park School was selected for several reasons; first, it utilized a widely known mathematics scheme, *Mathematics for Schools*; secondly, it was a primary school rather than an infant or a junior school, thus facilitating a study of the mathematics curriculum for children aged 5–11; thirdly, previous knowledge of the Headteacher, Harry Jarvis, led me to believe that he was particularly interested in mathematics and might regard my research in a favourable light. On the basis of this information I therefore decided to approach the Headteacher as the initial contact in gaining access. In this sense Harry Jarvis became the gatekeeper for my research at Elm Park, granting permission for me to observe and interview teachers in the school (*cf.* Burgess, R.G., 1980 and 1982). However, this raises a number of questions discussed by Robert Burgess (1982) concerning the right of individuals to grant or withhold access where other people are concerned, and the identification of the researcher with the gatekeeper which may create suspicion among the researched.

Making Classroom Observations

Access to the school, therefore, was initially granted by the Head but subsequent negotiations and renegotiations were necessary to gain entry to classrooms. For example, both Gillian Pritchard (the Deputy Head and a fourth-year junior teacher) and Mary Shipston (a mixed reception and middle infant teacher) seemed unaware that I wished to observe a series of their lessons, while I understood that this had been negotiated by the Headteacher before my first visits to their classes. Consequently, I had to explain my research in more detail to these teachers and renegotiate entry to their classrooms. In the case of Gillian Pritchard, after discussion about what I intended to do, I was able to negotiate observation of a series of lessons over half a term. However, Mary Shipston was less happy about my presence in her classroom for a long series of lessons but did agree that I could visit her classroom on three consecutive occasions. In addition, Mary arranged for me to observe one lesson in each of the other infant classrooms. In this way, although I had to revise my original plan, I was able to gain a broad view of the way infant teachers taught mathematics at Elm Park Primary.

Classroom observation proved to be a major source of data as I examined how the teachers defined and interpreted the mathematics curriculum in practice compared to the definition of mathematics presented in the school syllabus. Although Gold (1958) outlined four 'master roles' for collecting data by participant observation: the complete participant, the complete observer, the participant as observer and the observer as participant, I found I needed to take a particular role which suited the style and time period of my research. I selected the role of observer as participant where the researcher does not enter into a sustained relationship with the researched. This approach seemed ideal considering the limited amount of time I had available for conducting the research and as an overt[2] role it did not restrict me from communicating with those being researched. In this way, I was able to collect data by talking with the children, and with the teacher in each class, and by observing the teachers and their classes. It was these data that were subsequently used in framing questions for unstructured interviews with teachers and for preliminary analysis. For example, after observing Gillian Pritchard teaching division I decided to include a question on the way individual teachers taught this topic, in order to obtain a school-based view on the teaching of division. I also included questions on lesson organization and the use of practical apparatus in mathematics after my observations in Mary Shipston's classroom.

Using Diaries

My classroom observations were recorded in my field diary and included the dates, times and contents of the lessons observed. However, I found several difficulties involved in keeping such a diary. I had decided, before beginning my classroom observation that I would not take notes during the lessons as I thought the teachers might find this threatening. My first difficulty, was, therefore, accuracy of memory, although I found this did improve during the course of my field work! Another difficulty with my field diary, was my failure at the early stages, to record in as much detail as possible informal conversation held with teachers in the staffroom and while walking to the classrooms. However, as I realised this error at an early stage in the research little data were lost.

Field diaries were kept both by myself as the researcher and by some of the staff at Elm Park. The latter were used as informants' diaries (*cf.* Burgess, R.G., 1981 and 1984) and proved useful for collecting data which I could not collect by making observations. To ensure that relevant data would be recorded in the diary, teachers were encouraged to note the length of the lesson, its location, what particular aspect of mathematics was being studied and the kind of events which took place. Initially, I intended asking all the members of staff at Elm Park to keep a diary. However, after a discussion with the Headteacher, he suggested that he would ask the teachers himself.

We agreed that I should bring the books to be used as diaries into the school on my next visit and he would ask the teachers to complete them. However, on my following visit the Head explained that the staff were unwilling to keep such detailed diaries in the style advocated by other researchers (*cf.* Burgess, R.G., 1981 and 1984) as they were too time-consuming. Accordingly, I adopted a different approach by devizing weekly diary sheets. I sub-divided an A4 sheet of paper into sections so that teachers could provide details of their mathematics timetables together with comments on individual lessons. The diary sheets were designed to cover the mathematics lessons in one week as shown in figure 1.

This adapted version of the diary worked as teachers felt they would be able to adequately complete it without too much of their time being consumed. However, the space provided for comments by teachers obviously limited the amount they could write and in turn limited the data that were available to me. Accordingly, teachers tended to confine their comments simply to what both they and their pupils did in the lesson rather than what actually happened. For example, one teacher filled in the 'Monday' section as follows:

Monday
Number bond sheets, two letters chosen, thus 40 facts. Time test over two minutes. First child finished in fifty-three seconds, by two minutes all except five had completed. I gave answers, the fastest completed result entitles the child to go out of the classroom first all day as the champion. Introduced section 7 book 3 Fletcher revising product word, talked about the two rules making figures larger, talked about patterns in tables quoting 9 table. We then did p. 35.

While this passage may be sufficient for the teacher who wrote it to recall in detail Monday's mathematics lesson I found it difficult to visualize this particular lesson in progress without talking to the teacher concerned. However, as most of the diary sheets stated adequately the topics being taught in mathematics during one week they did assist in the overall analysis of mathematics teaching at Elm Park Primary. On the other hand, the Headteacher kept a fuller diary together with an interesting commentary that concerned the reasons for involving himself in the mathematics teaching in the school. He wrote as follows:

The purposes of my involvement [in mathematics teaching] are:

Figure 1:   A Diary Sheet

Class _____   Teacher _____

It would be helpful if you could give me some details about what actually happens in your mathematics lessons.

Week Beginning _____

Monday

Tuesday

Wednesday

Thursday

Friday

> (i)   to enable me to see children in a teaching situation;
> (ii) I can influence by example, I hope, the way to teach maths; and
> (iii) it gives teachers preparation and/or marking time.

As I wished to obtain further data about some of the areas he had mentioned I included some questions relating to this diary entry in my interview with him as shown in the following example:

HB: In your diary you listed a number of reasons for your own involvement in maths teaching. Your second reason was 'I can influence by example, I hope, the way to teach maths'. Does that mean that the teacher remains in the classroom with you?

HJ: Sometimes they do — it depends on how things are working out. Sometimes they do and sometimes they don't but the influence may not be just looking at me as a practitioner but looking at the end results of what you have done. For instance, the six sheep with six square centimetre question was left on the board so that not only the children looked at it after I had gone but staff did too and perhaps there is a chance for me to develop that sort of thing. In many ways I suppose it is a subtle approach. Sometimes I use the sledge hammer approach where I want to but people are open-minded enough to see, I think, that you can challenge the children to think creatively about maths, and you can. It is a firm belief of mine that you can.

In the interview I hoped to gain more data on how the Headteacher specifically influenced the mathematics curriculum in the school and the procedures he adopted with teachers in order to achieve his aims in mathematics. By linking together the Head's diary with an interview question I was able to obtain such data as shown in the above extract where the Head discusses the way in which he provided a practical example that the teachers could follow. Through challenging the pupils to work creatively in mathematics he hoped to challenge the teachers to be creative in their own mathematics lessons.

Problems of Interviewing

Interviewing proved to be a major source for obtaining data, and therefore, interviews were conducted not only with the Headteacher but with all members of staff. The interviews were intended to be informal and based, as far as possible, on my classroom observations.

I began by making a list of topics and particular questions which I wished to ask every respondent. In this way it would be possible for me to cross-check data to discover whether answers were individualized or reflected a common theme in Elm Park Primary.[3] All the interviews conducted with the teachers included questions concerning their particular class: the age of the children, the number in the class, the composition of the class and seating arrangements in the classroom. Other questions, however, were intended to illuminate the overall aims and policies for mathematics in the school such as:

> What aims do you have for teaching maths in Elm Park primary?;
>
> Do you have any specific aims for your own class?; and
>
> Do you think these aims fit with the Fletcher approach to teaching maths?

Here, the use of a tape-recorder proved invaluable for keeping a full and accurate record of the interviews as the majority of staff gave me permission to record our conversations. However, the four teachers who did not wish to be recorded consented to written notes being taken, although this did not result in such detailed data as it was not possible to record fully in note form the replies which these teachers gave. A further disadvantage of note taking was that it took a lot of time to obtain a small amount of data resulting in the interviews becoming stilted and formal compared with the interviews where a tape recorder was used (*cf.* Stenhouse, 1984). Indeed, in the tape recorded interviews it is noticeable that once teachers had answered the initial questions and settled to the interview conversation many talked fluently about mathematics and mathematics teaching with their class. However, as tape recorder batteries are inclined to 'go flat' I always checked them before setting out to avoid this happening in the middle of a taped conversation, and carried a spare set of batteries with me to cover all eventualities. Furthermore, I was also aware of some of the other difficulties which I might face while interviewing.

One particular aspect that I considered was the reactions of teachers being interviewed by another teacher. Text books, such as Smith (1975) dealing with interviewing as a research strategy, discuss situations of structured and unstructured interviewing where the interviewer and respondent are unknown to each other and where they have different occupations. It is also implicit in this type of interview situation that the interviewer is at an advantage over the respondent as the interviewer can 'set' and 'manage' the talk. This issue is discussed by Platt (1981) in relation to interviewing her own peers. She discovered that this involved a more complex approach than the 'traditional' interview. She maintains that when interviewing peers the interviewer no longer has the advantage of possessing superior knowledge or techniques. Equally, assumptions are made by the respondent that certain things do not need to be explained and therefore gaps can appear in data. Certainly some of the teachers at Elm Park made assumptions about the knowledge I needed to be given and knowledge which they believed to be 'common' to all teachers. For example, when I asked Judith Clay, a top infants teacher, about how she assessed the level of mathematics ability of new pupils who came into her class part-way through the year, she responded as follows:

JC: Well you are a practising teacher yourself.

HB: Yes, I know that. It is very difficult to ask these questions because I know what *I* (emphasis in taped interview) think . . .

JC: It is a mental assessment. You look at the child, you have to see their work to begin with. You have to try and see what they can do and then you find out that they aren't capable of something, well then of course you have to start back there. You have to make that assessment yourself — your own personal assessment. There are no real guidelines. You find that if children come with records which is very, very rare.

HB: Rare for them to come with records!

JC: Well records don't usually arrive until . . . (for example) I have had two new children within the last month. One (child) had his records — well they were given to me, I didn't happen to see them and that was about a fortnight afterwards. The other child's only arrived this week and there has been no sign of any record. I would hope that by the end of the first week I would have made an assessment.

HB: Would you find it easier if records came promptly with the children, would you use them?

JC: Oh yes. I would very much appreciate it if they arrived before the children because then you know exactly where you slot that child in and if the child is going to need remedial help well then you have got to make arrangements.

The pattern of Judith Clay's remarks indicate that she believed I ought to possess this 'common knowledge' and that individual teachers all approach the assessment of a new pupil in the same way. When I replied that I knew how *I* would assess a new child she began to expand on her initial comment. However, her remarks, although more explanatory, are still those of one teacher talking to another when she uses phrases such as 'You can look at the child'.[4] The school records which are kept on pupils are of little help to teachers in making an assessment. As Judith Clay points out, records may be several weeks behind the child's arrival at the school and therefore the teacher has to make a personal assessment. Accordingly, it would appear that where the interviewer and the respondent may be regarded as peers both should be aware that there may be a shared 'common knowledge' which should not be taken for granted.

As I was responsible for the research and the questions being asked it was difficult for the staff of Elm Park to regard me impartially during interviews. Indeed, having been given permission by individual teachers to tape record their interviews, some became concerned after discussion with each other as to where the tapes were going and who was going to listen to them. I assured those members of staff that what I had said concerning confidentiality and anonymity before recording their interviews was entirely genuine and that the secretary who transcribed the tapes and myself would be the only people listening to the tapes. However, I am not certain that all the Elm Park teachers were completely convinced, and indeed I think in some cases my research was regarded with suspicion from the comments made to me during my time there. For example, towards the end of my initial talk with Harry Jarvis about doing research in his school I asked if he would mind the school secretary providing me with the names of the teachers and showing me the school timetable. He replied, half jokingly, that he would rather I did not as he did not know whether I would be selling the information to the newspapers — but added 'of course, I'm sure you wouldn't'. Similarly, on a later occasion, an informal conversation with one of the teachers revealed that the Head and Deputy Head had been questioning what I was looking at in the school, to which this teacher told me she replied 'She (HB) knows what she's looking for. Why can't we just let her get on with it?' Other teachers such as Kate Dugdale, also talked to me informally about the tape recordings I had made. Kate's main worry concerned the use of these tapes within the authority and the possibility that other teachers or advisers would be allowed to listen to them. However, when I reassured her on this point she seemed satisfied. At this stage though, it is necessary to consider other sources of data which were used in conjunction with the interview material and my observational work, such as documentary evidence.

Hilary Burgess

The Use of Documentary Evidence

At Elm Park Primary a variety of documentary materials were available in connection with the mathematics curriculum. Some material was available in the classrooms and around the school on various display boards. Here, it was possible to note the value that teachers attached to making mathematics work prominent in their displays. In particular, the infant classrooms reflected an emphasis on mathematics as, for example, in Mary Shipston's classroom all the boards covering one wall were devoted to mathematical displays concerning shapes, sets and numbers. Furthermore, data were also obtained from the variety of mathematics text books used in the school such as Fletcher, Alpha/Beta and the pupils' workbooks. Each of these sources of data contributed to the overall picture of how mathematics was taught in the school (see Burgess, H. M. M, 1983, especially chapter 2). Further evidence was obtained through studying written documents on mathematics: the school syllabus,[5] 'patter sheets',[6] 'NUPE' sheets[7] and Mr Coggan's books.[8] These provided a comparison of the different methods and styles of teaching in Elm Park Primary School with those suggested in *Mathematics for Schools*, and revealed the way Fletcher mathematics was utilized in the school as part of the mathematics curriculum. Studying these documents also provided an insight into the ways the present mathematics curriculum had evolved and provided data concerning aims, methods and curriculum content. For example, several of the documents provided an outline of the way in which addition, subtraction, multiplication and division should be taught in the school. As the fourth-year class I was observing were studying division in mathematics I decided to analyze the teaching of division as presented in the documents and as taught by individual teachers. This observation together with my research strategy, therefore, led to the teaching of division becoming a major theme in the case study. The initial problem was to discover how teachers, in whose classes I was not observing, taught this topic. This was resolved by including a question on division in the interviews. I was, therefore, able to analyze the progression of the teaching of division throughout the whole school. The analysis of division in the Fletcher mathematics series, Mr Coggan's books and the 'patter sheet' provided some comparison with the teacher accounts. It was possible, therefore, to see how the staff at Elm Park Primary School redefined their mathematics teaching in this area compared to the 'official' methods, outlined in various texts and documents in the school.

Multiple Strategies of Investigation

The use of documents in relation to observation and interview is illustrated by the following example on the teaching of long division in Elm Park Primary. Gillian Pritchard, a fourth-year junior teacher, began by explaining to her class the method for long division and illustrated this with an example on the blackboard. The process by which Mrs Pritchard taught long division is outlined below:

$$
\begin{array}{r}
22 \text{ r } 10 \\
\hline
12)\overline{274} \\
-24 \\
\hline
34 \\
24 \\
\hline
10
\end{array}
$$

How many 12s in 27? — 2. Put the answer above the line, 2 12s are 24, take 24 away from 27 and you are left with 3. Move the 4 units next to the 3 tens. How many 12s in 34? — 2. Put the answer above the line, 2 12s are 24, take 24 away from 34 and you are left with 10. How many 12s in 10 — none. Therefore, the answer is 22 r 10.

Throughout her explanation pupils were invited to comment on what the next stage should be, as the class had already started this topic in an earlier lesson. However, before the children began the long division examples from their textbooks, Gillian explained some of the mathematical language used in the Fletcher pupils' book such as, divisor, dividend and quotient. It would appear, though, that the use of mathematical language was not regarded as important by Mrs. Pritchard as she had not used these terms during her explanation of long division from the blackboard.

During a discussion with me Mrs Pritchard pointed out that I had probably noticed that the method which was used to teach long division was not one which is used in Fletcher mathematics. Gillian explained the difference in approach by saying that Mr Jarvis believed the Fletcher 'way' was too complicated and had, therefore, produced a sheet suggesting a method of his own. However, the method for teaching division which she used bore more resemblance to the traditional approach suggested in Mr Coggan's books than to the Fletcher method or the method suggested on the 'patter sheet'. Indeed, in a later lesson, multiplication squares were used to assist pupils in finding the answers, a technique suggested by Mr Coggan but not by the authors of *Mathematics for Schools* or the 'patter sheet'. In this respect Gillian had redefined the teaching of long division, using a method of her own which was a combination of Mr Coggan's method, the Fletcher method and her view of the 'patter sheet' method. This example contains data derived from classroom observation, an interview and documentary evidence and highlights the necessity of combining different techniques of investigation in order to provide an account of the activities that occur in a social situation.

Without the documentary analysis of the teaching of division it would have been easy to accept Gillian's method as the version used in the school. However, when viewed in context alongside the school documents a totally different picture emerged concerning the way division was taught at Elm Park Primary. However, combining techniques can be fraught with difficulties as Gans (1962), Sieber (1982), and Davies *et al* . (1985) have noted, resulting in a profusion of data which can cause problems with data analysis. Certainly, the case study I conducted at Elm Park Primary resulted in a wealth of data and involved careful selection on the basis of particular themes.

One form of analysis which I applied to the data was the concept of multiple realities in the Elm Park mathematics curriculum. This concept is derived from Schutz's (1972) idea of human beings having the capacity for living in different worlds of meaning which he called multiple realities. Indeed, King (1978) also employed the concept of multiple realities in his study of infants' schools. At Elm Park the 'reality' of the mathematics curriculum became evident at three different levels: the local authority; the school syllabus on mathematics; and the individual views of teachers. Thus, the mathematics curriculum transmitted to pupils was redefined by the teachers in terms of aims, objectives and to a certain extent, content. In this sense, 'mathematics' for the teachers, was seen at the level of achieving competence in computation which necessitated practice in the four rules. Therefore, the meaning of 'mathematics' for Elm Park teachers was arithmetical and through their actions became a reality within the school.

Ethical Considerations in Research

Finally we need to consider the ethical questions which arise during case study research. Indeed, unexpected problems arose particularly during my observations in classrooms which involved me in attempting to resolve ethical issues. For example, one fourth-year mathematics lesson I observed consisted of the pupils drawing circles with pairs of compasses, but in this instance my attention was not only upon the lesson content but upon the children's use of the equipment. Here, the majority of pupils having used their pair of compasses to draw a circle proceeded to straighten them out in order to write with the pencil which was still attached. This action by the pupils appeared to be unnoticed by the class teacher as she made no comment on it. However, from my point of view as a teacher, a potentially dangerous situation had arisen as at least twenty sharp compass points came within a couple of inches of pupils' eyes; a playful 'shove' or an accidental bump from a pupil moving around the classroom could have resulted in a serious eye injury to one or more pupils. If an accident occurred who would be responsible? The class teacher, as the person in charge of the class, and myself as the only other adult in the room, were the only individuals who could be considered liable. I was faced with a dilemma: Should I as a teacher speak to the class and ask them to remove their pencils from the pairs of compasses before writing with them? Should I as a researcher simply observe the situation and await the outcome of events? After a few moments thought I decided to follow the latter course of non-interference and thankfully, the lesson passed without incident. However, I also decided that the teacher concerned should be alerted to the potential dangers inherent in such situations and therefore, during an interview I mentioned the incident. She agreed that it was dangerous to use pairs of compasses in this way and explained the situation by saying that the school pencil order had not arrived and therefore there were insufficient pencils for every pupil to have two each. Yet despite this explanation I still felt that the teacher was rationalizing an event that I had observed as she appeared embarrassed by my remarks.

This particular example also highlights the need for confidentiality and anonymity both for the sake of the researcher and the researched (Barnes, 1979). Implicit in any form of research is the need for trust in the researcher's integrity. If this aspect of the research is neglected the data that would be subsequently available to the researcher might be of limited value if those being researched felt betrayed. Denzin (1970) states 'It is impossible not to take ethical and value stances in the process of research' (Denzin, 1970, p. 332) and concludes that it is up to the conscience of individual researchers to ensure that their informants are safeguarded. Accordingly, Denzin is in agreement with Becker (1970) who argues that it is impossible to do research which is value free and suggests researchers need to ask themselves the question: 'Whose side are we on?' (Becker, 1970, p. 99). Indeed, I often found myself in conflict trying to decide whether I was on the 'side' of the teachers, the pupils, the school curriculum or my own research. Finally, I decided that while I wanted to see the research from all these points of view it was important to take a research perspective. In order to safeguard those involved in my research I adopted pseudonyms for the local education authority, the school and the teachers in the case study. While I am certain that I have guaranteed their anonymity in the wider sense I consider it an impossible task to disguise members of the same institution from each other.

As a teacher researching in Elm Park Primary, therefore, a number of issues and problems arose which needed to be resolved during the research. It was more difficult to gain access to classrooms than I initially realized, involving negotiations not only with the Head but also with the teachers concerned. Difficulties also arose when interviewing peers as the respondents often rightly assumed that there was a shared common knowledge among teachers. This difficulty also manifested itself in the writing of the diary sheets making them in some cases impossible to use as research evidence. Indeed, a major problem overall proved to be the selection of material on the basis of particular themes for inclusion in the final report. In the process of this selection a wealth of data which had been collected was left undisturbed and unaccounted for.

Epilogue to My Research

It would be easy to believe that any piece of research ends with the production of a written report. However, in this particular instance the story of my problems as a teacher-researcher does not end here, as after having it typed and bound I took it into Elm Park Primary for the Head and staff to read. Their reactions and feelings concerning the written account of my research contribute to the conclusions of this chapter.

The first reaction of the Head to my research was that it was completely 'negative'. This was also the view of Gillian Pritchard who joined the discussion between myself and Harry Jarvis. They both agreed that while everything I had written was true I could have written up my account in a more positive way by saying what I thought was 'good' about their mathematics curriculum and about the school. In trying to be objective in my written account I had avoided using value-laden terms and in their view, failed to present a positive account of the school and the mathematics curriculum. Accordingly, this raises the issue of whether the research should be discussed with the researched before the final account is written. Undoubtedly, the final version of my research into the mathematics curriculum at Elm Park Primary would have been different if each section had been discussed and amended as it was written. But would this have resulted in an abridged version of my study?

The use of quotations from the taped interviews in the final report had surprised both Harry and Gillian. Each considered that they would have expressed their comments more lucidly if they had realized that extracts were going to be used in the written account, and felt at a disadvantage alongside my 'prose' which had been drafted and redrafted before being finalized. Indeed, Gillian considered that 'People don't talk and think at the same time', and as I had time to think about questions that I wished to ask my respondents, so the staff at Elm Park should have been given a copy of the interview questions to think about before the interview.

The classroom observations which were written up alongside the documentary and taped conversations also became an issue during my discussion with Gillian and Harry Jarvis. Indeed, Gillian was obviously both hurt and angry about my written observations of her classroom mathematics lessons and said to me that she thought she came out of it looking like a 'mindless, gibbering idiot'. She thought I had not presented a true picture of herself as a primary school teacher and had not mentioned points such as the fact that her class was 'well-disciplined' and that there were 'good' displays up on the classroom wall. In this instance it was difficult to explain that it had not been my intention to provide 'all round' portraits of individual teachers as teachers, but detailed accounts of their work on one area of the curriculum. From these comments it was apparent that the issues and questions that these teachers had, were not the same as those that I had used.

The final criticism of these two teachers concerned the safeguard of anonymity. During the conversation it became obvious that they had identified most, if not all, the members of staff beneath the pseudonyms. Accordingly, they were worried that the school would be easily identifiable within the authority by anyone who read the report. Here, I was unable to reassure them although I repeated my earlier guarantees that I would not identify the school to others.

It seems ironic to me that the style of research, methods of social investigation and finalized account of my study should be held in high regard by my supervisors at the University of London, Institute of Education and yet only six weeks later were highly criticized by the teachers involved in the research. Obviously, there is a need to make the 'case' for the case study not only among researchers but also among those upon whom research is conducted.

Acknowledgements

I am indebted to Bill Gibby who provided much help and numerous detailed comments on the MA dissertation on which this work is based. I would also like to thank the teachers of Elm Park Primary who cooperated with this study and who must remain anonymous.

Finally I am grateful for the assistance of Robert Burgess in the preparation of this paper and would like to thank him for his helpful comments on the several draft copies I produced!

Notes

1 Pseudonyms were used for the school, the Headteacher, members of staff and the local education authority, to maintain confidentiality.
2 For a discussion on covert/overt research see, for example, HOMAN (1980), BULMER (1980). For material on the merits and demerits of covert participant observation see BULMER (1982).
3 This follows DENZIN (1970) and BURGESS, R. G (1982 and 1984), by using multiple sets of data. A process commonly known as triangulation.
4 For a similar situation where a common understanding is assumed by the respondent see FINCH (1984).
5 The mathematics syllabus listed the aims of the school in this subject and gave suggestions about work for individual years.
6 The 'patter' sheets were written after discussions by the staff and gave suggestions for teaching topics such as multiplication and division which varied from the methods suggested in the scheme *Mathematics for Schools*.
7 The NUPE sheets coordinated mathematics topics in the Beta mathematics series, Fletcher series and other mathematics aids which were available in the school. This particular set of documents were called NUPE because they were prepared during a strike by the National Union of Public Employees.
8 Mr Coggan's books were a series of handwritten books showing various stages, and containing examples of addition, subtraction, multiplication and division. Mr Coggan was a previous Headteacher of Elm Park Primary.

References

ADELMAN, C., JENKINS, D. and KEMMIS, S. (1980); 'Rethinking case study', in SIMONS, H. (Ed.) *Towards a Science of the Singular*, Norwich, Centre for Applied Research in Education, University of East Anglia.
BALL, S.J. (1981) *Beachside Comprehensive: A Case Study of Secondary Schooling*, Cambridge, Cambridge University Press.
BARNES, J.A. (1979) *Who Should Know What?*, Harmondsworth, Penguin.

BECHHOFER, F. (1974) 'Current approaches to empirical research: Some central ideas' in REX, J. (Ed.) *Approaches to Sociology: An Introduction to Major Trends in British Sociology*, London, Routledge and Kegan Paul.

BECKER, H.S. (1970) 'Whose side are we on?', in DOUGLAS, J.D. (Ed.) *The Relevance of Sociology*, New York, Appleton-Century Crofts.

BULMER, M. (1980) 'Comment on the ethics of covert methods', *British Journal of Sociology*, 31, 1, pp. 59–65.

BULMER, M. (Ed.) (1982) *Social Research Ethics: The Merits and Demerits of Covert Participant Observation*, London, Macmillan.

BURGESS, H.M.M. (1983) 'An appraisal of some methods of teaching primary school mathematics', unpublished MA dissertation, University of London, Institute of Education, Department of Curriculum Studies.

BURGESS, R.G. (1980) 'Some fieldwork problems in teacher-based research', *British Educational Research Journal*, 6, 2, pp. 165–73.

BURGESS, R.G. (1981) 'Keeping a research diary', *Cambridge Journal of Education*, 11, 1, pp. 75–83.

BURGESS, R.G. (Ed.) (1982) *Field Research: A Sourcebook and Field Manual*, London, Allen and Unwin.

BURGESS, R.G. (1983) *Experiencing Comprehensive Education: A Study of Bishop McGregor School*, London, Methuen.

BURGESS, R.G. (1984) *In the Field: An Introduction to Field Research*, London, Allen and Unwin.

DAVIES, B., CORBISHLEY, P., EVANS, J. and KENRICK, C. (1985) 'Integrating methodologies: If the intellectual relations don't get you, then the social will', in BURGESS, R.G. (Ed.) *Strategies of Educational Research: Qualitative Methods*, Lewes, Falmer Press.

DENZIN, N. (1970) *The Research Act*, Chicago, Aldine.

FINCH, J. (1984) '"It's great to have someone to talk to": The ethics and politics of interviewing women', in BELL, C. and ROBERTS, H. (Eds) *Social Researching: Policies, Problems and Practice*, London, Routledge and Kegan Paul.

GANS, H.J. (1962) *The Urban Villagers*, New York, The Free Press.

GOLD, R. (1958) 'Roles in sociological field observation', *Social Forces*, 36, 3, pp. 217–33.

GOULDNER, A.W. (1971) *The Coming Crisis of Western Sociology*, London, Heinemann.

HARGREAVES, D.H. (1967) *Social Relations in a Secondary School*, London, Routledge and Kegan Paul.

HARGREAVES, D.H. (Ed.) (1980) 'Classroom Studies', *Educational Analysis*, 2, 2, pp. 1–87.

HOMAN, R. (1980) 'The ethics of covert methods', *British Journal of Sociology*, 31, 1, pp. 46–59.

HOWELL, A.A., WALKER, R. and FLETCHER, H. *et al.* (1979) *Mathematics for Schools* (2nd. edn.) London, Addison-Wesley.

KING, R. (1978) *All Things Bright and Beautiful? A Sociological Study of Infants' Classrooms*, London, Wiley.

LACEY, C. (1970) *Hightown Grammar: The School as a Social System*, Manchester, Manchester University Press.

MacDonald, B. and Walker, R. (1975) 'Case study and the social philosophy of educational research', *Cambridge Journal of Education*, 5, 1, pp. 2–11.

Platt, J. (1981) 'On interviewing one's peers', *British Journal of Sociology*, 32, 1, pp. 75–91.

Pollard, A. (1979) 'Negotiating deviance and "Getting Done" in primary school classrooms', in Barton, L. and Meighan, R. (Eds.) *Schools, Pupils and Deviance*, Driffield, Nafferton Books.

Schatzman, L. and Strauss, A.L. (1973) *Field Research*, Englewood Cliffs, New Jersey, Prentice Hall.

Schutz, A. (1972) *The Phenomenology of the Social World*, London, Heinemann, originally published in 1932.

Sharp, R. and Green, A. (1975) *Education and Social Control: A Study in Progressive Primary Education*, London, Routledge and Kegan Paul.

Sieber, S.D. (1982) 'The integration of fieldwork and survey methods', in Burgess, R.G. (Ed.) *Field Research: A Sourcebook and Field Manual*, London, Allen and Unwin.

Skilbeck, M. (1983) 'Lawrence Stenhouse: Research methodology', *British Educational Research Journal*, 9, 1, pp. 11–20.

Smith, H.W. (1975) *Strategies of Social Research: The Methodological Imagination*, Englewood Cliffs, New Jersey, Prentice Hall.

Stenhouse, L. (1984) 'Library access, library use and user education in academic sixth forms: an autobiographical account', in Burgess, R.G. (Ed.) *The Research Process in Educational Settings: Ten Case Studies*, Lewes, Falmer Press.

10 Doubts, Dilemmas and Diary-Keeping: Some Reflections on Teacher-Based Research

Gordon Griffiths

Emanating from the changing directions in the sociology of education during the 1970s, new approaches in educational research moved away from statistical survey-based methods to research frameworks which focused upon the details of school life — an approach which has concentrated on the interactions between teachers and between teachers and pupils. In doing so it has illuminated the complex web of experiences which are the essence of school life. While the majority of studies, so far, have been conducted by researchers from outside of schools, recent years have seen a growing emphasis on teacher-based research, particularly as a result of large-scale curriculum development projects and in-service first and higher degree courses.[1] Teachers have been encouraged to acquire research skills and knowledge so that they may investigate their own schools and classrooms and attempt to identify and understand their own and their pupils' experiences.[2] This chapter discusses an attempt to carry out such an investigation that focused on some methodological issues in teacher-based research. The emphasis of the study was on diary keeping as a tool of enquiry; its use in studying the learning situation; and an analysis of the position of the teacher as a researcher. Each area of study highlighted a number of problems, doubts and dilemmas which will be examined and discussed.

Location of the Study

The school in which I work and where I conducted the study is a purpose built, 11–18, coeducational comprehensive school which was opened in 1967. It is located within a mile of Sunderland's town centre though its catchment area covers a wide spectrum of the town's urban development, ranging from the redeveloped heart of the old town, and through established residential areas to post-war council developments on the edge of the town. The school has a ten-form entry and the pupils are sub-divided into five vertical house groups but are taught in horizontal year groups. There are approximately 100 full and part-time teaching staff who are members of both a house and department. The pupils are members of a house group and a teaching group, and for those in the first three years these two groups generally coincide, though in each year there are twelve teaching groups, two of which provide for pupils with learning difficulties. In the fourth year and beyond the pupils remain in the same house groups but are taught in groups according to their option choices, ability, and core curriculum provision. My area of responsibility is the Remedial Department, whose pupils are drawn from all the house groups.

Starting Points

This exploration in teacher-based research arose from the acceptance of two propositions: first, that teachers should become researchers or involved in research in their own schools; and second, that ethnographic methods of investigation might be the most suitable to use in the pursuit of this research, because they help to create more detailed pictures of what has actually happened or is happening. The reasons for accepting these propositions were: to see if a study could be done in which I took a teacher-researcher role; what implications there might be for the teacher acting as researcher; what aspects of the learning situation might be highlighted; and what insights might be gained into other studies and published work about schools.

The aim of this study was to look at daily or familiar events in the school and attempt to identify the issues involved rather than just experience them. To do so it was necessary for me to stop taking for granted the normally taken-for-granted and to regard the familiar as unfamiliar for it is within such events that the themes and issues are embedded. This point is well made by James and Ebbutt (1981):

> In the same school he (Ebbutt) had also accepted differential treatment of boys and girls unquestioningly; but the implications of this, that large parts of the school were, in fact 'no-go' areas for one sex or the other, was not appreciated. Even the

assembly hall had a male and female half, a feature that was obvious, but which had actually gone unnoticed for ten years. (p. 90).[3]

For me, the question of where to look rested on the premise that what happened in the classroom could not be divorced from what was happening in the rest of the school, and as a result, data collection could not be restricted to one location but had to draw on the wider context in which the classroom was located. On this basis, the focus of the investigation was not only an exploration of the events which belong to the classroom but also the events which contribute to the milieu or context in which the classroom and the work of the teacher are located; both of which can influence the teachers' and pupils' performance, approach and conduct during a lesson.[4]

My intention was to conduct the investigation by adopting the role of participant observer and recording my observations in a field diary. Subsequent analysis of this record of events could then be used to highlight any recurring themes, specific issues, and possibly illuminate aspects of the learning situation which had hitherto gone unnoticed.[5] In this respect, the exploration in diary keeping was being applied at the level of initial site investigation.[6] But from the start, it became obvious that it was not going to be possible to record *everything* which I was, or might become involved in. It was therefore necessary to re-focus the study in order to manage the task and to be as comprehensive as possible in collecting data in the selected areas rather than concluding the period of observation with a little data about a wide variety of events and activities. Consequently I decided to concentrate on one class which I was timetabled to teach every day except Thursdays (Diary I), and to keep a separate record of events of those things which happened around me or in which I was involved, other than teaching (Diary II). This would then give an example of events in the classroom and lesson context and also an example of events in the wider context of the school. This strategy has been endorsed by Hamilton and Delamont (1974) who state:

> In the search for the key to the classroom 'black-box' there is a danger that research will cease to consider the wider educational and social context of the classroom ... While for research purposes, it may be possible to regard the classroom as a social unit in its own right, it is only with difficulty that it can be regarded as self-contained. An adequate study must acknowledge and account for both the internal and external aspects of classroom life. (p. 8)

If being able to recognize the 'familiar' or 'taken-for-granted' is one of the major problems for teacher-researchers then another of similar magnitude, must be data recording. Not only is there a problem of making notes as soon as possible after the events observed or experienced, but also the problems involved in writing up the chronological account from the notes.[7] Time is the key factor[8] as data recording must be accommodated alongside, or in addition to, all teaching commitments and school responsibilities. The researcher may, therefore, also be working against the physical problem of tiredness.[9]

Getting Started

In getting started, perhaps one of the most important considerations centres around one of the fundamentals of the research process — negotiation of access. In one respect, I had no problems in getting on to the research site because I was employed there and was an integral part of the scene to be observed. But this is where the dilemmas began to emerge. The question to be considered was, did automatic presence signify freedom to research? What other negotiations, if any, needed to be entered into? A general research intention had already been discussed with the Headteacher as a prerequisite for the in-service course which had generated this study. While permission had been granted in general terms, the nature of this particular study made the declaration of intent and negotiation much more difficult to contemplate. The dilemma centred around three questions:

With whom should the negotiations take place?

How should the negotiations take place?

What was there to be declared and negotiated?

In the first instance there were ninety-eight members of staff and the only time they all meet together in the common room is after school once per half-term for staff meetings with the Headteacher. While many meet together in the common room at morning break at least one-fifth of the total staff are absent because they are involved in playground, house-base, and corridor supervisory duties. Other methods of mass communication are the common room notice board and personal letters to each member of staff. But, from an insider's point of view it would need very careful consideration as to which of these vehicles would be the most appropriate to use, as each situation has its own unique dynamic. For example, it has often been commented upon that while staff meetings are a necessary forum for communication in the school, they are too large to promote really effective discussion. With regard to the notice board, only one section is avidly read by the majority of staff, and that is the section which contains the daily supervision timetable which shows who has to supervise which classes for absent members of staff. But, while notices or letters can be used to notify staff of an intention they do not provide for the two-way process of negotiation. The question of what there was to be declared also proved difficult to pursue because short of declaring an intention to conduct a research exercise and keep a field diary it was not possible to say what would be recorded or who it might involve.

These problems did not arise with later research exercises in school because each had a definite focus; they involved only small numbers of staff, who were each approached individually and asked to cooperate; and negotiations were easy because there were concrete proposals. But these features were lacking from this investigation. Ultimately, it was decided not to publicly declare my particular research intentions for a number of reasons. First, it was an exploratory study in which I tried to survey the scene and isolate significant issues. If this was successful and if the pursuit of any of these issues was possible through later research exercises then this would be the time to formally negotiate with those who would be involved. Secondly, there were still the logistical problems to experience and if these were found to be impractical then the exercise could be abandoned without having to renegotiate with staff about its closure. Thirdly, reporting-back strategies could not be adequately planned because it was not possible to define the specific direction of the exploration. Fourthly, the advantage of not declaring my research intentions would, I thought, avoid a situation where others might feed things into the data collection which I would not normally have experienced. Finally, any other dilemmas which might arise during the course of the investigation could at least be dealt with privately, thus avoiding any unnecessary embarrassment to either the researcher or others who might become involved in the study. While the foregoing reasons were related to Diary II (events other than teaching), similar dilemmas can also occur when the research centres upon the classroom (Diary I) and involves the pupils.[10] Again, in this study negotiations were not entered into, partly for the reasons outlined above and also because the emphasis at this stage was on recording the teacher's experiences in the lesson rather than those of the pupils.

Data Collected — Diary I

For Diary I to be used in any substantive account or for the significance of the events to be appreciated or understood, the observations need to be located in their physical and organizational context. To say that the diary contains a record of events which occurred in the lessons with a class of third-year (14-year-old) pupils in the Remedial Department of my school indicates very little without the following considerations:

— The location of the Department within the organizational structure of the school.

— The location of the class within the Department.

— The composition of the class and the ability range of the pupils.

— The content of the lessons observed within the overall scheme of work.

These considerations on their own raise a number of issues for separate debate and include:

— The rationale behind remedial teaching; is it to identify and overcome specific learning difficulties experienced by any pupil, or has it just become 'D-stream' syndrome by another name with its attendant low status and air of defeat?

— Its position in relation to the general aims and work done in the rest of the school; is there equality of curriculum provision and opportunity or complete segregation and differentation?

— How is the Department perceived and reacted to by other teachers in the school? While some have commented on its value and necessity other comments have referred to 'a lost cause' or 'Wooden-top Farm'.

— How is it perceived and reacted to by pupils? Some have commented 'It's best because I'm not very good at school work'. While others have said 'We're 'ere 'cos we're not brainy'; 'They say you must be thick if you are in that class'.

— Definitions of 'remedial' and remedial work by teachers both inside and outside of the Department with comments ranging from 'striving to overcome learning difficulties' and 'trying to create a stable working base' to 'she must be remedial, her handwriting is terrible', and 'I don't know how you stand it, all day and every day'.

Set against this background of contextual considerations and perceptions, an analysis of the events recorded in Diary I began to show a complex web of issues and activities. While many belonged exclusively to the lessons recorded, others originated or reached far beyond the neatly timetabled seventy minute lesson allocated to the class in that particular room. Some of these activities were connected with my pastoral role as a house tutor, while others involved my responsibilities as a head of department and the diary shows how these various responsibilities impinged upon and interrupted a number of lessons. The first of these impingements was in relation to my pastoral role and was the initial entry in the diary:

> Four minutes late for the start of the lesson after investigating a member of my tutor group (fifth year). Persistent latecomer — so late not getting to registration before end of tutor group period (8.50–9.15am.). Checking late-boards.

The late-boards are left in the entrance foyer beside the school office and if a pupil arrives at school at the end of or after the registration period they sign-in on the board and then go straight to their lesson. The purpose of this procedure is to save time by removing the need for the pupil to go around the school searching for their tutor to announce their presence and then proceed to their lesson. The amount of pupil time saved by the late-board procedure is quite considerable, because of the size of the school and because not all teachers teach in the same room which they use for their tutor groups. But, this process can be time consuming for the tutor when it becomes necessary to find out whether the pupil is in school and to contact them before the end of the session. It was to one of these occasions which the diary extract above refers. I needed to see that particular pupil for a number of reasons. First, so that absence at the end of the previous week could be checked upon, as there had been a suggestion of truancy made by another member of the group ('I called for her, but her mam said that she had already gone. But I didn't see her in school all day'). Secondly, so that an urgent message from the school librarian could be passed on before the pupil went home at lunch-time, and thirdly, so that the register could be completed and returned to the school office by 9.30am.

Pastoral business continued to impinge upon the beginning of that lesson. While establishing the start of the lesson, that is, bringing the pupils into the room, seating, 'settling down', rapport, emotional negotiations (finding out what mood each other are in) and generally reaffirming 'methodic practices' (*cf.* Payne, 1976, p. 34) one pupil asked a question about a form which had been issued during their tutor-group period. These were application forms for new cheap travel passes that could be used on public transport locally. The pupil was still unsure how to apply for the pass, and what geographical area the concession covered. While this pupil was asking questions, several others produced their forms also asking for points to be clarified. Several minutes were spent in discussing the information on the forms before beginning the actual planned content of the lesson.

In many respects it was not unusual to experience aspects of pastoral impingement upon lesson time but in saying so it is interesting to note the change in organizational and role emphasis with the suggestion of demarcation. Previously in secondary teaching, especially in secondary modern schools, a teacher registered and taught his or her own class for a large proportion of the timetable, and this is still the case in most primary schools. In these situations the pastoral and academic roles of the teacher are all in one, whereas the predominant comprehensive school experience is for pupils to be responsible to one particular member of staff for registration, pastoral care, guidance, welfare and well-being, and to many others where the emphasis is on academic development. While the main advantage of this system has been that the pastoral tutor has followed the pupil through their school career and provided a stable reference point for the pupil during the daily and annual changes of subject teachers, the disadvantage has been the limited amount of contact that the tutors have had with their groups. As a result, many colleagues have remarked that in the initial stages they often have a greater knowledge of the pupils in their teaching groups than their tutor groups, though recent changes have gone some way towards alleviating this problem.[11] The organization of the remedial work is, however, in many ways, similar to the primary or old secondary modern school system alluded to above. Although the teachers in the department do not register the pupils, (that is done in their tutor groups) they are responsible for teaching basic subjects to their own main group of pupils for just over half of the total time-tabled time. As a result of the length of time spent by these pupils with one teacher the overlapping of the pastoral and academic spheres is much greater, and it has often been found that some pupils will consult and talk more with their class teacher than with their tutor. Contained within this short commentary, however, is a whole debate about the organization and grouping of pupils, incorporated into which is the debate about how the provision for pupils with learning difficulties may be structured.

In addition to pastoral impingements upon the lesson the diary shows other interruptions which were connected with my role as Head of the Department. One particular incident not only provides an example of the type of interruption to the lesson but also brings into focus some of the problems of communication in a large school. Near the end of the period before lunch on the second day, a pupil in one of the other classes in the Department had used abusive language and had sworn at the teacher. The incident occurred in a teaching room some considerable distance from mine and the member of staff had immediately reported the offence to the Deputy Headteacher, whose office was near to that classroom. The teacher informed me of what had happened when we met in the staffroom at lunch-time. I went and saw the Deputy Head who arranged to meet again later in the lunch break when we could discuss the incident with the pupil's Head of House. Unfortunately, at the time arranged the teacher who had been sworn at was involved in supervisory duties in one of the house base areas and therefore could not be present. By the time the meeting had finished the bell had rung for the start of afternoon school and it was not going to be possible for me to contact the member of staff personally before having to attend to my tutor group registration and the start of the first lesson. The only alternative was to write a brief note explaining the result of the discussion and outlining what action was to be taken, which I did, and then asked a member of my tutor group to deliver it on the way to their lesson. Approximately twenty minutes after the start of my lesson with the third-year group the member of staff, who had a non-teaching period, arrived to say that they had received the note and to enquire about the substance of the meeting. This discussion took approximately ten minutes, but unfortunately it had occurred at a point in the lesson where the activity was in transition from oral work (that is, discussion, questions, answers, explanations) to practical application so that time had to be spent in recapitulation in order to re-establish the continuity of the work. On reflecting about the whole incident the situation was made more complicated than it should have been by two major factors: the distances between the various locations in the school, and the availability of the different participants in the events which took place. Furthermore, it also illustrates the often conflicting demands of a teacher's roles and responsibilities, which, in this case, were the demands of being in particular places at particular times yet still being required to deal with other events at the same time, but elsewhere.

Among other interruptions recorded during subsequent lessons there were two incidents of pupils arriving from other classes in the Department with requests for new exercise books, and one incident caused by the school secretary. She had come into the room enquiring about a particular pupil, but unfortunately she had misread her timetable and had come to the wrong class in the wrong room. In order to save her time and a long journey back to the office to check the timetable there, I had to get my copy of the school timetable out of the stock room and look for the correct information. Although these three incidents were only brief interruptions they again nevertheless broke the continuity of the work being done in the lesson so that time had to be spent re-establishing the activities which had been interrupted. But impingements upon, and interruptions to, the lesson was only one of many issues and themes to emerge from the analysis of the diary entries. Others included:

— Patterns of classroom management and organization; for example, how the pupils were arranged in the room; how materials and resources were distributed; and variations in organization in relation to lesson content and activities.

— Communication between staff and the complications caused by distances and availability.

— Communication between the teacher and pupils and differences in projection in various situations within the classroom; for example, conversation, instruction, communicating with individuals, small groups and the whole class.

— Non-verbal communication; for example, the significance of the glance, the raised eyebrow, the cough, hand and arm gestures, standing postures and sitting down.

— Meanings attributed to teacher words like 'busy', 'satis-factory', 'problems with work', and 'unsettled'.

— How pupils organize their time or devize strategies for avoiding work set during the lesson.

— Systems and forms of discipline and sanctions which are operated within the classroom as part of the management of the lesson and learning activities; for example, encour-agement and caution, approval and disapproval, the de-vices or strategies used and their place within the school's overall policy regarding discipline and sanctions.

— Classroom negotiations. Devices used by both the pupils to modify the aims and achievements of particular lessons, (for example, 'If we finish this (piece of work) can we do some pictures for the frieze for the rest of the lesson?'), and the teacher, in order to achieve the aims of the lesson.

Each of these issues is a separate debate in itself and all are additional to any analysis of the subject content of the lessons from which they emerged. Furthermore, they may be explored beyond the classroom which was the focus of my observations and linked to other areas in the school. For example, how other work areas which these pupils experience are organized and managed; what other forms of negotia-tion are entered into; and how others define the vocabulary such as 'busy' and 'satisfactory'.

The further exploration of these themes also introduces another element of this type of research (though not used in this exercise) — that of pupil perceptions and definitions and drawing upon their experiences in school and in lessons.[12] But in doing so it introduces questions about the position or status of the teacher-researcher. In this case, from the pupils' point of view, they have seen the teacher-researcher fulfilling several different roles as teacher, as pastoral tutor, a head of department (to whom some of them had been sent in the past for misbehaving in other teachers' lessons) and have built-up perceptions based on those experiences. Also, where, within this structure of perceptions and experiences do situations in which some pupils have addressed this teacher-researcher as 'Dad' (or in the case of one confused soul 'Mam') fit in? The question is, therefore, how far can the teacher-researcher hope to depart from these images when attempting to gather data from pupils about their experiences in the classroom and in other parts of the school, particularly where this might imply 'checking up on', or criticisms of other members of staff? This is especially relevant when any attempts by the pupils to comment about members of staff in the past had been rebuked. Similarly, in any other follow-up work or research with other teachers, how inhibiting is the researcher's formal school role and status? For example, to take one of the themes outlined above and explore how other work areas are organized and managed; what other forms of negotiation are entered into; and how others define the vocabulary of 'busy' and 'satisfactory' — could this be seen as a head of department 'checking' on other teachers?[13] Such an exploration to ascertain and capitalize on the degree of consistency of approach could, however unintentional, be interpreted as 'threatening' by the teachers being questioned.[14] Consequently, of the many issues to emerge from initial observations, the teacher-researcher may find the choice of those issues to be followed, the avenues of pursuit and the mode of enquiry could be limited because of professional or occupational considerations, and these restrictions may be heightened by the lack of a research tradition in the school.

Data Collected — Diary II

Diary II contains a record of events which happened around the researcher or in which he was involved, other than teaching in the classroom. The Diary includes examples of administrative tasks and of being involved in issues in a head of department role and in others in a pastoral tutor role. It also provides a picture of daily events, including timetabled and after school activities. It located the time when the Diary notes were recorded in school and it contains a record of conversations and a record of a staff development interview. From this record of events various themes emerge which could be the focus for further or future exploration. They include links and cohesion between the academic and pastoral structures; an exploration of the extent and expectations of the teacher's role as pastoral tutor;[15] the use of sanctions, areas of responsibility in their use, together with 'support' systems; and the division and relationships between administrative and teaching tasks. But, as with some of the issues which emerged from Diary I, the implications involved in their exploration need to be carefully considered. For example, an enquiry into how teachers organize their day and cope with administrative tasks alongside their teaching tasks could, seemingly, appear less contentious than an exploration of the links and cohesion between the academic and pastoral structures. Both structures emphasize and are responsible for different aspects of the pupils' membership of the school, but involve the same members of staff — though often occupying different positions of responsibility in them. Because of the difference in emphasis, conflicts of interest can occur, and in fact were evident during the period when the Diary record was kept. A direct research focus on this aspect of school organization at that particular time could have been interpreted as more than just a quest for greater understanding of what happens in our schools.[16] If the research had been undertaken and had resulted in showing some areas lacking in cohesion or that the links were only tenuous where the opposite should have been the case, would this have been seen as the teacher-researcher making accusations of inadequacy towards the personalities involved? Similarly, what 'threats' are suggested by the teacher-researcher in an exploration of how they and other teachers perceive and define their roles as pastoral tutors, or to what extent they operate in that role? Would this be seen as another case of 'checking up on', especially where one has previous knowledge of staffroom conversations which have alluded to some members of staff being 'good' tutors and others not? Consequently, in situations like those outlined above, perceptions of the research exercise could easily move away from the descriptive to the judgmental. This possible change in emphasis was summarized by a colleague during an interview which was part of a later and separate investigation.

> ... basically we are insecure and afraid etc., we're afraid of admitting our faults and failings ... and the only way we can evaluate ourselves ... is to do it anonymously ... probably until the overall climate of the school, teaching permits us to confess our faults and failings etc ..., and them not to be seen as criticism ...[17]

The Teacher-Researcher

The themes to emerge from the analysis of the data have highlighted a number of aspects of the research situation which the teacher-researcher must carefully consider. A re-examination of the issues contained in and emanating from the diaries could suggest a series of categories arranged on a scale of increasing sensitivity, depending on who or what is involved, how the data might be collected and treated, and for what purpose. This assessment possibly provides one of the keys to teacher-based research — that is, sensitivity towards how particular issues are treated and the data handled. Perhaps one of the most sensitive issues to arise from Diary II relates to the recording and use of conversations and discussions. While all material gathered during an investigation can assist in the analysis of the issues there is a danger of the teacher-researcher abusing what is essentially 'privileged' access to events merely by being there. This not only includes membership of informal or social groups within the school or staffroom, but also participation in meetings which have restricted access, like, for example, heads of department meetings. Though a speculative point here is that two sets of 'rules' or considerations appear to operate in that in both cases the proceedings may be relayed orally to others with seemingly less pause for reflection than if they are transmitted in writing. However, in this exercise the conversation and discussion material has not been directly used because its collection was not negotiated. To release such data would be a betrayal of trust and an abuse of access. Herein probably lies another key to the research position, and that is the need for an understanding of the difference between research and voyeurism.

In many respects the degree of sensitivity involved will probably depend on the purpose of the research and the audience to which the findings are directed, or who will eventually have access to them. For example, an investigation which is conducted by a teacher-researcher for his or her own enlightenment or professional development may be seen as much less threatening than an exercise aimed at wider audiences, particularly those closely involved with the school or the careers of those upon whom the focus of the research falls. The issue here is that research which might be done as part of an in-service degree or diploma course can be less threatening because there is restricted access to the data by people who are not usually connected with the school. Whereas, research exercises which might be conducted for the purposes of internal policy making with their attendant reports and possible revelations, could carry political implications in either the reward and advancement structure of the school[18] or in the delicate credibility structures amongst one's own colleagues.[19] The realization of these implications can present the teacher-researcher with some considerable dilemmas to resolve — not least his or her own position within those structures. In seeking guidance about these dilemmas from established researchers one finds that 'the ethical issues raised by these problems are incapable of simple resolution' (Hargreaves, 1967, p. 199), while Burgess (1980, p. 171) states that '... the way in which a teacher-researcher resolves these problems may involve him knowing more about himself ...'. On the other hand Woods (1979, appendix 1) described himself as an 'involved' observer and stated that he had no ties with the school, he was not dependent on it for his livelihood, he did not have to teach or be taught to keep order and had no official role (and hence no role conflict). But, because the teacher-researcher is an integral part of the scene being researched they have more at stake than the outsider-researcher. Though it could be said that Woods (and possibly other outsider-researchers) underplays his dependence on the school because if the products of outsider-researchers are seen by those inside schools to be too contentious then any future requests for access may be denied.

However, it is not a case that teachers cannot do research or use qualitative methods while conducting research. Perhaps an indication of the teacher's position lies with the more philosophical considerations involved in research methods and research approaches in that each researcher brings to the research site his or her own stock of knowledge and while much of this knowledge will overlap with each other there will be facets which will not. Consequently, how the research exercise is approached will depend as much on the shared stock of knowledge as on the unique facets. If this is the case, what does the teacher bring to the research situation? First, there is an intimate knowledge of the context; secondly, a knowledge of contextual features or events; thirdly, teacher-researchers are in a position to view both the obvious links between situations and events and also to understand the more subtle or diffuse links; and finally, they are also in a position to assess the implications of following particular avenues of enquiry. Accordingly, the specific context and the specialized knowledge which the teacher has will determine how the research situation is approached. The teacher's approach will be different from the outsider researcher's approach even though they are working within the same methodological framework. Both will be approaching the research situation with the intention of producing a picture of 'what is happening here' but perhaps the key to the situation is to stress the notion of 'picture' as opposed to 'photograph' in that with a photograph it is the viewer of the finished product who selects the images to concentrate their attention on, whereas with a picture it is the artist who highlights particular images for others to see. Consequently, just as two different artists will approach the same scene with the same materials yet produce different pictures, so the same may be said about two different researchers approaching the same scene with the same methodological tools. Neither can be judged in terms of right or wrong even though the images which they identify may well be different. The picture which the teacher-researcher may produce and the images which are emphasized should be seen in the light of considerations about the purpose of the research and its intended audience.

Conclusion

By examining the issues involved in keeping field diaries, an attempt has been made to highlight potential problems for the teacher-researcher. The exercise and the report were not embarked upon with the intention of providing definitive answers to particular problems. There are probably no 'answers' because each research location is different, and each researcher will approach particular issues in different ways. But, by outlining the exercise from its inception, by reporting the issues to emerge from data analysis, and by indicating how a number of them were handled, it is hoped that some of the issues and dilemmas which may confront teacher-researchers have been brought into clearer view. Of particular concern have been: the breadth and depth of initial negotiations; the pursuit of particular issues and consequent threats to others; the political implications of research projects; the handling of data and the fundamental position of the teacher-researcher. However, the catalogue of issues contained in my report is by no means exhaustive. On the contrary, many of the notions and considerations are still in their exploratory stages, as is, in many respects, the rationale behind teachers researching. But, if the activity is to grow and develop there should be a place in the wider debate about research methods and research strategies that can be developed with particular reference and relevance to teachers as researchers, especially in their own institutions.

The position of the teacher as researcher is unique and the benefits which may be accrued can be extremely valuable not only to the teacher, but also to his or her colleagues, pupils, school and the research community in general. Perhaps the most obvious benefit is the development of the teacher's own professional expertise and improved practice through informed analysis of their own teaching style, lesson content and pupil techniques. Though a further equally important, but less definable benefit may be summarized as 'a greater awareness of others'. In the context of the school, that is a greater awareness of both colleagues and pupils, and an increasing sensitivity towards their individual needs, problems and perceptions. This may not only help towards improving classroom practice, but can also lead towards more sensitive support for one's colleagues and pupils. More obviously, teachers who engage in research can develop the ability to contextualize and critically analyze situations and events which occur in schools. This can, in turn, lead to more informed policy-making at all levels in the school (for example, in the classroom, department, house or at whole school level) rather than having to rely on a consensus of well-meaning opinions or notions. Allied to this, the teacher-researcher is in a position to engage in informed analysis of published work about or concerning schools. From this position he or she is able to bridge the gap between the theorists and practitioners, and provide an informed link between outsider research and everyday school practice.[20] But, if teacher-research is to grow and flourish it is to be hoped that these links would not just be at the level of collaborators or key informants,[21] but as partners in the research process.

Notes

1 The original exercise which is the basis of this paper was conducted as part of an in-service MEd course.
2 For example, see BURGESS (1978).
3 Similarly, see Kelly's chapter in this volume with reference to the teaching of science to girls.
4 For example, PARSONS (1981) remarks:

> One of the basic flaws is ... '... the assumption that teachers are committed to generating learning in all pupils for whom they have responsibility'. (p. 57)

and SIMONS (1981) states:

> ... in the last analysis teachers cannot be held to be entirely accountable for what pupils learn or fail to learn. There is no accounting for the fact that some children may choose not to learn or not to tell what they have learned. (p. 136)

5 See also HAMMERSLEY (1980) who states:

> ... much of our action is of a routine, taken-for-granted character. Indeed it is only out of this routine background that problems emerge nd strategies are developed. (p. 56)

6 See BURGESS (1982), especially p. 15.
7 ENRIGHT (1981, p. 37) states that the task of writing up the daily diary took between two and three hours each evening. My experience was very similar.
8 The problem of time has been considered to be the main constraint against teacher research. See the report of the Fourth Annual Conference

of the Classroom Action Research Network in ELLIOTT (1982, p. 77).

9 For example, DAVID HARGREAVES (1982) writes

> When I became a don I found myself working very much longer
> hours than when I had been a school teacher, but I did not
> experience at the end of the day that curious sense of numbness,
> of being emotionally drained and empty, which can overwhelm
> the teacher. (p. 203)

10 For example, see SADLER (1980).

11 First and second-year pupils are now timetabled to spend one period (1
hour 10 minutes) per week with their tutors. They engage in a specially
created Foundations Course, the core of which is social and
environmental education.

12 See BALL's paper 'Participant observation with pupils', and MEASOR's
paper 'Interviewing and ethnographic research', with reference to the
problems of image and interviewing pupils, in BURGESS (1985)

13 See BURGESS (1980, p. 167) where he quotes a similar situation involving
the Deputy Headteacher of a middle school.

14 For example, see the experiences of JAMES and EBBUTT (1981):

> Even research confined to one's own classroom is sometimes
> interpreted as threatening by others. For example, MJ was
> charged by a colleague and friend with undermining her own
> professional status and, by implication, that of her colleagues.
> By looking at her own practice so openly was not MJ publicly
> confessing to her own shortcomings, and was this not likely to
> lower the image of the profession? (p. 82)

15 See BURGESS (1983).

16 *Ibid.*, p. 59.

17 Extract from a transcript of one of a series of interviews with different
colleagues during an exercise which explored teachers' perceptions and
definitions of evaluation in schools.

18 For further discussion see HOLT (1981, p. 120). Although HOLT is
writing in the context of evaluation and accountability, the same
sentiment applies here:

> ... what risks does a school and a staff run in bearing its soul to
> those who are the gatekeepers of professional advancement?

19 For a summary see HAMMERSLEY (1980, pp. 52–5).

20 For a discussion of this topic see THREADGOLD's chapter in this volume.

21 For a discussion of this topic see BURGESS' paper 'Key informants and
the study of a comprehensive school' in BURGESS (1985).

References

BURGESS, R.G. (1978) 'Preparations for teacher-based research: a report of
an in-service course', *British Journal of In-Service Education*, 5, 1, pp.
14–19.

BURGESS, R.G. (1980) 'Some fieldwork problems in teacher-based research', *British Educational Research Journal* , 6, 2, pp. 165–73.

BURGESS, R.G. (Ed.) (1982) *Field Research: A Sourcebook and Field Manual*, London, Allen and Unwin.

BURGESS, R.G. (1983) 'Teacher-based research and pastoral care', *Pastoral Care in Education*, 1, 1, pp. 52-60.

BURGESS, R.G. (Ed.) (1985) *Strategies of Educational Research: Qualitative Methods*, Lewes, Falmer Press.

ELLIOTT, J. (1982) 'Action-research into action-research', *Classroom Action Research Network*, Bulletin No. 5, Cambridge Institute of Education, pp. 68–80.

ENRIGHT, L. (1981) 'The diary of a classroom', in NIXON, J. (Ed.) *A Teachers' Guide to Action Research*, London, Grant McIntyre.

HAMILTON, D. and DELAMONT, S. (1974) 'Classroom research: a cautionary tale', *Research in Education*, 11, pp. 1–15.

HAMMERSLEY, M. (1980) 'Classroom ethnography', *Educational Analysis*, 2, 2, pp. 47–74.

HARGREAVES, D.H. (1967) *Social Relations in a Secondary School*, London, Routledge and Kegan Paul.

HARGREAVES, D.H. (1982) *The Challenge for the Comprehensive School: Culture, Curriculum and Community*, London, Routledge and Kegan Paul.

HOLT, M. (1981) *Evaluating the Evaluators*, London, Hodder and Stoughton.

JAMES, M. and EBBUTT, D. (1981) 'Problems and potential', in NIXON, J. (Ed.) *A Teacher's Guide to Action Research*, London, Grant McIntyre.

LACEY, C. and LAWTON, D. (Eds) (1981) *Issues in Evaluation and Accountability*, London, Methuen.

PARSONS, C. (1981) 'A policy for educational evaluation', in LACEY, C. and LAWTON, D. (Eds) *Issues in Evaluation and Accountability*, London, Methuen.

PAYNE, G.C.F. (1976) 'Making a lesson happen: an ethnomethodological analysis' in HAMMERSLEY, M. and WOODS, P. (Eds) (1976) *The Process of Schooling*, London, Routledge and Kegan Paul.

SADLER, P. (1980) 'Personal decisions in classroom research ethics', *Classroom Action Research Network*, Bulletin No. 4, Cambridge Institute of Education.

SIMONS, H. (1981) 'Process evaluation in schools', in LACEY, C. and LAWTON, D. (Eds) (1981) *Issues in Evaluation and Accountability*, London, Methuen.

WOODS, P. (1979) *The Divided School*, London, Routledge and Kegan Paul.

11 Qualitative Research in the Infant Classroom: A Personal Account

Carol Cummings

Why should teachers engage in classroom research? Indeed, why classroom research at all? As an infant teacher, my day is busy and overfull, I make frequent choices about how and where to spend time — why do I also attempt to step 'outside' the situation and look at what appears to be happening in the classroom? Of what interest could such 'data' be to others? Does it have sufficient methodological rigour and theoretical underpinning to be 'legitimate'? Need any of these questions concern me as I work in the classroom and reflect on that work? It is my concern here to examine notions of the 'teacher-as-researcher' in the light of my own work in the classroom, which has followed two distinct avenues that bear comparison in terms of methodology and outcome. The first involved tape-recording and transcribing teacher/pupil and pupil/pupil classroom talk, and the second was an attempt at collaborative research with an 'outside' researcher, into the daily events of my own classroom.

The Teacher as Researcher

Why classroom research at all? Certainly, until comparatively recently, the questions which were being asked about education by such people as Douglas (1964), Halsey, Floud and Anderson (1961), Barker Lunn (1970) and others included:

— why do some children succeed and others fail?

— which children can best benefit from continued education?

— how can we best equip society with an appropriately-trained workforce?

Such questions were asked with little or no reference to what actually happened in schools and were often the result of demands for 'answers' from policy-makers. Research was largely in terms of an input-output paradigm — the relationship between social class and low achievement, language and delinquency, education and the economy, and the status of the teacher in the wider society. There was little or no emphasis on what happens in the days, months and years when the child is in school and in the classroom. It would seem to have been taken for granted that because a child was in school, he or she was, *ipso facto*, being educated and, perhaps an even greater leap of faith, that 'being educated' was a valuable and valued state in which to find oneself.

Research, until comparatively recently, has also striven primarily for legitimation in terms of validity and reliability, and on generalizability based on sampling. But have the findings of such research reached the chalk-face? And if they have been placed on the staff room table, have they been critically reviewed and used to further understanding and effectiveness? I would argue that all but a few teachers (and those tend to be on formal in-service courses, as were the teachers in Nixon's (1981) book, or on the 'promotion trail') do not come into more than cursory contact with research findings, and when they do, tend to reject them out-of-hand, as irrelevant to the particular situation in which they find themselves for a number of diverse reasons. It is for this reason that Margaret Threadgold (in this volume) calls for greater liaison to the benefit of both communities.

The Background

It was Lawrence Stenhouse (1975) who outlined the need for a move towards teachers becoming researchers in his critique of curriculum research and development. His emphasis is heavily based upon what Hoyle (1972) characterizes as the teacher as 'extended professional', viewing his or her work in terms of the widest possible context, extending educational interests beyond the door of the classroom and school, concerning him or herself with the link between theory and practice and having a commitment to some form of evaluation. Stenhouse (1975) pushes the characterization further than Hoyle, and adds:

> The commitment to systematic questioning of one's own teaching as a basis for development; the commitment and the

skills to study one's own teaching; the concern to question
and test theory in practice by the use of those skills. To these
may be added as highly desirable, though perhaps not essential, a readiness to allow other teachers to observe one's work
— directly or through recordings — and to discuss it with
them on an open and honest basis. (p. 144)

Calls for teachers to take up the gauntlet by researching their
own practices (Nixon, 1981) have followed an increasingly strong
move to augment quantitative, large-scale surveys looking at:

antecedents and consequences but never once into the classroom to see how the teacher actually teaches or the pupil
learns. (Medley and Mitzel, 1963, p. 247)

There have also been demands for teachers' concerns to be recognized, for classroom data that record teachers' and pupils' perceptions
to be seen as important and for teachers to become increasingly self-
aware and self-critical.

The Ford Teaching Project can be seen to have followed fairly
close on the heels of Stenhouse's Schools Council Humanities
Curriculum Project which called for new teacher-roles and a radical
new pedagogy, coupled with the study of controversial issues in the
classroom. The 'neutral' teacher, along with enquiry-method learning
created 'new' classroom situations, 'new' attitudes and an increased
awareness of the significance of what happens beyond the classroom
door. A variety of other groups have also been established with
similar concerns. For example, the Classroom Action Research
Network was established in 1976, and the Leicestershire Classroom
Research and In-Service Education Project set up in 1980. My own
involvement has been primarily with the Schools Council Action
Research Project, Programme 2, Teacher-Pupil Interaction and the
Quality of Learning (TIQL) coordinated from the Cambridge Institute (see also Ebbutt in this volume).

Methods of Investigation

Nixon's (1981) collection of papers by teacher-researchers illustrates
how methodologies can be disparate and numerous. There is no one
agreed way of going about classroom research and the choice will rest
on both practical and philosophical criteria.

The American emphasis on interaction analysis was initially

based on the core assumptions of behaviourist psychology, and an observation schedule was used to reduce classroom behaviour to manageable proportions. Flander's schedule (FIAC) sets us a check-list of possible interactions which the researcher can use to produce a systematic and tidy study of the interactions which have taken place (see Delamont, 1983, for commentary).

Whilst recognizing that many of the early objections to interaction analysis have been overcome, and similar, more refined, schedules have been employed in projects such as ORACLE (Galton, Simon and Croll, 1980), Delamont and Hamilton's (1976) critique is still persuasive. Their comments are clearly stated:

(i) The nature of the system ignores the spatial and tem-poral context of the data.

(ii) There is an over-emphasis on overt and observable behaviour.

(iii) An expressed concern with the measurable leads to dismissal of the immeasurable.

(iv) The focus on 'small bits of action or behaviour rather than global concepts' (Simon and Boyer, 1968) which must be linked to global concepts provides unnecessary circularity.

(v) Pre-specification of categories assumes the truth of what they are explaining.

(vi) The static nature of the categories creates initial bias and leaves the researcher within a straight jacket of concep-tualizations. (pp. 8–9)

Although each point carries considerable weight, the third 'speaks' most strongly to me. As I see classroom practices as both active and reactive, as a learning environment for both teacher and children, I feel that I would find categorization both intrusive and constraining. It might force me to look at my classroom through Flanders' eyes and direct me to 'what is important' before the event, allowing me to ignore other facets. Much of what happens in the classroom is unforeseen, and it is these features that provide the main focus of my interest. I could not, by definition, pre-specify these events and would, therefore, be in danger of overlooking them. If pre-specification of categories was considered to be of significance adding to the research process then I would prefer to evolve my own list, but such constraints, I feel, would alter the outcome to the extent that the work would no longer be of interest to me.

'Anthropological' investigation would seem to offer more to the teacher-researcher, who is, by the nature of the job, already immersed within, and participating in the object of the enquiry. It is, rather, the mental act of stepping outside the familiar setting that becomes a research problem. The necessity of divorcing the research role from that of the participant involves a rather uncomfortable step 'in order to adopt an attitude of 'anthropological strangeness', which Schutz (1971) describes most lucidly. His formulation of the notion of the 'stranger' might help to resolve some of the tensions inherent in the apparent mutual exclusiveness of the role of researcher/researched, in that he provides a framework through which to evolve an approach to the data, to adopt the relevances of the outsider. Nevertheless, several questions remain — which outsider, whose relevances, and are they more valid and useful (and to whom) than 'insider' relevances? Such research need not be straight-jacketed by pre-specified observation categories, but, if they are to be used, they can be generated out of data so that they will be temporarily and situationally specific and used to clarify and order what is seen to be happening. Derek Sharples, at the Manchester Polytechnic Action Research Conference (March 1983), characterized the nature of teacher-researching as being generated by and informing teachers' concerns and interests involving shared discourse and collaboration, but not being con-cerned with replication, with reliability and generalizability except in terms of deepened insight and increased awareness.

Much of the discussion that followed this paper and the papers by Griffiths and Threadgold when they were originally presented at the Whitelands Conference in 1983, revolved around the different sorts of research undertaken by teachers and the professional research community, the varied audiences and the expressed need for two strands of educational research. There was considerable feeling expressed that the 'utilitarian' approach might sterilize much of the valuable work undertaken by sociologists of education, whilst feeling was also strongly expressed that the dissemination of such research might be widened to the benefit of the classroom practitioner and the educational policy-makers. The theories that are generated in the classroom might be incomplete and frequently adapted but are, nevertheless, working models which have the potential to solve problems. Can we any longer afford to split the educational com-munity? Must we not use such funds as are available to disseminate *all* research as widely as possible?

It is vitally important for the teacher-researcher not to lose sight of the nature of his or her research, not to aim for ends which might destroy his or her own purposes whilst still striving to eliminate unexplicated bias and to make visible that which was previously obscure. The generalizability of such work is questionable, but need not be of concern, so long as it provides some insight into teachers' 'problems'. To follow Michael Bassey's heuristic dichotomy, class-room action research falls into the area of 'the study of singularities', concerned with description and possible explanation and evaluation, rather than 'the search for generalities', which could, and often does, lead to spurious predictions. It is not the concern of the teacher-researcher to work towards either generalization or prediction: to do so would be to adopt an altogether different role.

How then to proceed in a quest for self-knowledge and an attempt to evaluate the taken-for-granted. I have travelled along two distinct routes, interwoven though they were in terms of both time and personalities, and found both of value and satisfying in their own ways. It is to a commentary on these research experiences that we now turn.

The Research

Getting Started

I became involved in the neurosis-inducing process of the systematic analysis of my classroom practice through in-service work and a growing desire to monitor the taken-for-granted daily routines in which the children and I are involved, and which, arguably, are as potent a force in the children's lives as any intended and planned curriculum projects. I became increasingly convinced that 'the medium is the message' and that many of the unnoticed features of classroom life constitute 'what school is' for children whose first experience of school is provided by me. They do not question that this is what school is about any more than they question the family model in which they have grown up as being what 'a family' is. They will be involved with schools and schooling directly for twelve years and the effects may well last throughout life. It is then, perhaps our duty to look at the model which we as teachers present to them, the attitudes we try to engender (and those we engender without even trying) and life skills that are encouraged.

I had come to look for a more systematic way of monitoring the events of the day and therefore joined the Manchester Polytechnic-based outer network group of the Schools Council Action Research Project, Number 2. This was, at first, a loosely-knit group of people, both teachers and college staff, in search of a methodology and direction. In terms of methodology, the commitment of some of the group to ethnomethodology and, in particular the analysis of tape-recorded data, provided a starting point.

For the first few sessions, when group membership was 'flexible' when people came and left, or came and decided it was for them and stayed, those of us who felt that we had found at least a way to move towards our own ends, towards a more methodical and conscious way of looking at our classrooms, started to tape record, transcribe and bring our data to be furiously pulled apart by our colleagues. The initial meetings, in retrospect, were disquieting both for the 're-searcher' and for everyone else, concerned as we were not to offend or drive people away. We became tougher as we became more of a group. The joint commenting on papers helped immeasurably when we later came to analyze our own transcripts and began to think about the 'action' side of the research we were undertaking.

Our 'problems' were and are as varied as our working life. Indeed, it never ceases to amaze me that such disparate activities as sixth-form poetry analysis, the class teaching, transmission-style of history 'facts' to a class of 14-year-olds and making clay models with two 5-year-olds can come under the umbrella-term 'teaching'. In a sense, though, our 'problems' seemed to be very much on the same lines — how to assess children's learning, knowledge acquisition, development of cognitive skills and attitudes, so that our teaching and interaction with them can become more appropriate and effective.

I was the only infant teacher for much of the time and found the comments of those involved with older students refreshing, as the world of the infant school can easily become insular and lack wider perspective.

Tape Recording

I shall look at the transcript of the three different types of pupil talk with a view to highlighting similarities and differences. I shall look at interaction in a relatively unstructured early morning session (see Appendix: Transcript 1); in a more structured storytime session (see Appendix: Transcript 2); and an 'eavesdropping' session when the children were talking without adult presence (see Appendix: Transcript 3).

Two of the transcripts are 'mine'. I was the teacher, I recorded and transcribed the material. The third transcript was recorded by others but transcribed by me. My approaches to these different types of data are of necessity, different. In the case of the first two transcripts, I was there. I can remember much of the background and circumstances of the sessions, the personalities of the children, and can, therefore, find *my* reasons for what can be seen by all to have happened. Nevertheless, the dangers inherent in such knowledge must be acknowledged. The fact I was there makes the assumption of a position of anthropological strangeness doubly difficult to achieve. Not only do I 'know' what everybody knows about classrooms, about teachers and about children, but also have more explicit knowledge about these particular children, this particular teacher, and the circumstances within which this episode occurred.

My peculiar relationship with this data raises all sorts of questions about qualitative studies and the classroom-research findings of others. I feel conclusions are too easily reached, and all too rarely is the basis of reasoning examined. I am here making some claims to 'insider knowledge' because of my actual presence, because of my ability to reflect on my own thoughts and intentions at the time. However, I must admit almost complete defeat in terms of what I had intended by particular utterances or actions, or the perceptions of the children. Yet, so often, researchers claim that 'this utterance demonstrates' or 'here we can see that the teacher was doing ... '. If 'the teacher' herself cannot make such claims, one wonders about calls for reliability and validity.

My concern to 'get at' the different ways children might present themselves to each other without the presence of adults (and how different a picture we gain of some children on playground duty than in the constraining classroom!) led to the third transcription. Because of the nature of the data, interpretation and comments are open to all. The end result of this type of research is not generalized 'findings', but deepened awareness, sight of the 'seen-but-unnoticed', 'answers' which, though personal, may well be of inherent value to those who share the same world of common-sense reality, a different perspective on the taken-for-granted which may lead to changed practices and must lead to heightened awareness.

The Transcripts Compared

Two of the transcripts (1 and 2) are of my own class at the beginning and end of typical days. I was interested to compare the talk at these times — the first an unprepared and relatively unstructured informal session drawing 'the class' together as they arrived and the other a planned and intentionally orderly end to an 'integrated' day.

Transcript 1, despite the frequent interruptions of children arriving, messages being received and given and parents seeking the teacher's time and attention, seems to exhibit the same sort of organization and coherence as does Transcript 2, which is pre-planned and teacher-directed. The storytime session, whilst calling for child-involvement, is dominated by the teacher's plan to tell, share and enjoy a particular story to encourage the children to find the book for themselves in subsequent free-choice time. Transcript 1 is the record of an intentionally child-centred session, but, organiza-tionally it is very similar to Transcript 2.

What of children's learning — in 'hidden curriculum' terms — as demostrated in these two transcripts? Both show a degree of order-liness, of social training, of teacher domination, that I found disturb-ing, and at the same time gratifying. Like the spokes of a wheel the conversation, wide-reaching and diverse as it became on both occa-sions, seemed to have to return to the hub for validation. Is this desirable? Is it inevitable? The first question begs a philosophical answer, the second demands action and reassessment. Is it in the nature of the school setting-in the nature of the 'normal' relationship between adults and children that this pattern appears? Is is, perhaps, a device used, unconsciously or consciously by those *with* power to retain that power?

There is, certainly, a measure of overt social control, of teaching children to become pupils that is apparent in the transcripts. In Transcript 2, utterance 48, the teacher quietens all those desiring to speak, and nominates just one — her choice. This is not questioned by the children, who accept the legitimacy of her right to do so. Speier (1976), looks more closely at the nature of adult-child con-versational interaction and the status achieved by the child in such situations. He looks at the methodic 'turn-taking' practices of any conversation, the taken-for-granted nature of dialogue, which, al-though generally unnoticed must be accomplished for a 'conver-sation' to take place. No-one notices the pattern of conversation unless one party feels unable to enter the conversation, unless the 'naturalness' breaks down.

Not all conversationalists though are accorded equal rights in conversation — some may enjoy privileges due to their social position within the group (the boss with a group of workers; Sir Robin Day on *Question Time*!) or to the nature of the conversation.

Speier quotes the privileged rights to speak accorded by the situation, place and system to the judge — in a court of law — perhaps here it is appropriate to add the teacher in the classroom, who may interrupt children's conversation, impose topics, but feels aggrieved if children attempt to do the same. Children, when engaged in conversation with adults, are in a subordinate position and have restricted conversational rights (Sacks, 1966).

Speier identifies several features of adult-child interaction which accord with the data presented here:

1   Adults can exercise their rights to enforce silence upon a child or a group of children (Transcript 2, lines 56 and 104) — even at a distance! (Transcript 3, lines 2, 4, 7, after 21).
2   Adults can exercise their right to terminate a particular aspect of the conversation (Transcript 1, line 114; Transcript 2, line 76), or to introduce their own choice of 'new' topic (Transcript 2, lines 28 and 76; Transcript 1, lines 102 and 171).

Mary Willes (1981) looks at the process by which children learn appropriate interaction strategies as they become pupils. Her particular concern was with those children who could be seen not to participate to an acceptable degree in class discussions, and her attempts to 'teach' them to do so reveal some of the processes by which 'normal' children uproblematically achieve and take on the role of pupil and come to accept their status-relationship with the teacher. She used a story book about children and their teacher, and in asking children to supply the story and dialogue, uncovered the necessity for children to be able to predict what is going to happen next in discourse, (vital for the child if his or her participation is to be appropriate) and as understanding of the situational rules of the classroom and of turntaking, so that he or she has the tools to enable his or her participation.

We take for granted the idea that if a child can and does speak before coming to school he or she will be able to participate in classroom life. We are so used to what constitutes 'normal' classroom behaviour that we rarely look at the rules that govern the orderliness which seems to be routine.

George Payne and Ted Cuff (1982) in their introduction to *Doing Teaching*, examine the nature of 'routine' and 'ordinariness', and following Sacks' point about the degree of work that the achievement of 'ordinariness' requires and paradoxically what this achievement requires for ordinary competent members of society. What is perhaps amazing is that most children of 4 or 5 also find this achievement unproblematic, and we, as teachers, spend most of our time, energy and emotion on the few who do not. We expect children to accomplish 'being ordinary pupils' with ease. It is only those who do not that cause us to pause and consider what is happening (Transcripts 1 and 2). For instance, their previous experience has done little to prepare them for their new role as one of many, yet we assume that they will quickly learn to share, to take turns, to play by the rules. Both transcripts contain direct teaching episodes (Transcript 1, lines 291–315; Transcript 2, lines 84–102). Opportunities are provided for children to display knowledge (Transcript 1, lines 139–48, Transcript 2, lines 3–6) and to recall past experiences (Transcript 1, line 75; Transcript 2, line 72).

Despite the fact that the 'subject matter' for Transcript 1 originated from the children and Transcript 2 from the teacher, remarkable similarities become apparent on closer examination. The organization of talk, power structure and competences of the parties are similar, there are control episodes and both transcripts are readily recognizable for what they are: large numbers of children in a fairly structured environment with one more powerful adult.

Transcript 3, perhaps surprisingly, also shows a great deal of control (see utterances 4 and 7). The children seem adept at turn-taking (perhaps more so than when competing for an adult's attention) and at cooperating to achieve the degree of fantasy they desire. The organization of 'parts' is taken for granted and unproblematic, and 'what-to-do-next' seems to present no difficulties as episodes follow one another and the children disregard the 'noises' of others.

After utterance 21, there is a sound of adult footsteps, the 'battleplay' calms down and the children are silent until the sound of footsteps has disappeared. Then play is resumed as though no interruption has occurred and without comment. Nevertheless, it is as though an adult were present in this transcript — in utterances 1 to 7 the teacher's authority is there without her physical presence. The children have learnt 'the rules' and have adapted their behaviour in terms of those rules.

Collaboration

The second piece of research undertaken was an attempt at outsider/ insider collaboration (for further discussion see Threadgold in this volume). Dave Hustler, a lecturer at Didsbury School of Education, and a co-member of the Didsbury based teacher-research group, was fortunate enough to receive a one-term secondment linked to his involvement in the Polytechnic's MEd (with special reference to young children) and it seemed to provide an ideal opportunity to at least briefly try out in practice some of the ideas associated with action research which seemed so appealing on paper. We envisaged a collaborative teacher-as-researcher, researcher-as-teacher project in which we could both add to our perceptions and depth of under-standing of the daily routine of *a* particular classroom.

One implication that we read into this, was that Dave had to involve himself in the classroom. He had to participate in some sense as a teacher, so that at least up to a point, he could come to share, through experience, some of the concerns of being *this particular* teacher. To operate as a detached observer was not a viable basis for collaborative action-research as we viewed it here. A second feature, we felt, is that action-research cannot be pre-planned or prestruc-tured in the way, for example, that traditional experimental pro-cedure demands. As the research develops, so ideas develop which can lead to action of some kind, which leads to more data and analysis and more ideas and so forth. Action-research as we saw it, is to do with discovering hypotheses and ideas as well as with attempting to test them out. One implication of this for our own work was that we would need to spend a lot of time discussing the research and possible next moves, as the research developed. Another implication, given our attempt at a collaborative project, was that we should monitor fairly closely our own collaboration — our own perception of the work as it developed. We monitored our collaboration in a variety of ways: for example, initial thoughts and anticipations written down separately, tape recordings of discussions and a technique whereby we interviewed each other and tape-recorded the interview.

In retrospect, I can look back upon the experience with a little detachment. Initially, my fears were numerous, overcoming the enthusiasm which thoughts and plans for this research had engen-dered. They took four distinctive avenues. The first was personal. How would I react to an ever-present adult, and one who, for much of the year, evaluates student teachers? How would my 'perfor-mance' stand up to the test? And, as Dave had been a tutor on an in-service course on which I was a student, we had exchanged views, theories, of teaching — did I, in fact, *do* what I *said I did*?

The second cluster of concerns was, perhaps, more of a problem, and one which was in fact, easier to talk through and resolve. How would the presence of an outsider affect the children? Would they react with 'difficult' behaviour, with lack of application to the tasks set — would the 'normal' life of the classroom be upset and, perhaps be difficult to retrieve? We resolved this problem with the under-standing that, should Dave's presence in the classroom lead to any major problems of this type, we would abandon our attempts at collaborative research.

The third consideration and worry was purely practical. In an already busy life, where would we both find time to discuss what we felt was emerging, a part of our joint enterprise which we both thought was central to our concept of collaboration. In fact, we managed lengthy discussions which began to clarify what we agreed were issues that we might profitably look at, and I personally found these discussions helpful and illuminating, both as an opportunity to talk to someone 'outside' the infant world about my own concerns, and to hear a 'stranger's' reactions to my daily experience.

Finally, as a member of staff at school, I could not act in isolation. Although Dave's presence would not have any direct impact on other classrooms and other teachers and children in the school, his anticipated presence inevitably provoked questions and discussion and I worried that his presence in the staffroom might be seen as a 'burden' that the staff would be called upon to carry. Colleagues were bewildered by the open-endedness of what we planned, by the relative lack of quantitative techniques, by our inability to pre-specify the 'problems' we were hoping might emerge. Nevertheless, their support and encouragement were ever present.

The anticipated problem of the staff room was resolved in much the same way as the problems of the 'stranger' in the classroom, and Dave's presence became no more noticeable than that of a frequent and familiar visitor, although I do not think that he was ever party to the most relaxed and informal 'in-house' discussion that occasionally takes place. Unlike children, adults never quite seem to 'let go' in the presence of an outsider. As time progressed, my feelings of being evaluated largely disappeared. Indeed, Dave became almost a 'fly-on-the-wall' during class time — although an increasingly useful 'fly'.

At first, I felt that I should attempt to provide 'jobs' for him, but this initial unease soon vanished and as the children began to use him as a resource, he soon became part of the classroom routine. They revelled in the luxury of two adults to whom they could go and talk, for information or for approbation. And, as Dave became more of an insider in the classroom, feelings of collaboration grew and our discussions began to move towards defining possible 'problems'.

From an initial feeling of 'being researched' an atmosphere of us both teaching and researching developed, although, of course, the balance reflected our different areas of 'expertise' and we both felt it important that my role as the class teacher must be maintained. The children, at first interested and questioning, soon accepted Dave as an integral part of 'our' classroom, and, although the tape-recorder never really ceased to provoke comment, the presence of another 'teacher' was more an added resource than an intrusion.

We were both initially concerned about the unaccustomed presence of a man in the all-female adult world of the infant school. This was never mentioned by the children and Dave managed to disguise his towering height by adopting the semi-crouching (and incidentally, back-breaking!) stance of most teachers of young children.

The research itself gradually began to focus on how children of different ages participated in the classroom, and how their activities were differentially structured by both me and the rest of the class. Tape-recordings of storytimes and news-times, as well as the morning and afternoon setting-up of activities, led to this interest, and provided the initial data on it. At half-term (in the middle of the research) a new group of children started school and entered my class and their integration into the group and into classroom activities received particular attention. Qualitative and quantitative data-gathering techniques were used, the former, for example, providing details of the way I oriented to the different age-groups within the class, and how the children identified themselves as 'oldies' and 'middles'. Dave used time-sampling to establish a picture of participation in the class oral work and a regular schematic profile displayed shifts in friendship allegiances.

The focus of this part of my research has been very much on the process, but, some of the issues can be conveyed using three examples. The first is illustrative of matters we pursued linked to the central focus of the research: the mixed-age character of the class, which is semi-vertically grouped, with children 4½ to 6 years, spending the first four-and-a-half terms of their school life with me.

It became increasingly clear to Dave that at different stages in the term, there was increased or decreased emphasis placed by the children and me on the age-groupings within the class. As half-term, and the transition of the 'oldies' to other classes approached it was noticed by Dave, and hotly disputed by me, that not only was age-status a frequent referral point, but also that I spent considerably more time with the oldest group of children although they did not form a classroom 'group'. This provoked considerable discussion mostly centred around my belief that the children were, in fact, being treated 'as individuals'.

Nevertheless, such differentiation can be seen to have served various purposes. It perhaps, provided an entry into a new status for all three groups of children: the oldest as future members of a new class, the middle group as future 'oldies' and the youngest as now competent members of the class, ready to accept and help a new group of novitiates. One matter for concern, however, was how, for one particular child, his approaching transition led to a structuring of activities which were probably inappropriate for him.

The second example is illustrative of several issues which emerged as a result of data-gathering techniques used to investigate the children's perceptions of their status in the class. They arose out of the taping of conversations with individual children and were amusing, sometimes disquieting and, on occasion, led to action. For example, a 'new' child, when asked to relate his attitudes about his class and teacher, replied that, he 'quite liked school', but, that he 'didn't like his teacher a lot'. When asked why, he said, 'because she's always telling me off'. On listening to the tape this raised a laugh, but also questions. Is it true, and, if so, why? Indeed, on reflection, this child was right: he certainly did come in for much more teacher-control than many other children. Why? At the time I identified him as 'immature' and 'excessively mobile' — he does not 'fit' the organizational pattern of the classroom, and can therefore disrupt the taken-for-granted orderliness of the classroom.

This is the sort of problem that most, if not all, teachers face daily, but we rarely start from the child's perception in defining the 'problem' and moving towards coping. Although overtly happy to come to school, and 'growing' visibly under praise, this child feels persecuted, perhaps justifiably so, and, surely, no caring teacher could ignore this issue. The realization has led to a greater awareness and an attempt (frustrating though it often is!) to reduce negative control and substitute more praise.

The third example is one of the many by-products of the research. Dave noticed fairly early in the term, that when I was writing for the children to read or underwrite, I placed myself behind them so that they saw the writing appear, letter by letter, before them, as it would appear when they wrote it themselves. This is justifiable on many grounds, but had previously occurred spon-taneously and with no prior thought. How many teaching practices are, in fact, like this? how conscious are we of the minutiae of daily life? The simple and straightforward insight into something which happens daily and the opportunity to verbalize reasons for almost unconscious activities leads one to look ever more closely at what occurs in the classroom, and to 'justify' or change it.

In conclusion, what was gained by this collaboration? Firstly, for us both, insights into a situation with which one was familiar and the other entered as a stranger. This was an illuminating experience and engendered scrutiny of the routine practices of the classroom with which, in our different ways and for different reasons we are both centrally concerned. Secondly, it was an enjoyable experience, an opportunity to collaborate and for the children, an additional adult — and a man at that! — with whom to interact. And, thirdly, through our discussions 'problems' emerged, were discussed, and clarified and added to our perception of how this particular classroom, 'my' classroom, works.

Conclusion

To return then to my original question — why classroom research at all? — Surely it is part of the professional responsibility of every teacher to attempt some assessment of what they are teaching, not only in terms of direct curriculum content, but also in terms of what has frequently been called the 'hidden' curriculum. It is common practice to prepare lesson notes and to evaluate the outcomes, be they in terms of the interest the children have shown or more tangible 'work' produced but, if *how* is at least as persuasive as *what*, we must, at last, take up the challenge of evaluating this aspect of our work.

Can such evaluation be of use to others? Is it generalizable? Is it academically respectable? To tackle the last question first, perhaps it can be dismissed as irrelevant. Is it of concern to the practitioner? If what I do speaks to me and, perhaps, to others whose daily life bears some resemblance to mine, then surely that is adequate justification for the exercise. After all, the value of any study is likely to be most felt by those most involved. So the question of academic respectability may be a problem for others — but not for me. Of what use then, are these particular strategies for classroom research? Is the notion of 'teacher-as-researcher' of use to the practitioner at the chalk face?

Self-evaluation can be frightening. Some teachers will feel that they have, through lengthy experience, 'found' the 'answers'. The less confident might perceive the whole notion as a threat, and those who vary approach and method in an attempt to follow ever-changing trends might see self-evaluation as yet another 'solution'. It requires some degree of courage and a desire to look more closely at what happens in one's classroom to overcome the initial trepidation. The threat is probably greatest to those who feel most confident in their teaching; honest evaluation of what has actually taken place may provide some surprises and disappointments — it may shake confidence. However, it cannot be denied that for any teacher it may also provide a basis for change and pointers towards greater effectiveness.

This type of self-evaluation may be valuable and enlightening, but following it does not bring easy solutions. It requires no initial change of approach, but may point the way to modifications that the individual teacher hopes will remedy perceived shortcomings. It cannot be seen as a universal panacea; it leaves the evaluation and any consequent changes to the individual. Perhaps though, such changes might better suit the individual; the 'take-up rate', so often the despair of large-scale curriculum developers might be higher than with blanket-changes in philosophy and practice imposed by White Papers or evolved in 'ivory towers'.

It is probably true that the majority of teachers look at what they are doing, judge their effectiveness and plan future strategies based on their evaluation of past successes and failures anyway. But they generally do this work almost sub-consciously, often haphazardly and most frequently unsystematically. Perhaps tape recording, transcription, discussion and evaluation might provide an answer to these criticisms.

For my own part, no major changes in practice or philosophy have resulted from this research. But I have become increasingly aware of myself as both participant and 'stranger' within the classroom. Most teachers become more consciously 'the good teacher' when an observer is present — when one becomes one's own observer, hopefully, this effect is not too diluted. I have become increasingly aware of what I say and do, and attempt, limited though this may be, to assess the children's reactions and understandings of classroom life. I feel that I have become a more thinking teacher, more 'open' to what the children experience, and more self-conscious, but also more paranoic! Self-evaluation is not for the faint-hearted!

Appendix

Transcription 1

Class: Reception and younger middle infants. Twenty-six children.
This is a transcription of twenty-three minutes of classroom talk at the
beginning of the day as children arrive, often with mothers, in the classroom.

1	C	Me cousin found this when we went for the day.
2	T	Where?
3	C	Um near Dunham Park.
4	T	Oh — who's your cousin?
5	C	Claire.
6	T	How old's Claire?
7	C	Seven.
8	T	Very good. Does she live near Dunham Park?
9	C	No.
		(approximately one minute untranscribable background chatter whilst T attends to child from another class)
10	C	Mrs Cummings.
11	T	Yes.
12	C	Watch this.
		((laughter))
13	T	Oh. Where did that come from?
14	C	A (bollin) shop.
15	T	A what shop.
16	C	A bollin shop.
17	T	What's that?
18	C	Um — uh — you — you can buy strawberries there.
19	T	Oh. Do you go and pick your own strawberries there?
	C	((shakes head))
20	T	No. Oh. Let me finish doing this writing.
21	C	( )
22	T	Right — are you ready to do a job for me? Can you go and take that ((a piece of paper)) to Mrs A or Mrs F — please //
23	C	//Can I go with her?
24	T	Yes.
25	T	Now then, what have you got here? *Buckingham Palace* by Rebecca ((reading from paper with child's drawing)) Who are these then?
26	C	Guards.
27	T	Aren't they *lovely*. Are they the guards at the palace gate.
	C	((nods))
28	T	Very nice.
29	C	Can I go and take it to Mrs H ((Head))
30	T	Not at the moment lovey because I think she's quite busy, we've got some visitors today.
31	C	( )

32	T	From America.
		((C holds up chopsticks))
33	C	Look at my chopsticks.
34	T	What are chopsticks then.
35	C	Chopsticks. Watch this.
36	T	What are they?
37	C	To eat with.
38	T	You eat with them? Well they don't look much like a kn-knife and fork to (hh) me.
		((Interruption of another teacher with changed plans for the day))
		((Ch crying))
39	T	Now what's the matter?
40	C	I bumped my knee.
41	T	Well that was a very silly thing to do — Where did you bump?
42	C	( )
		((Mother comes in asking for permission for child to come to school on his bike))
43	C	((Showing badge)) ....hospital//
44	T	// What's that now //
45	C	// mummy's hospital
46	T	((Reading)) new born infancy care unit — is that where your mummy works?
	C	((nods))
47	T	Is it? With all those new babies?
	C	((Nods))
48	T	Oh, does she?
49	C	At Park Hospital.
50	T	Well *that* doesn't say Park Hospital. That says St Mary's Hospital.
51	C	Well it *is* ( )
52	T	That's not the same hospital as Park Hospital because St Mary's is in Manchester.
		((to another child with earrings))
53	T	I see you've got your crosses on again — in your ears. I think they're lovely, those. ( ) aren't they.
54	C	( )
55	T	Now then ... let's see.
		((Child comes in from another class with party invitations))
56	T	Have you got one for me?
57	C	I forgot — ((big smile))
58	T	Have you forgotten mine?
	C	((nods and giggles))
59	T	// Ja:yne ((laughter))
		((Parent comes in to tell T about taking a child to dentist in the afternoon. Child looks reluctant to let mother go))

60	T	Morning. A nice smile. Special smile. Special smile today ((cajoling))
61	M	If she's falling asleep this afternoon, she went hiking yesterday so she's rather ( )
62	T	This afternoon?
	M	((laughter))
63	T	Right. So long as we know it's not till this afternoon we'd better work *very* hard this morning ( ) ((to child)) Try to keep awake this morning — then you're allowed to sleep this afternoon.
64	T	C'mon. See you later ((referring to mother — taking role of child)) Sit down now.
65	C	(older sister) David won't be coming to school today. He's got a tummy pain.
66	T	Oh right. Thank you for letting me know, Jenny.
67	CC	( )
68	T	Right boys and girls. Are you going to sit down? (Ch looks like crying) *Don't* start now mummy's gone — ((Ch smiles shyly)) Right. Better? — What are we going to do with you when all the new little ones start? You'll make them think they've got to cry — and that won't do at all.
69	C	My friend's coming to this school —
70	T	When?
71	C	September.
72	T	Really — who's your friend?
73	C	Karen — and Paula //
74	T	// Yes (to another child) Where do you know Karen and Paula from?
75	C	From my play school.
76	T	Oh smashing. Have you told them all about it?
	C	((Shakes head))
77	T	*No?* ((Child brings in registers))
78	T	Thank you.
79	CC	( )
80	C	My tooth started bleeding last night //
81	C	// I've got one there.
82	T	Did it? Is it going to be wobbly?
83	C	(I've got one there) //
84	C	// Yes.
85	T	Have you got one too? Oh yes it's wobbly too. Very good.
86	C	( )
87	T	Why do you think your teeth fall out?
88	C	Because we eat too much sweets.
89	T	Not *those* teeth, do they?

90	C	My daddy's got ( ) //
91	T	// Do you get new ones instead?
92	CC	( )
93	T	Yes. Why do you think those baby teeth come out?
94	CC	( )
95	T	Why do you *think* they come out?
96	C	Because they're bad.
97	T	Are they bad, though?
		((Parent comes in about asthma inhaler for child))
98	T	Hello Darren. Are you better? ((C nods)) Good. Don't forget not to go ((for inhaler)). Don't go at lunchtime for it. Right.
99	T	((Counts children on carpet)) 1, 2, 3, 4, 5, 6, 7, 8, 9, 10, 11, 12, 13, 14, 15, 16, 17, 18, 19, 20.
100	C	( )
101	T	He *should* be. Yes I wonder if he's ( ) Where was he. Where's he been ((referring to a child who's been on holiday and should be returning to school today)).
102	CC	France // France // France // Abersoch.
103	T	He's been to France on his holidays. He's not been to Abersoch.
104	C	I'm going to France //
105	C	// I've been on a boat //
106	C	// He went in his holidays — and he went he's — he's been on a boat.
107	T	Boys and girls d'you think we — boys and girls could you close your books up. D'you think we could just talk *one* at a time. Just *one* at a time — Lee, put your book away. Put them away. Put the books *away*. Sara Jane *wake* up — Put it away Lee — Kim is that your biscuit money. Well where does it — // No.
108	C	// ( ) change.
109	T	Well put it in — there's your change. Put it in your pocket.
	C	((hiccup))
110	T	Oh — hiccups — Oh.
111	T	Now I want to know about these teeth because Rebecca here says — that — your teeth go wobbly and come out because they're bad because you've had too many sweets. Is that right?
112	CC	No. // No. // No. // Yes. // No.
113	T	Lee.
114	C	Because there are new teeth growing.
115	T	Because there are *new* teeth growing. I wonder why you don't have your new teeth when you're very small then. Why don't you have the — the new teeth when you're very small. Why do you have two lots of

		teeth — Jonathan.
116	C	( ) (because — can grow — little teeth) ( )
117	T	Yes, that's right. When you get bigger your little teeth *do* get more wobbly but — why do you have to have two lots of teeth. Why don't you just start and grow your big teeth — straight away — Nicholas.
118	C	Because you haven't got a big mouth.
119	T	*Good boy.* Good thinking. Your mouth wouldn't be big enough would it for those *big* teeth. Wouldn't be big enough for *my* teeth — when you were very little //
120	C	// Little babies grow bigger and then — and then — then we're big and then they come out //
121	C	(//)
122	T	Do they. I didn't know that was what happened.
123	C	( ) baby teeth. ((Child comes in with register.))
124	T	Right, let's do the register. Mark sit down please. Timothy isn't here. Perhaps he's not — perhaps he'll be here tomorrow. ((T goes through with register and children answer names))
125	C	Nigel's always late. ((Child holds up something she's brought to school))
126	T	Well put them down. We'll look at them in a minute.
127	C	( ) ((T carries on with register))
128	C	Who's missing. Kelly, Timothy.
129	C	David.
130	T	Oh — and David, Yes. He's just coming.
131	C	( ) Mrs. Cummings.
132	T	Pardon.
133	C	( )
134	T	Yes I did too. Should be back but he might not get back till late.
135	C	I'm going to France with Jonathan Lamb.
136	T	I know, you *told* me. Aren't you lucky. ((T counts numbers for dinner))
137	T	Oh well, we'll send down what we've got. Er — Stuart — Oh Lee isn't it. Can you take it on your own, Lee.
138	C	Yes.
139	T	Can you manage it ((dinner money box and register)).
140	T	((counts dinner money envelopes)) Shouldn't there be another one — Who has dinners? //
141	C	// David.
142	C	// Alan.

143	T	No, David doesn't have dinners.
144	C	He has sandwiches.
145	C	Nigel. //
146	C	// Nigel.
147	T	Oh it's Nigel. Have I put Nigel here and he's not. Hold that a minute — go and get a pencil from over there for me will you.
148	T	( )
149	T	Here we are. Thank you.
150	C	Mrs Cummings, can we show — um —
151	T	Yes — we can — indeed. Come on. I still want to know where you got it from — Now then, I wonder what it could be ((laughter)) Don't show them yet (exciting) I wonder what it could be.
152	C	I know.
153	C	(A puppet)
154	T	Katrina.
155	C	( )
156	T	Could be.
157	C	A ( ) doll.
158	T	How d'you think you'll get to see it.
159	C	Pull it down.
160	T	What down.
161	T	Go on.
162	C	((Pulls down stick to reveal pop-up doll)) *Oh* ((Laughter))
163	T	Isn't it beautiful.
164	C	I've got one //
165	T	// Now I still want to know *where* you got it from. Tell me again.
166	C	Shop.
167	T	A shop. Can you remember what sort of shop — Because you told me once before and I didn't understand. Try again.
168	C	( )
169	T	( ) shop. Is that the name of the shop.
170	Parent	It's called the Bollin Craft Shop // ( )
171	T	Oh // Oh, I see. Very ( ) isn't she //
172	C	(going round)
173	C	dances
174	T	She dances doesn't she ((T makes doll dance)) *Oh* ((laughter)) Isn't she beautiful //
175	C	// I've got one.
176	T	Have you //
177	C	( ) //
178	T	// Look what happens to her — pigtails — There you

		are. Are you going to keep the paper bag to keep her safe — Now what's this Laura?
179	C	Feather.
180	T	Feather. Where did you find your feather.
181	C	(Dunham Park)
182	T	Oh. Is it from one of the ducks there — d'you think. Where did you find it?
183	C	On the ( )
184	T	*Could* it be a duck feather d'you think.
185	CC	No.
186	T	No. Very clever things feathers you know. Push them the right way they all stick together — can open them out, but if you push them back again — push them back again they all — stick together again. Really very clever. It's lovely that. If you put it on the half hexagon table in the other room — for people to look at — and to feel — and to be — *gentle* with 'cos it feels beautiful and silky — //
187	C	( )
188	T	Did she really. Oh — I can't imagine that. Go on, off you go. Now what's this. It's very small. Couldn't you find a bigger one.
	C	((shakes head)) ((child shows huge whistle))
189	T	No. Why did you buy such a small whistle.
190	C	Got it from a party.
191	T	Whose party?
192	C	Er — can't remember now.
193	T	Have you had it a long time?
	C	((shakes head))
194	T	D'you think it's a very small whistle?
195	CC	No.
196	T	It's *huge* isn't it?
197	C	I know it //
198	C	(Blow it)
199	T	That'll be a good idea. Go on.
	C	((blows whistle)) ((laughter))
200	T	Go on ((blows again))
201	T	Oh it's not got a very big noise. I wonder if you can — find out — during the day — What makes it make the noise. You'll have to blow it and somebody else'll have to look down that little hole —
202	C	( )
203	T	Don't think so Paul.
204	C	Ball //
205	T	Don't think so //
206	C	Ball //
207	T	There's a little ball in there. But have you seen what

		the little ball does when you blow it?
208	CC	No.
209	T	Well you'll have to have a try during the day. Go and put it on the half hexagon table.
210	C	( )
211	T	Don't *tell* them, then. They've to find out for them-selves. What have you got there Kim — What's that?
212	C	( )
213	T	It's from Jane. What is it?
214	C	( )
215	T	Just a minute. I want to know if Kim knows what it is because it says — *Kim* on it. What is it Kim — what *is* it?
	C	((nod head))
216	T	It's not a nod of your head is it? What's inside here — what's inside — what's this?
217	C	( )
218	T	Pardon.
219	C	Going to Jayne's party.
220	T	You're going to Jayne's party — what's this called then — what's it called when somebody asks you to their party — what's it called — Paula.
221	C	A invit- invitation.
222	T	An *invitation*, yes. Jayne is *inviting* you to her party — on the seventeenth — I think it's on Friday — after school. Can you read what it says. Come here. ((Child brings invitation to T))
223	T	((reading)) Dear
224	T+C	Kim.
225	T	Here's an invitation — at 1 Delamere Road. Date seventeenth of the seventh — that's July // ((Child brings letter into classroom))
226	T	Thank you. Oh for Adrian in class 6 — 1981 time four o'clock till 6 o'clock from Jayne please — let — me — know — if — you — are — coming. Very good. ((Child enters late with mother and dinner money))
227	Mother	Sorry we're late but I had to ( )
228	T	Could you take it up to the other end because it's gone ( ) //
229	Mother	Where shall I take it to?
230	T	Up to the — to the office to Mrs Spencer please. OK Thank you. Thank you.
231	T	There you are ((handing invitation back)) Have you — have you got a *coat* with you today?
	C	((nods))
232	T	Well go and pop it in your coat pocket. And that's for Adrian — Er Carolyn come and get this lovey.
233	C	( )

234	T	Oh you have. Just — sit down with it for a minute Carolyn cause Rebecca's got something to show ( ) her little box. She's been working very hard this weekend haven't you. I wonder who can tell us what this might be a picture of
235	CC	Castle.
236	T	No.
237	C	It's Buckingham Palace.
238	T	Buckingham Palace — and — What's this?
239	CC	Guard
240	T	The Guardsman.
241	C	Been there.
242	T	And what have you written up here then Rebecca.
243	C	*Buckingham Palace.*
244	T	*Buckingham Palace* by Rebecca Robinson. Have you seen a picture of Buckingham Palace? — When are you going to see pictures of Buckingham Palace? — When do you think you'll see them? — Who can think when they're going to see pictures of Buckingham Palace? Lee
245	C	When it's the Wedding.
246	T	When it's the Wedding. Where will you see the pictures then.
247	CC	On tele // On the tele.
248	T	On the television for the Royal Wedding won't you //
249	C	I've been there.
250	T	Tell me what Lady Diana's going to go to her Wedding in.
251	C	Coach //
252	C	Silver — silver coach.
253	T	I think it's a *golden* coach actually.
254	C	It's silver.
255	T	Is it. Well you'll have to watch and see. She not going in an *ordinary* car is she.
256	C	Mrs Cummings.
257	T	Yes.
258	C	I might be in France then.
259	T	Might you. I expect they'll have it on the tele even in France.
260	C	( ) Prince Charles in the middle
261	T	You're going to —
262	C	Wear when I go — wearing Prince Charles tee shirt in the middle of France.
263	T	Oh you'll have to. Yes. And I think you'd better take a flag //
264	C	And my — and my brother's got one the same as me.
265	T	Has he. Good. Well everybody'll know where you

		come from won't they.
		Yes love.
266	C	They haven't seen my chopsticks.
267	T	They haven't. Right Rebecca. You pop and sit down with that thank you.
		Now, Lee's brought these sticks. Say's they're chopsticks.
268	C	They *are* — chopsticks.
269	T	Told *me* they were to eat with and I said they don't look like a knife and they *don't* look like a fork and they *don't* look like a spoon so I don't know how you can eat with *those*.
270	CC	I know // I do // I know.
271	T	Do you. Well — just a minute just a minute lets — let Lee show you how you eat with them. Can you do it —
272	C	I don't know.
273	T	You don't know. It's not easy is it.
274	C	( )
275	T	You have — yes.
276	C	( )
277	T	For spaghetti. Well. I don't think it's quite spaghetti 'cos where does spaghetti come from? — where do they eat lots and lots of spaghetti? — Elizabeth.
278	C	Italy.
279	T	Italy. Are chopsticks from Italy?
280	C	Yes.
281	T	Are they?
282	C	Yes. I've seen //
283	T	// Is that Italian writing up here?
284	C	I can't read it.
285	T	You can't read it. No. That *is* writing. D'you know where chopsticks are used?
286	C	No.
287	C	China.
288	T	*China*. Yes, that's a long way from Italy and that's Chinese writing up there — Very hard to understand.
289	C	( ) brought them back.
290	T	Who did?
291	C	(Jim big)
292	T	Who's (Jim big)
293	C	One of my daddy's cousins.
294	T	And where did he come from?
295	C	(Australia)
296	T	Well that doesn't sound like England does it.
297	C	No.
298	T	Or even Italy. You'll have to find out *where* he comes from and find out all about it //
299	C	( ) a big bag of sweets.

300	T	Did you.
301	C	Yes special ones.
302	C	Yea — No.
303	T	No.
304	C	( )
305	T	Who's been to eat Chinese food — in a Chinese restaurant —
	C	((puts hand up))
306	T	Now then Kelly, d'you have spaghetti in Chinese restaurants? — can you remember? — because I'm still not clear what you eat with these and *I* don't think it's spaghetti — Daniel.
307	C	You have rice with them.
308	T	You *do* have rice — yes. Is it rice you meant?
	C	((nods))
309	T	Yes. D'you //
310	C	// I don't like that rice.
311	T	You don't like that rice but it's usually rice and meat and things and they're *very* hard to use. You have to keep them like that and try and move them together to pi- very hard to pick up little bits of rice with *those*.
312	C	I've got chopsticks at home.
313	T	Have you?
314	CC	And I have ( )
315	T	They're very smart. Thank you for bringing them. They're lovely. And Nicholas brought us something — also something lovely. What have you brought us Nicholas?
316	C	(Flowers)
317	T	What sort of flowers?
318	C	Roses.
319	T	Roses. Where're the roses from?
320	C	In my garden.
321	T	Have you got lots and lots in your garden?
322	C	((nods)) I've got loads of them.
323	T	They smell very delicate those roses.
324	C	*I've* got loads of them.
325	T	Um. Some roses have a very *strong* smell. Nicholas' roses you really have to smell very hard — they're a very *delicate* smell — now what are these, these aren't roses.
326	C	Cos they — they were — they were — I went walking into Derbyshire on Saturday — and we went — we went to see Michael and went to — wanted a walk ( )
327	T	Mark and Da- and Nigel stop it //
328	C	// And we found those grasses.
329	T	These *grasses*, that's what they *are* all sorts of beautiful grasses — they're lovely — unfortunately I don't

know very much about grasses, I think these look like wild oats, these very fuzzy ones — they feel lovely, very sort of spiky and rough feeling —
((Bell for assembly rings))
So we'll put them in a vase later on — and you can feel them yourselves — what *are* the little bobbles on um — on the grasses — now you should know by now — are they the flowers?

330	CC	No.
331	T	What are they? — Elizabeth.
332	C	Seeds.
333	T	They're the *seeds* aren't they. When will they start to fall off the grasses?
334	C	Autumn.
335	T	*Autumn*-time yes when they are — what's the word? When they are r-
336	C	Ripe.
337	T	Ripe. Very good. When they're ripe in the Autumn-time they'll fall off — and they'll stay — on the ground or under the ground till the —
338	CC	Spring.
339	T	Spring. Good. And then what do they do?
340	CC	Grow // They start growing.
341	T	They start to grow — Now, boys and girls, that was the bell for assembly so can you stand up *very* very quietly and go and make a line by *that* door. ((Children line up to leave the classroom))

Transcription 2

Class:		Reception and younger middle infants Twenty-seven children
Situation:		Large, bright classroom. Children on carpet, teacher on chair.
Choice of story:		A new set of class books had arrived for the children's free use. After a few days, I felt that we should look at them together.

1	T	Right. Let's have a look at this book — 'cause these are — smashing books. Are you enjoying them?
2	CC	Yes // Yes // Yes.
3	T	What's it called this one? Can anybody tell me?
4	CC	Splosh // ·
5	C	// Splish //
6	CC	// Splosh
7	T	Splosh not splish. It's got an 'o' in the middle. Splosh.
8	CC	Splish splosh //
9	C	// Splosh.

10	T	Splosh it says. ((Reading)) A dog, a pig, a cow, a bear, a monkey, a donkey, all in the —
11	T & CC	Air
12	T	((Showing pictures)) There's the dog and the pig and the cow and the bear and the monkey and the donkey all in the air. What are they in the air in?
13	CC	( ) //
14	T	// Put your hand up if you know. Vicky. ((Buzz of children trying to get in))
15	C	The cow's popped it //
16	Vicky	// A hot air balloon.
17	T	A hot air balloon.
18	C (as 15)	The cow's popped it.
19	T	What's the cow popped it with?
20	CC	Horn // horn // ear // horn // his horn.
21	T	His horn — it's not his *ear* is it — his ears //
22	CC	((laughing)) //
23	T	are down here. It's his horn that's sticking up.
24	CC	((laughing))
25	T	What does this mean then? ((showing stylized drawing of air escaping))
26	C	Air's coming out //
27	C	// Air
28	T	The air coming out of the balloon isn't it. Can you *really* see the air coming out of a balloon?
29	CC	No. No. No.
30	T	No — very often in cartoons it looks like that doesn't it.
31	C	I can see gas coming out of my mouth when I ( ) on the windows.
32	T	*When* can you see it.
33	C	When its steamed up.
34	T	Yes. And if //
35	C	// When its cold.
36	T	When its cold. When you hhh //
37	C	// When your breath — when your breath turns over and it steams on the — steams on the window.
38	T	Yes //
39	C	And it //
40	T	But only when its —
41	CC	Cold.
42	T	Cold. Only when its cold. Yes.
43	C	I saw a airship.
44	T	Did you. When? Where?
45	C	On the park.
46	T	Really.
47	CC	I have // I saw // Mrs Cummings
48	T	Shh — Yes, Luke.
49	Luke	When we — when the airship was- aft- when it was

finished and the Pope was on we took the telly outside —
and — we took the telly outside — and — and we saw —
we saw the good old airship.

50	T	Did you.
51	Luke	An air balloon as well.
52	T	It's not good *old* airship — it's good*year* — the good*year* airship.
53	CC	Goodyear // Mrs Cummings
54	T	Goodyear. Yes.
55	C	I seed the airship.

((Many children talking at once))

56	T	Just a moment because I can't hear Luke because other people are chattering. You'll have a turn in a minute.
57	Luke	I said Mummy, what's that thing with the 'X' on the back and she didn't answer me but when I ( ) it off ( ) an air balloon.
58	T	Yes. It was an airship. Yes. Actually I think we saw it at school one day last summer, didn't we.
59	CC	Yes.
60	T	We all went outside and had a look at it. It was going through the sky.
61	CC	( ) //
62	Luke	Mrs Cummings //
63	C	( )
64	T	U u h m — Ben
65	Ben	I remember that time when it came ( ) over the school.
66	T	Did you. Y-//
67	Ben	// ( ) the same one came over my house when I went home.
68	T	Yes. Paul.
69	Paul	I went to a airship where they did //
70	Luke	// It flew over my house ( ) //
71	T	// Just a moment Paul because Luke is now interrupting. We listened to him very carefully. Now it's his turn to listen to us.
72	Paul	I went to see a airship where they take off and when I —when I got there I saw ( ) going around.
73	T	Oh ... What keeps an airship up in the air?
74	CC	Air // air // gas //
75	Luke	Mrs Cummings.
76	T	Air or gas. Yes. If its air, its got to be *hot* air to keep it up — or gas. Now put your hands down for a minute and we'll have a look at the rest of the book.

((Reading)) Help said Pig. There he is saying help.
((There is a cartoon-like 'bubble' from his mouth with 'help' written in))
Help said —

| 77 | CC | Monkey |

78	T	Help said donkey. It's gone wonky.
79	CC	h-h-h ((untranscribable talk from several children))
80	T	Looks as though it had gone wonky once before. What makes me say that?
81	C	Because — because there's — something on the balloon.
82	T	Mmm. There's already a patch on it isn't there to cover up a hole — ((reading)) A bear, a cow, a pig, a dog, a donkey and a monkey *all — in — a* — and this is the word you got wrong before — all in a —
83	C	Bog
84	T	Bog — Who said it said dog at the end and it shouldn't?
85	James	Me.
86	T	*James!* James, what does it start with
87	James	'b' for bog.
88	T	'b'. It only goes to show how important it is to get them the right way round //
89	C	// Toilet
90	T	No. I don't think it means toilet.
91	CC	((Laughter))
92	T	I don't think they're in a toilet.
93	CC	((laughter))
94	T	What's a bog when it isn't a toilet?
95	Gavin	My brother calls it the bog.
96	T	Yes. Lots of people do — call a toilet a bog but I don't think that's what this means.
97	Paul	(fall in) something when — when it sticks to you.
98	T	Yes, you're quite right Paul. It's somewhere that's very sticky. If you fall in its very sticky //
99	C	( )
100	T	It's not glue
101	C	It's called a swamp.
102	T	Swamp is another word for it, good boy — but it's not glue, it's usually mud or somewhere. It's usually somewhere — somewhere in the countryside that's very wet. ((Many children talking))
103	C	Mrs Cummings what ( )
104	T	Just a moment you are forgetting to listen. You *are* remembering to think and to talk but you're forgetting to listen and take your turn. Now Olga
105	Olga	Once my daddy —

Transcription 3

Situation: Four children playing unsupervised in the corridor.

| 1 | | I'll tell |
| 2 | | I'll tell Mrs A that you're making a noise |

3	OK — I'll toss you ((sounds like a USA gangster inter-change)) (Aggressive noises)
4	We're making too much noise
5	(Child making gun firing noises)
6	Eeeah! you going to get ( ) ((Sounds like the soundtrack of Bugsy Malone))
7	We're going to get sent back to the classroom if we're not quiet
8	I see a planet
9	What, here?
10	Yeah a planet
11	It's two hours ( ) its two hours away
12	That space rocket. Look, its going fast
13	The space rocket
14	We're going two miles an hour now
15	A space rocket is faster //
16	( ) quick
17	( ) a race how
18	C'mon. You look up //
19	I can see it. I'll shoot it ((shooting noises continue through next utterances))
20	Get out
21	(Where would a planet do)

((Noise of adult footsteps. 'Battle' calms down a little and children don't speak until adult footsteps have gone))

(5 minutes later)

22	You could
23	Think about the ( )
24	I don't think
25	There's sixteen planets ahead
26	Yeah which ones ( )
27	Jupiter, Saturn
28	You count them when I say them
29	OK
30	( )
31	One
32	Jupiter
33	Two
34	Ee'er Uranus
35	Three
36	Then it's — Mercury
37	Mercury — Yes
38	The Sun
39	Five
40	There is Neptune
41	( )
42	Neptune, Pluto, Uranus

43	Eight
44	ET's planet
45	Nine
46	Er um um um um the coloured planet
47	The coloured planet Ten
48	Alpha (Tudor)
49	Eleven
50	The planet of colours.
51	Thir . . . Twelve
52	The planet of creatures
53	Thirteen
54	Two-headed monsters . . . and, er, secret planet
55	Secret planet! (with excitement)
56	That's not a planet
57	That's sixteen . . . and the last one is ( )
58	The space ships going to take off now ((followed by organization of take off, planning etc). ET becomes highly involved, much gunfighting.

References

BARKER-LUNN, J.C. (1970) *Streaming in the Primary School*, Slough, NFER.

DELAMONT, S. (1983) *Interaction in the Classroom*, London, Methuen.

DELAMONT, S. and HAMILTON, D. (1976) *Explorations in Classroom Observation*, Chichester, Wiley.

DOUGLAS, J.W.B. (1964) *The Home and the School*, London, MacGibbon and Kee.

GALTON, M., SIMON, B. and CROLL, P. (1980) *Inside the Primary Classroom* London, Routledge and Kegan Paul.

HALSEY, A.H., FLOUD, J. and ANDERSON, C.A. (Eds) (1961) *Education, Economy and Society*, New York, Free Press.

HOYLE, E. (1972) 'Educational innovation and the role of the teacher', *Forum*, 14.

MEDLEY, D.M. and MITZEL, H.E. (1963) 'Measuring classroom behaviour by systematic observation', in GAGE, N.L. (Ed.) *Handbook of Research on Teaching*, New York, Rand McNally.

NIXON, J. (Ed.) (1981) *A Teachers' Guide to Action Research*, London, Grant McIntyre.

PAYNE, G.C.F. and CUFF, E.C. (Eds) (1982) *Doing Teaching*, London, Batsford.

SACKS, H. (1966) UCLA Lectures No. 2.

SCHUTZ, A. (1971) 'The stranger', in COSIN, B.R., DALE, I.R., ESLAND, G.M., MACKINNON, D. and SWIFT, D.F. (Eds) *School and Society*, London, Routledge and Kegan Paul.

SPEIER, M. (1976) 'The child as conversationalist: some culture contact features of conversational interaction between adults and children', in

HAMMERSLEY, M. and WOODS, P. (Eds) *The Process of Schooling*, London, Routledge and Kegan Paul.

STENHOUSE, L. (1975) *An Introduction to Curriculum Research and Development*, London, Heinemann.

WILLES, M. (1981) 'Learning to take part in classroom interaction', in FRENCH, P. and McLURE, M. (Eds) *Adult-Child Conversation*, London, Croom Helm.

12   Bridging the Gap Between Teachers and Researchers

Margaret W. Threadgold

There is frequently a gulf between theorists and practitioners in any sphere of work. This probably results from suspicion on the part of the practitioners that theorists are out of touch with the everyday reality of a situation and an assumption on the part of the theorists that the practitioners are incapable of seeing general trends and patterns while immersed in the detail of specific events.

In educational studies I am aware that the relationships between those concerned with educational research on the one hand and teachers on the other, has been subject to these difficulties. There has been a significant problem of communication between the two which has resulted in teachers often ignoring relevant research or regarding the findings with cynicism. From the teacher's point of view, researchers often focus their attention upon irrelevant or inappropriate issues.

In this chapter I intend to examine the use of qualitative studies in schools within the context of the relationship between teachers and researchers. At the outset, however, I must emphasize that I am expressing views and recording observations from the standpoint of a teacher.

Clearly, the relationship between teachers and researchers is complex. Teachers are concerned primarily with the practical aspects of education, whether it be interaction within the classroom or management of an institution. It is my experience that their expectation of research is that it should address itself to matters which inform and refine practice: frequently this expectation is not met. Within this chapter I shall, therefore, attempt to establish some of the reasons for what has been referred to as this apparent 'lack of fit between research and practice' (Walker, 1980, p. 41) by examining the nature of educational research and the issues with which it has concerned itself. Secondly, I shall look at the development of qualitative studies which appear to focus upon issues and problems that are part of the day to day process of education and schooling and, therefore, have relevance for teachers. Finally, I shall examine the means whereby teachers can involve themselves in the definition of research problems and work with researchers in their investigations, and discuss whether or not such collaboration would be the most effective means of bridging the gap which currently exists.

The Nature of the Problem

Whilst the problem of communication between teachers and researchers is a significant factor in creating a gulf between the two, it would be too simplistic to regard it as the only difficulty. The fundamental issues are rather to do with questions concerning who should nominate or define potential areas of research and why, together with questions about the audiences to whom the findings are addressed.

These questions are a component of what Andy Hargreaves refers to as the micro-macro problem in the sociology of education (see Hargreaves in this volume). He expresses it in terms of research being segregated into 'studies of the schools and studies of the system', the former being typified by small-scale projects focusing, for example, upon interaction between teacher and pupil and the latter concerned with 'grand theoretical explanations of the relationship between schooling and society'. Hargreaves' analysis of the link between theory and evidence as one interpretation of the micro-macro problem has application to the connection between the teacher and the researcher; the teacher as the practitioner being involved with the evidence which should interact closely with the theoretical knowledge and 'macro' perspective of the researcher.

From the teacher's standpoint, the researcher frequently operates outside of, and in isolation from, the mainstream of educational practice, the school. Even when researchers are working within schools, carrying out case studies or ethnographic work, they are often defining their own problems with an audience of fellow researchers rather than teachers in mind. For example, David Hargreaves in his preface to *Social Relations in a Secondary School* (1967) states that the research on which his book was based was part of a project whose aim was 'to provide an analysis of the school as a dynamic system of social relations through an intensive study of interaction processes and day-to-day behaviour within my school'. Such aims would seem to contain little space for teachers' interests.

This view has been discussed on several occasions. For example, in 1965 a conference concerned with 'Educational Research and the Teacher' expressed the view that much research was not meeting the needs of teachers (Van der Eyken, 1965). Fifteen years later it would seem that little progress has been made. Walker (1980) and McCutcheon (1981, p. 188) raise similar points concerning the origin of the subjects of research, the audience to which findings are directed and the purpose behind the choice of both. Perhaps, historically, part of the explanation as to why such a state of affairs has come about is related to Young's expression of Seeley's (1966) distinction between the 'making' and 'taking' of problems (Young, 1971, p. 1). Young discusses the distinction in the context of research concerned with the class determinants of educational opportunity, which raised significant questions about selection but did not treat as problematic such matters as the organization of knowledge. The sociologist took what appeared to be the educator's problems, interpreting them as concerned with the system, rather than looking beyond such an explanation to what may be giving rise to the problems, that being practice within the institution: an analysis relating to Hargreaves' 'micromacro' problem.

Traditionally, research has been based in institutions of higher education or commissioned from research groups such as those based at the National Foundation for Educational Research. The process has carried with it overtones of academic elitism which have reinforced the division between researcher and practitioner and introduced feelings of threat. On the occasions when teachers have been involved in field work it has been frequently in a menial capacity and often the courtesy of communicating the findings of the project has not been paid (Van der Eyken, 1965, p. 9). It is not surprising, therefore, that attitudes of cynicism and impatience have developed.

Among the criticisms that teachers often make of research and researchers in sociology and education are those that refer to researchers as people living in ivory towers, discussing theory detached from reality in a language understood only by themselves. Frequently, it is also stated that few researchers have practical experience of teaching and are, therefore, not qualified to comment upon the processes and practices involved in a manner that commands the respect of the community of practitioners. Altogether, such criticisms are not indicative of a desire on the part of teachers to engage in a dialogue with educational researchers.

Until the early 1970s much educational research was concerned with the 'taking' of problems and had often been carried out in isolation from schools. Moreover, the researchers were working within disciplines distinct from education, such as sociology and psychology and appeared to be using education as a vehicle to discuss issues that were of central concern in their discipline. For example, much of the work conducted by sociologists was closely linked to studies of social class and debates in their discipline concerned more broadly with social inequality. Important though the work of such people as Floud, Halsey and Martin (1957) and Douglas (1964) may be for education, they are not concerned with areas of research generated from inside schools nor of immediate interest to teachers. Whilst teachers could read about cultural deprivation, for example, or the linguistic handicaps of working class children together with their subsequent impaired performance in school (Bernstein, 1971), there appears to have been little collaboration between teachers and researchers in identifying the problems within the classroom and developing compensatory programmes in an attempt to minimize the disadvantages experienced by some children. That is not to ignore the fact that compensatory programmes were developed, nor to ignore the fact that some teachers did use the findings of Bernstein to legitimate their own common sense knowledge despite the fact that he stated that he did not have sufficient evidence to make recommendations to teachers (Bernstein, 1971, p. 19). In each case, however, programmes were devized by practitioners following the researchers' accounts of their findings rather than by the two working together; a situation which potentially could have produced greater and more effective benefits.

Not only did the researchers originate from such disciplines as sociology and psychology but the language which they employed was peculiar to their own subject and, at best, unfamiliar to the majority of teachers. All subjects generate their own technical language, and their own analytical concepts which are understood by their adherents. To those outside, however, who are not fluent in this language, it can be regarded as a protective shell, creating an obstacle which the teacher has not the time nor the inclination to surmount. Teachers' impatience with technical language is recognized by David Hargreaves in his preface to *The Challenge for the Comprehensive School* (1982). He acknowledges the difficulty of writing for different audiences and states that on this occasion he is writing particularly for teachers.

Whilst increasingly some sociologists who have published research in the field of education have had the experience of teaching, the conceptual frameworks of their studies have tended still to be those of their own discipline. Broadly speaking, the focus of their studies has been the social processes within the social system of the school. David Hargreaves (1967) explores the development of two opposing sub-cultures in Lumley Secondary Modern School by focusing on the structure of informal groups of pupils and the influence of such groups on the educative process. He comments that the two sub-cultures persist, year after year because the system within the school remains unchanged, thus drawing attention again to the fact that it is the nature of the processes and procedures within the school which should be regarded as problematic. Colin Lacey, in his study of the performance of working class boys in grammar schools, (Lacey, 1970) uses the concepts 'differentiation' and 'polarization' in relation to the development of the 'pro-school' and 'anti-school' group sub-cultures. He demonstrated how, at the time when he was carrying out his research, these two sub-cultures were associated with class differentiation and further influenced by the attitudes of working-class 'scholars' and middle-class 'fee payers'.

Both the study of Lacey and that of Hargreaves have implications for the way in which the academic and social groupings within a school should be structured. They also shed light upon the unintentional outcomes of the way in which teachers approach their pupils. Neither of these matters, however, are of immediate concern to the teacher in the classroom. The former may be of interest to those senior staff reviewing the academic organization of the school and the latter should be of interest to all teachers. Teachers, however, are extremely defensive about criticism implied or expressed, and I suggest that only the minority of particularly self-critical teachers would be able to recognize something of themselves in the teachers portrayed.

Whilst such studies are valuable, more recent work such as Ball's study of Beachside Comprehensive (Ball, 1981) and that by Burgess of a Roman Catholic comprehensive school (Burgess, 1983) can be seen more easily to be of direct relevance to practising teachers and hence more readily used. At the outset, from their titles, the potential reader is aware that the studies are set in the context of today's reality, the comprehensive school, not that of the erstwhile system of grammar and secondary modern schools. Thus, the appeal is immediate. Secondly, whilst dealing with overarching concepts, such as innovation in the case of Ball, and, in the case of Burgess the way in which teachers and pupils define and redefine situations, the level of focus is such that the educational processes and procedures are documented in a depth of detail which produces an image recognizable to the teacher. Thirdly, the degree to which both authors interact with the teachers in the studies themselves, lends significant credibility to their work.

Each of these authors implies that their findings are relevant to school organization. As a Headteacher and previously as a Deputy Headteacher, I find their work illuminating and particularly helpful, firstly by providing a different perspective from that of the person initiating the innovation and secondly, by providing additional data against which decisions about organization and curriculum may be made. For example, in Ball's account of the management of the change from banded to mixed ability teaching groups at Beachside I recognize the three categories of perspective held by the teachers; the academic, the disciplinarian and the idealist. Having experienced this change in two very different schools, the three perspectives were visible, only the proportion of the staff committed to each differed. Had I been able to analyze the reactions of staff in this way whilst being involved in these changes I may have been helped, firstly, by having the support of knowing that these reactions were typical and secondly, by being prepared for such attitudes, I may have been able to develop better strategies for dealing with them. For example, whilst considering the introduction of mixed ability grouping in a school where pupils were being taught in streamed classes, I was aware that several staff were expressing support for the change because they thought that it would break up the groups of lower ability pupils which they found difficult to teach. In my view, this support was being offered for the wrong reason and I felt sure that these teachers would be those least able to organize learning for mixed ability groups. I considered that while such attitudes were in evidence it would be unwise to go ahead with the innovation. After further thought, however, I began to introduce the change and in some cases initially, my worst fears were realized. Fortunately, however, the situation did not remain so negative. Many of these teachers were encouraged by what they perceived to be 'improved behaviour' on the part of pupils who previously, as part of a large lower streamed group, had been extremely disruptive. They became gradually more interested in the learning difficulties of their pupils and eventually began to organize their lessons around learning rather than teaching. Had I delayed the introduction of mixed-ability grouping on account of these 'disciplinarians' I may not have initiated the change at all. Having read Beachside after implementing the change, I was aware, retrospectively, that the study could have provided an extremely useful reference against which I could have compared my own situation.

Schools, and in particular, classrooms, are extremely private places in that it is unfortunately rare for teachers in the normal course of events to spend any significant period of time either working alongside or observing other teachers in their work. Consequently, they are unable to experience the practices and processes of another establishment and bring such experience to bear upon an evaluation of their own work. Both the studies of Ball and Burgess provide the opportunity for teachers to look, as it were, inside another school and apply the observations of the authors to their own situation. Burgess's work is particularly interesting from the point of view of the headteacher in the way it exposes the manner in which policies formulated by the headmaster are not always carried through by the appropriate staff. Although Burgess does not suggest that strategies for monitoring the implementation of policy should have been initiated by the headteacher, the inference is there for the reader to take.

The studies by Ball and Burgess have significance not only for those teachers involved largely with organizational matters but also for the teacher in the classroom. If researchers wish their work to be applied within education and have relevance for teachers it is vitally important that more consideration should be given to the matter of accessibility and perceived relevance. I would suggest that Burgess's study *Experiencing Comprehensive Education* (1983) is accessible to teachers in that both the language and concepts it employs are readily understood by teachers and are part of their experience. Similarly, Ball's study, which deals with school and classroom practice in relation to the central issue, has credibility in the eyes of teachers because it deals in detail with matters which are easily recognizable and which are continuing subjects of discussion for teachers. In contrast, I would argue that Woods' study *The Divided School* (1979) is too obviously rooted in sociological theory to be of significant value to teachers. Its analytical structure together with its use of complex technical language produces an almost insurmountable barrier to the uninitiated at the outset. Perhaps, as I shall argue later in this chapter, the practitioners themselves should be more closely involved in defining the problems which are directly relevant to their work and which would benefit from extended study.

Margaret W. Threadgold

Methods of Investigation

Closely allied to the field of enquiry selected by researchers are the research methods employed. Nixon (1981) asserts that the real problem with reference to teachers and researchers is not inadequacy on the part of either group but the inappropriateness of the research method frequently applied to education (p. 195). Until relatively recently emphasis has tended to be placed upon measurement in education rather than an exploration of the processes and interactions within schools and classrooms. Consequently, the subjects of educational research have tended to be those which lend themselves to quantification. Nixon states that:

> The need for a research tradition which measures qualitatively rather than quantitatively, which explores specific instances rather than generalities, and which treats as at least problematical the supposed 'objectivity' of the researcher is now widely acknowledged. (p. 195)

He maintains, however, that the development of such a tradition is only likely to emerge if teachers are positively involved in the research process.

Some criticism of the traditional quantitative model is also made by Nisbet (1980) who sets out a 'spectrum' of research methods, expressing aspects of the agricultural model, which he refers to as 'Experiments to improve your products by manipulating treatments' to the anthropological model which he describes as 'Go and live there and see what it is like' (p. 3). Within this framework Nisbet identifies five stages or methods, ranging from experimental, exploratory survey, through curriculum development and action research to open-minded enquiry. Nisbet suggests that the best researcher will not use one of these methods to the exclusion of others, but that each has strengths which can contribute to more effective research in education. This point also emerges from Burgess's (1982) detailed discussion of the use of a range of research methods in relation to field research (pp. 163–7).

Increasingly, however, some educational researchers are using the medium of ethnographic study for their work. These researchers are not so much interested in aspects of 'the system' but are concerned rather with actors' meanings and behaviours. As a result of this the appropriate research methods employed by ethnographers include participant observation and unstructured interviews, which involve a close relationship with teachers and pupils. Such situations enable researchers to become better acquainted with the concerns of teachers and also creates a context within which teachers begin to appreciate the benefits which may accrue from such an involvement.

The development of a closer relationship between the researcher and the practitioner is seen by Walker (1980) as a possible conse-quence of adopting a democratic approach to research (pp. 11–12). In turn, MacDonald defines three types of evaluation: bureaucratic, autocratic and democratic: the key concepts of the latter being confidentiality, negotiation and accessibility. Walker (1980) argues that the democratic approach facilitates the accessibility of the method of research to practitioners and creates the opportunity for them to acquire skills, which will allow them to continue the work themselves (p. 43). He also maintains that this involvement of practitioners could result in a shift in emphasis from the concerns and problems of researchers to those of practitioners thus echoing the concept of the 'taking' and 'making' of problems.

In practice, however, what does happen to the dialogue between the teacher and researcher once the study has been completed? Do teachers make use of the techniques observed, the contacts made or the findings of the research to evaluate their own teaching or the workings of their schools?

Teachers and Research

From Stephen Ball's account in 'Beachside reconsidered' (1984) it would appear that some teachers did involve themselves with his work, reading and commenting upon the papers produced during the course of the study. One teacher was 'always keen to discuss research methods' and another became involved in some teacher training work. These teachers were, however, those who had identified themselves as Ball's informants and, therefore, one would assume, were teachers with some interest which predisposed them towards his work. Others, however, were unable to accept the aims of the study or to understand the fact that Ball was not addressing individual teachers but issues and principles through them. His account of two seminars held to obtain feedback from staff on two chapters of his study illustrate this clearly (pp. 84–9).

The inability of teachers to relate to overarching issues is one which I experienced during the course of a study which I undertook. This was devoted to an investigation of the response from teachers and schools to demands for accountability through the process of school evaluation (Threadgold, 1982). The purpose of this project was to look closely at how individual teachers within one school were responding to the current demands for accountability. I chose to look at the school in which I was working as a Deputy Headteacher and which I was about to leave. In the course of the study I interviewed a sample of staff from each level of the organizational hierarchy. Out of a total staff of eighty-eight, the sample included the following: The Headteacher, one out of two Deputy Headteachers, two out of three Heads of School, two out of six Year Heads, four out of thirteen Heads of Departments, four assistant teachers (scale 2) and four assistant teachers (scale 1). Part of the study involved questioning some staff about the extent to which they were familiar with literature concerned with self-assessment and school-based evaluation. I found that few of them, apart from those in the most senior posts, had either read articles in journals or books on the subject. In answer to the question: What do you see as the main issues involved in evaluation? none of the staff I interviewed were able to discuss what they considered the main issue without prompting. Following suggestions from me that these might be concerned with accountability, identification of future policy or informing outsiders, only half the senior staff saw this as concerned with policy-making. In those cases where an attempt was made to answer the question the context in which the reply was given was that of the classroom and the evaluation of pupil progress.

On the basis of this evidence I deduced that the teachers were not aware of the issues relating to evaluation. Further questioning, however, revealed that this was not the case. Much of what I was seeking to discover had been internalized by the teachers and was being articulated in practice, in the classroom, if not overtly in discussion. In most cases, as the interviews which I held with staff progressed, they discussed the same issues in a specific context. For example, in response to my questions asking how they would use data gathered on their teaching they expressed the view that it would help them to make decisions for future lessons. I asked a further question as to why data should be gathered on such matters as school organization and relationships with parents and the community. They said that they saw this as a means of evaluating current procedures with a view to future improvement, thus expressing their accountability in professional terms (Becher *et al.*, 1981, p. 20). At the same time they made clear that in practical terms they had an understanding of the concepts of evaluation and accountability although they were not able to articulate these freely in discussion.

In the course of my research I discovered that not only were many teachers unable to identify themselves with whole school policies and curriculum issues but also they were unaware of the overall structure of organizational procedures within the school although I felt that these were clearly visible. Apart from four of the senior staff, none of the teachers I interviewed acknowledged an awareness of the processes of curriculum evaluation operating within the school. Of these staff eight had been present at the senior staff meetings when the annual curriculum plan had been presented and each Head of Department had been interviewed by the Headteacher about departmental progress and future plans. In addition to this the terms of reference of the curriculum working parties which always either explicitly stated or implied an evaluation of current practice had been published to all staff annually. I was also aware that at least two of those interviewed had served as members of such a working party. Four of the staff interviewed knew that their Head of Department discussed the work of the Department with the Head-teacher on a regular basis and saw this as a particular strategy for evaluation.

When the teachers were asked how their teaching was assessed, six of those questioned said they did not know. One mentioned the fact that 'the Headmistress moves around to see what people are doing' — echoing an earlier comment from a Head of Department on the Headteacher's informal system of checking up: rather in the nature of 'trouble spotting' as part of the problem solving aspect of evaluation identified by Becher *et al.* (1981, p. 80). One teacher with a scale 2 responsibility post indicated that unless a teacher was having problems she did not know how teaching was assessed. One person only mentioned examination results and a junior member of the Physical Education Department answered that she assumed that she was assessed by the Headteacher and Deputies observing her lessons and also by her Head of Department's knowledge of her work. As someone who had recently completed her probationary period within the school she was alert to the process and, it seemed, saw this monitoring as continuing beyond probation.

Apart from the senior staff of the school, the staff's impression of how the pupils' overall welfare was monitored was vague. One teacher suggested that lack of success could be evaluated by the number of pupils referred to outside agencies and another teacher said that she was aware of the reference machinery for problem children but was not aware of any overall system for other pupils Two Heads of Department confessed to being aware that 'things went on' but found it difficult to say what the systems were, if any. A third Head of Department said that she knew that overall everyone was evaluated through the 'year system' but was unhappy about the lack of feedback on individual cases; a similar criticism to that made earlier by the tutor concerned with her pupils' academic progress. Only one junior member of staff made reference to the school's pupil record cards at this point.

It seemed as far as the evaluation of the pupil's overall welfare was concerned, the staff were confident that something of this nature took place and it would have been surprising had this not been the case given the pastoral orientation of the management structure. The staff did reveal ignorance, however, of the way in which this evaluation was carried out, except perhaps in the case of a minority of pupils whose problems necessitated reference to outside agencies.

Although the teachers could not discuss aspects of school evaluation freely, it was evident from their answers that they were aware of the issues and were constantly evaluating their own performance as teachers and also that of their pupils. From the questions which I posed concerning teachers' awareness of the procedures of evaluation in their own school I had, in part, a similar impression. There was a considerable ignorance of existing procedures in all of the areas in which I posed questions. It was obvious, however, from the course of my conversations that, for instance, each of the four Heads of Department were evaluating progress of their respective areas in terms of curriculum development, assessment techniques and teacher expertise although they did not mention this in answer to any of the questions. As Form Tutors several of the staff I interviewed were known by me to be concerned for their pupils' academic progress and general welfare and capable of acting upon this concern. As subject teachers also many of the staff had expanded their answers to an earlier question concerning pupil assessment to include detailed discussion of how they assessed their pupils' achievement in terms of skills and conceptual development. Perhaps in answer to my questions concerning their awareness of procedures and processes they were focusing at school level and were omitting to mention or even recognize the part which they themselves played.

Since carrying out this research I have been aware of similar issues in my present school. In an attempt to develop teachers' awareness of issues which are common to all subject areas, I have established committees, chaired by coordinators, where each member has a brief to liaise with a particular subject area. Currently, two committees exist to monitor pupils' personal development and careers education respectively, across the curriculum.

One of the criticisms which these committee members may have to face as their work takes them into the classrooms of colleagues is that which was raised by the Head of Science at Beachside when he queried the researcher's qualification to criticize a chemistry lesson because he was not a science teacher (Ball, 1984, p. 88). Indeed, it is a criticism with which I have been faced as a new Headteacher in a school where, previously, concern about what actually was happening in classrooms had not been manifest. Unfortunately such a response highlights the problem that teachers are still concerned, by and large, with the specific and differentiating subject content of the curriculum at the expense of cross-curricular processes and methodology.

Extrapolating from the evidence gathered during the course of my study one could conclude that studies concerned with organizational concepts, broad curriculum issues or social relationships couched in theoretical terms are of limited interest to teachers. Their focus is on the classroom rather than on the school.

The Value of Ethnographic Studies to Teachers

How valuable, therefore, are ethnographic studies to practising teachers? Are they used to clarify thinking and/or improve practice? In order to make a comprehensive assessment of the usefulness of particular studies it would be necessary for researchers to return to schools after an interval of time and examine the extent to which any change had been influenced by the results of their work.

The extent to which this type of large-scale ethnographic study can be of wide benefit to schools, however, depends upon the degree to which it is possible to generalize from the particular case in so far as it deals with concepts which can be adapted and applied to the reader's own immediate situation. Some of the benefits which can accrue to teachers from such work are in terms of support by explaining some of the phenomena which occur in schools. David Hargreaves' exploration of the effect of sub-cultures, Lacey's concepts of polarization and differentiation and Burgess's exploration of how information and situations are defined and redefined within the school are all examples of occurences which, I would submit, are common features of most schools. Studies can also be helpful to teachers by documenting the life of the school in such a way that the evidence is available for them to draw out the implications and make their own assessments. For example, in *Experiencing Comprehensive Education* (Burgess, 1983) one is able to construct quite a detailed picture of the Headteacher from references to his philosophy, his aims for the school, his reactions to situations together with the reactions of others to his aims and the procedures which he adopts to realize these. The evidence is there for readers to draw out the management problems with which the Headteacher was faced, evaluate his strategies, if any, for dealing with these and then consider how they themselves would have reacted to similar problems. Other readers may relate, for example, to the varying ways in which the House Heads carried out their responsibilities.

One of the prime advantages of a large-scale ethnographic study is that it can subject a situation to analysis in depth which could not be carried out by teachers alone. Researchers are able to bring to the study resources such as time and specialist knowledge of research methods which would not otherwise be available. In the normal course of events full-time teachers have little opportunity within the school day to pursue the planning and follow-up of research, nor do they have the necessary expertise in research methods. Researchers also bring to bear upon the subject a fresh view which has not been affected by previous involvement with the subject. There is always the risk, however, that the researchers' observations may challenge the vested interests of some teachers.

Whilst from the researchers' point of view it is important that their work does not unduly influence the subject of the study, I would argue that the processes of observation, interviewing and questioning must, on occasion, give the people involved cause for thought and assessment. During the course of my research (Threadgold, 1982) I found that several staff commented that the dialogue which we were engaged in was concentrating their thoughts upon aspects of evaluation which they had not considered previously. The teachers appeared to be grateful for this stimulation and an opportunity to 'think aloud' and in some cases expressed an intention to explore the matter further. In reply to my question about who should be involved in evaluating school organization and management, two staff chose to take their consideration of the question further than initially required and speculated as to how such an exercise could be carried out so as to include groups external to the school such as parents and governors. On reflection, at the conclusion of the project I felt that the ground had been prepared for the seeds of an integrated policy of school evaluation to be established. Whether or not this took place I have no way of knowing without further study. Such follow-up work is difficult for practising teachers but should not be so difficult for those outside the profession. Unlike most research which, if properly structured, should not directly influence the subject of the study, the stimulation which the questioning process causes is an important by-product.

In the light of the increasing size and complexity of organization in secondary schools it must surely be advantageous to the smooth operation of the institution for all teachers to have an understanding of such matters. Associated with the increased complexity of schools has come an increasing democratization of their organization. If staff wish to participate in policy formulation then they need to have a sphere of reference beyond the classroom. Participation brings this about to a limited extent but more knowledge is necessary if the maximum benefit is to be gained. The main difficulty for the Headteacher, however, lies in persuading the teacher in the classroom that both the studies in themselves and the research methods which they employ are relevant to their work.

Teacher-Based Research

How, therefore, can one convince teachers of the value to them of research findings and the research process? How can researchers become more fully acquainted with the concerns of teachers? The answer, I think, lies in teacher-based research where the teacher is either involved in a project guided by the researcher or is working alongside the researcher on a school-based project. In this way the participants are directly involved in exploring issues which they encounter every day in the course of their classroom work. Here the dialogue between the teacher and the researcher is on-going and interactive, maximizing the theoretical skills of one and the practical skills of the other.

The Cambridge Accountability Project (Elliott *et al.*, 1981) is one example of a research project which although concerned with a broad issue, not only identified a field of study which teachers seemed to regard as being directly relevant to their work, but also set out to establish a two-way communication with teachers through which the teachers' views were able to influence the next stage of the research. Accepting that many schools were trying to involve more people in the discussion of what should take place in schools, one of the aims of the Project was to:

try to understand the problems which arise when schools adopt this 'responsive' approach, and its potential for influencing decision making in schools. (p. 13)

Furthermore the document circulated to local education authorities and schools explaining the purpose of the Project, stated that:

It is hoped that case studies compiled by the Project team will be used by participating schools in the further development of their own procedures. (p. 14)

In an attempt to ensure that this would occur, each of the six schools involved in the Project received a first draft of its case study for discussion with the intention that it should be scrutinized for 'relevance and validity'. It was also made clear that the team wished their communication to influence teachers' thinking as well as to assist schools. In the light of staff reaction to the draft case studies the team found themselves

either collecting data around new theories which teachers felt we had neglected, or probing certain issues more deeply, or trying to clarify new concepts and ideas which had arisen from our discussions with teachers. (p. 15)

It is obvious that the original draft had met with considerable critical discussion. This is not surprising given the diversity of viewpoints represented by any group of teachers. Whilst ideally the interaction between teachers and researchers generated by this particular procedure should positively affect the work of both, questions need to be raised about how representative such a response can be of the staff as a whole.

In his introduction to the Ford Teaching Project, Elliott (1975) maintains that the central problem associated with curriculum reform in the late 1960s were

the clash between the theories of the reformers and those theories implicit, often unconsciously, in the practice of teachers.

He suggests that the reason why so many of these projects were less than successful in schools was because neither the reformers nor the teachers found themselves able to reflect critically on their own theories in relation to their practice. Taking this as a problem, Elliott (1975) and his team set up a research project which involved teachers in what he termed 'Action Research' to collaboratively develop a practical theory of 'enquiry/discovery teaching' (p. 2). Through the medium of the Project, teachers were introduced to the language and methods of research in structured situations and were able to develop confidence in their application. For educational research to have maximum effect upon teachers it must not be presented as a *fait accompli* 'originating in expertise and technique which are beyond the comprehension of those to whom it is directed' (Sheard, 1981, p. 176) but must involve teachers themselves actively and practically. Sheard maintains that those who are engaged on action research in the classroom are likely to be affected by it more deeply than anyone reading about it (p. 176). During the course of such work the perceptions of the teachers are sharpened and by involvement in discussion and questioning they develop the ability to assess them-selves as well as their pupils (Nixon, 1981, p. 189). Hopefully, teachers involved in such a Project would not only be able to use the techniques which they had learned for their own purposes in the future but would also be more ready to facilitate both future research and apply the results to their own work.

Implicit in the work of Elliott and those involved in action research is a recognition of the fact that in order for educational research to be of value to researchers and teachers alike, the two must interact closely and initiate each into an understanding of the work of the other. Increasingly, as teachers are required to respond to demands for accountability from external agencies, to assess their own work and participate in an evaluation of that of the school, they need to acquire the skills of the researcher in order to enable them to gather the evidence upon which to make judgments. Involvement in research within the classroom also provides the teachers with the opportunity to offer their own work to the scrutiny of others, representing what Nixon (1981) refers to as 'a serious response' to the demand for professional accountability (p. 198).

One of the most effective ways of acquiring any skill is by working alongside those who have expertise in that area. As in the case of any learning situation where teachers learn from pupils and are constantly adjusting their approach in the light of new knowledge, researchers can learn much from teachers which may influence their approach to future projects. By this means the work of those engaged in large-scale ethnographic studies is rendered more accessible to teachers and hence can more easily influence their work. This is not to say, however, that all research related to education should be of this nature. Different problems and different audiences may be better addressed by other styles of investigation.

Margaret W. Threadgold

Conclusion

One of the most unfortunate factors in education is the fragmentation of the groups involved. They are frequently isolated, one group from another, and there is little interchange of personnel between them. Administrators, inspectors and advisers, teachers, researchers and those involved in teacher education all operate within the boundaries and constraints of their own particular area. McCutcheon (1981) maintains (p. 193) that everyone involved in each aspect of education must work together creatively in an attempt to solve the issues and problems within the whole area. Indeed, McCutcheon argues that many perspectives are needed to understand the nature of the educational process whether it is in terms of decision making, or developing teaching strategies or whatever.

Barriers need to be broken down within the education service and the views and expertise of the practitioners need to be fed into other parts of the system, to inform judgments, facilitate decision-making and to influence initial teacher education. Research carried out by teachers in schools could inform others in this way, giving 'a realistic notion of the nature of schools, teaching and teachers' (McCutcheon, 1981, p. 190). Thus, a dialogue could develop with far-reaching consequences.

In the past it would seem that areas of research have been identified almost exclusively by groups or individuals outside the schools. Whilst not suggesting that such an approach is no longer valid, perhaps a better balance should be created between those problems which are 'made' and those which are 'taken'. Teachers could identify more frequently the subjects for research, based upon their own findings and commission the extended research from those with greater expertise within the field. This would involve some change in the approach to educational research, casting the researcher more often in the role of consultant or problem-solver (Becher *et al.*, 1981, p. 70).

Already in situations where teachers and researchers are working closely together, appreciating each other's expertise, the gap between the two is in the process of being bridged. Hopefully, from such co-operation, misunderstandings and suspicions will be replaced by a mutual respect. Teachers will begin to recognize the point at which the researchers' skills become necessary to assist them in defining and investigating an issue and welcome the contribution of a different perspective. Researchers, brought closer to the practical activities within schools and the education service generally, may see priorities differently and recognize that if they really wish their work to have some validity in the eyes of the practitioners, research areas must be mutually defined and teachers themselves must be involved in the project in a meaningful way. Meanwhile, teachers should acknowledge that researchers must also address their work to their academic colleagues and may use the field of education in order to engage in this activity. Nor should they regard the work of the researcher as a utilitarian service. The way forward lies, I would suggest, in the growth of mutual respect between the researcher and the practitioner and an understanding of each other's aims which can only be brought about by working together practically, to ensure a continuing dialogue.

Acknowledgements

I would like to thank those friends and colleagues who, through discussion, helped me in the preparation of this chapter. In particular I would like to acknowledge the assistance of Stephen Ball and Robert Burgess whose comments on an early draft were extremely helpful.

References

BALL, S.J. (1981) *Beachside Comprehensive: A Case Study of Secondary Schooling*, Cambridge, Cambridge University Press.

BALL, S.J. (1984) 'Beachside reconsidered: reflections on a methodological apprenticeship', in BURGESS, R.G. (Ed.) *The Research Process in Educational Settings: Ten Case Studies*, Lewes, Falmer Press.

BECHER, R.A. (1980) 'Research into practice', in DOCKRELL, W.B. and HAMILTON, D. (Eds) *Rethinking Educational Research*, Sevenoaks, Hodder and Stoughton.

BECHER, T., ERAUT, M. and KNIGHT, J. (1981) *Policies for Educational Accountability*, London, Heinemann.

BERNSTEIN, B. (1971) *Class, Codes and Control, Vol. 1. Theoretical Studies Towards a Sociology of Language*, London, Routledge and Kegan Paul.

BURGESS, R.G. (1982) 'Multiple strategies in field research', in BURGESS, R.G. (Ed.) *Field Research: A Sourcebook and Field Manual*, London, Allen and Unwin.

BURGESS, R.G. (1983) *Experiencing Comprehensive Education: A Study of Bishop McGregor School*, London, Methuen.

DOUGLAS, J.W.B. (1964) *The Home and the School*, London, MacGibbon and Kee.

ELLIOTT, J. (1975) *Ford Teaching Project*, Cambridge, Institute of Education.

ELLIOTT, J. *et al.* (1981) *School Accountability*, London, Grant McIntyre.

FLOUD, J., HALSEY, A.H. and MARTIN, F.M. (1957) *Social Class and Educational Opportunity*, London, Heinemann.

HARGREAVES, D.H. (1967) *Social Relations in a Secondary School*, London, Routledge and Kegan Paul.

HARGREAVES, D.H. (1982) *The Challenge for the Comprehensive School*, London, Routledge and Kegan Paul.

LACEY, C. (1970) *Hightown Grammar*, Manchester, Manchester University Press.

McCUTCHEON, G. (1981) 'The impact of the insider', in NIXON, J. (Ed.) *A Teachers' Guide to Action Research*, London, Grant McIntyre.

NISBET, J. (1980) 'Educational research: The state of the art', in DOCKRELL, W.B. and HAMILTON, D. (Eds) *Rethinking Educational Research*, Sevenoaks, Hodder and Stoughton.

NIXON, J. (Ed.) (1981) *A Teachers' Guide to Action Research*, London, Grant McIntyre.

SEELEY, J. (1966) 'The "making" and "taking" of problems', *Social Problems*, 14.

SHEARD, D. (1981) 'Spreading the message', in NIXON, J. (Ed.) *A Teachers' Guide to Action Research*, London, Grant McIntyre.

THREADGOLD, M.W. (1982) 'An investigation of the response from teachers and schools to demands for accountability through the process of school-based evaluation', unpublished MEd dissertation, University of Warwick.

VAN der EYKEN, W. (1965) 'Educational research and the teacher', a report of a one day conference held at the University of London Institute of Education, Slough, NFER.

WALKER, R. (1980) 'The conduct of educational case studies: Ethics, theories and procedures', in DOCKRELL, W.B. and HAMILTON, D. (Eds) *Rethinking Educational Research*, Sevenoaks, Hodder and Stoughton.

WOODS, P.E. (1979) *The Divided School*, London, Routledge and Kegan Paul.

YOUNG, M.F.D. (1971) 'Introduction: Knowledge and control', in YOUNG, M.F.D. (Ed.) *Knowledge and Control*, London, Collier Macmillan.

Notes on Contributors

Hilary Burgess has recently been appointed Lecturer in Education at Westhill College, Birmingham. Previously she was a primary school teacher who worked for the ILEA and Coventry Education Authority. In 1983 she completed an MA in Curriculum Studies at the University of London Institute of Education. Her dissertation at the Institute involved case study research on the primary curriculum and was entitled 'An appraisal of some methods of teaching primary school mathematics'. She is currently interested in school-based self-evaluation in the primary school.

Robert Burgess is a Senior Lecturer in Sociology at the University of Warwick. His teaching and research interests include the sociology of education and social research methodology; especially field research. He is particularly interested in ethnography and its use in educational settings. He is the author of *Experiencing Comprehensive Education: A Study of Bishop McGregor School* (1983); *In the Field: An Introduction to Field Research* (1984); *Education, Schools and Schooling* (1985); and the editor of *Teaching Research Methodology to Postgraduates: A Survey of Courses in the U.K.* (1979); *Field Research: A Sourcebook and Field Manual* (1982); *Exploring Society* (1982); *The Research Process in Educational Settings: Ten Case Studies* (1984); *Field Methods in the Study of Education* (1985) and *Strategies of Educational Research: Qualitative Methods* (1985). He was Honorary General Secretary of the British Sociological Association, 1982–84.

Carol Cummings trained at Didsbury College, Manchester and has taught in primary schools. She is currently the Deputy Head of a primary school in Trafford and is also engaged in postgraduate studies at Manchester Polytechnic conducting research on the education of the young child (3–8 years). Her main research interests include: classroom interaction, teacher self-evaluation and the experiences of young children starting school.

Dave Ebbutt is currently the national evaluator for the Secondary Science Curriculum Review. In recent years he was a Research Fellow at the Cambridge Institute of Education where he worked full-time on two research projects: the Cambridge Accountability Project and Teacher Pupil Interaction and the Quality of Learning Project. Before this he taught science in schools in England, Nigeria and Uganda. He has published articles in various books on action research and school accountability.

Janet Finch is a Senior Lecturer in Social Administration at the University of Lancaster. She is a sociologist by background, and a former Chairperson of the British Sociological Association. Her main research and publications have been in the area of education and social policy, and in women's studies, her particular interest being in sociology of the family and family policy. Her publications include: *Married to the Job* (1983); *A Labour of Love* (1983) (with Dulcie Groves); and *Education as Social Policy* (1984).

Gordon Griffiths is Head of the Remedial Department at Thornhill School, Sunderland. He trained as a teacher at Bede College, Durham. Several years ago he gained his BEd degree through the in-service course at Sunderland Polytechnic. It was during this course that he developed a keen interest in the sociology of education. He is currently studying for an in-service MEd degree.

MARTYN HAMMERSLEY was previously Research Fellow in the Department of Sociology, University of Manchester. Currently he is a Lecturer in the Sociology Discipline in the School of Education at the Open University. His main research interests are the study of classroom interaction and the methodology of social research. He has written articles in both fields as well as a book on *Ethnography* (1983) with Paul Atkinson; *The Process of Schooling* (1976); *School Experience* (1977); and *Life in School* (1984) (all with Peter Woods); and *Curriculum Practice* (1983) (with Andy Hargreaves). His previous research project (working with John Scarth and Sue Webb) concerns the effects of different types of external assessment on teaching and learning in secondary schools. He is currently engaged in a comparative analysis of observational techniques (with John Scarth).

Andy Hargreaves, after being a primary school teacher and a college of education lecturer, has been a lecturer at the Open University and the University of Oxford. He is now a Lecturer in Education at the University of Warwick. He has published work on educational theory, teacher coping strategies, teachers' cultures and decision making, and educational policy. He is the author of a forthcoming book on *The Sociology of Educational Policy and Practice*; and coeditor of: *Middle Schools: Origins, Ideology and Practice* (1980) (with Les Tickle); *Curriculum Practice: Some Sociological Case Studies* (1983) (with Martyn Hammersley); and *Classrooms and Staffrooms* (1984) (with Peter Woods).

Alison Kelly is a Lecturer in Sociology at Manchester University and a director of the Girls Into Science and Technology (GIST) project. She has a degree in physics and taught maths and science for two years before moving into educational research. Most of her research has been concerned with the problems of girls' underachievement in science and she has published widely on this topic. She is the editor of *The Missing Half: Girls and Science Education* (1981), a collection of papers for teachers and student teachers.

John Scarth is a Research Assistant in the School of Education at the Open University where he has spent the last three years studying (with Martyn Hammersley and Sue Webb) the effects of different types of external assessment on teaching. Previously he has worked as a teacher and has been a Research Student in the Department of Educational Research at the University of Lancaster, where he studied for a PhD on the effects of examinations on curriculum decision-making. His current research (with Martyn Hammersley) focusses on a methodological analysis of observational research techniques.

Sue Scott graduated in sociology from Newcastle-upon-Tyne Polytechnic in 1974. She then worked as a Research Officer for the Health Education Council. In 1977 she moved to the University of Lancaster to do postgraduate research, and from January 1979 to January 1982 she was a Research Associate there in the Department of Sociology working on the Postgraduate Research Project. After completing the 1981–82 academic year in Lancaster as an Honorary Research Fellow she took up a post as researcher on the Mansfield Community Health Project. She is currently Assistant Director of the 'Women in Medicine' project at Lucy Cavendish College, Cambridge. She is a member of the British Sociological Association's Executive, and of the BSA'a Sex Equality Committee. She has written several articles on women postgraduates and postgraduate education.

Margaret Threadgold has recently taken up the post of Headteacher at Swanshurst School, Birmingham. Previously she was Headteacher of Erdington School and has served in a senior capacity in schools in other local education authorities. She has been engaged in work on aspects of comprehensive school management and was seconded to the University of Birmingham on a one-term fellowship for head-teachers. Her MEd dissertation at the University of Warwick was about teacher perceptions of the processes of evaluation in schools. She is particularly interested in in-service education and training and staff development.

Sue Webb was a Research Fellow in the School of Education at the Open University between 1982–83 working with Martyn Hammersley and John Scarth. She has also taught sociology and women's studies in sixth-forms, further education colleges and the University of Manchester. She is currently teaching in a sixth-form college. Her main research interests are organizational behaviour and the sociology of gender. She has written an MA thesis on 'Women and Class' and a PhD thesis entitled 'An Ethnography of a Department Store'. She has also written articles on adult education.

Peter Woods is a Reader in Education at the Open University. After graduating in history at the University of London, he taught at schools in London, Norfolk and Yorkshire, and studied education and sociology at Sheffield, Leeds and Bradford universities. He is author of *The Divided School* (1979) and *Sociology and the School* (1983) and co-author of *Changing Schools* (1984) and *Teacher Careers* (1985). He is currently researching pupil development in primary schools.

Author Index

Subject Index

ability
of pupils, 62–4
action research, 129–51, 152–74,
226–31, 266–7
see also classroom research;
educational action research
advantages of, 140–8
and change processes, 138–9
as cyclical process, 164–70
and data feedback, 136–8
definitions of, 129–33
disadvantages of, 140–8
as 'experimental social
administration', 129–30, 131,
132, 140, 142, 144
and implementation, 136
and knowledge, 134
and maxims, 172
and problem solving, 134
and research collaboration, 135–6
as school-based, *see* school-based
research
as sequence of spiral steps, 161–2,
169
and 'simultaneous-integrated'
approach, 129, 132–49
and social commitment, 144
societal context of, 147–8
and teacher competencies, 134–5
and teacher-researcher model, 8,
129, 130–2, 140, 145–7, *see also*
teachers, as researchers
and understanding, 138
*Action Research: A Framework for
Self-Evaluation in Schools*, 153,

161, 162, 164–5, 167–9, 170
Action-Research Planner, The, 153,
161, 162, 163, 168, 170
accountability
and school evaluation, 259–63,
264–5
adult-child interaction, 225
see also teacher-pupil interaction
Amadeus, 91
analytic induction, 28, 56–8, 61
anonymity
see confidentiality
anthropological approach, 219–20
art
as model for ethnographic work,
89–92
assisted places schemes, 21
audiences
for research reports, 11
see also writing up

Beachside Comprehensive [School],
55–6
'Beachside reconsidered', 259
Brave New World, 38–9
British Sociological Association
(BSA), 69

Cambridge Accountability Project,
265–7
Cambridge Institute of Education,
152, 218
case study
of mathematics curriculum in
primary school, 177–96

121, 122
historical sources, 3
see also documentary evidence

infants schools, 221–50
interactionism, 22–3, 24, 35, 48–9,
    104, 114, 218–19
interviews, 3, 10, 68–9, 70, 71–2,
    73, 74–80, 81, 115, 117, 126–7,
    178, 184–7, 189–90, 192, 193,
    260–3
    with peers, 10, 186–7, 192

Joseph, Sir Keith, 110

Lancaster, University of
    Department of Sociology, 69–71
Leicestershire Classroom Research
    and In-Service Education Project,
    218
life history approach, 71
Lighthouse, To the, 90
London, University of
    Institute of Education, 193
longitudinal research, 58–62
Lumley Secondary Modern School,
    255

macro theory
    see also micro-macro problem
    combination with micro theory
        of, 40–2
    and micro theory, 36–42
    as speculative, 37–40
    worth of, 37–40
Manchester
    Girls into Science and Technology
        Project in, 133
Manchester Polytechnic, 220, 221
    Action Research Conference
        (March 1983) at, 220
Marxism
    and empiricism, 112, 114
    and ethnography, 29
    and micro-macro links, 24–36
    and sociology of education, 22
mathematics curriculum
    methodology for research on,
        178–80

in primary school, 8, 177–96
Mathematics for Schools, 178, 179,
    188, 189, 194
micro-macro problem, 6, 21–47,
    51–2, 252, 253
micro theory
    see also micro-macro problem
    combination with macro theory
        of, 40–2
    and macro theory, 36–42
middle schools
    constraints on teachers in, 43
mixed ability grouping, 2, 256–7
moral issues
    and research, 119–21
Morgan, J.H., 96
mosaic model 50–6
Mozart, W.A., 91
multiple realities, 190

National Children's Bureau
    Intermediate Treatment Centres
        of the, 130
National Foundation for
    Educational Research, 253
Neptune [planet], 39–40
'NUPE sheets', 188, 194
nursery education
    research on, 109–28

observation
    see participant observation
Office of Population, Censuses and
    Surveys, 3
ORACLE project, 219

parents
    and collaboration in research,
        135–6
participant observation, 3, 115, 137,
    178, 180–93, 199–213, 226–31
    see also classroom research
pastoral role
    of teachers, 203–5, 207, 208–9
personal experience
    and the research process, 67–85
physical sciences
    and micro-macro problem, 22
playgroups